Nisar /

# Journalism in Retrospection

## Thirty Years of Reportage

**H**
HANSIB

The opinions, views and beliefs expressed by the author do not necessarily reflect those of the publisher or its representatives and agents.

The freedom of expression applies not only to information or ideas that are favourably received, but also to those that may offend, shock or disturb. It applies to all who wish to seek, receive or impart information and ideas of all kinds.

*"Everyone has the right to freedom of expression."*

Article 10 of the Human Rights Act

First published in Great Britain by Hansib Publications in 2023

Hansib Publications Limited
76 High Street, Hertford, SG14 3WY, UK

info@hansibpublications.com
www.hansibpublications.com

Copyright © Nisar Ali Shah, 2023

ISBN 978-1-912662-94-4
ISBN 978-1-912662-95-1 (Kindle)
ISBN 978-1-912662-96-8 (ePub)

A CIP catalogue record for this book
is available from the British Library

All rights reserved.

Without limiting the rights under copyright reserved above, no part of this publication may be reproduced, stored in or introduced into a retrieval system, or transmitted, in any form or by any means (electronic, mechanical, photocopying, recording or otherwise), without the prior written permission of both the copyright owner and the publisher of this book.

Design & Production by Hansib Publications Ltd
Printed in Great Britain

# Contents

Preface .......................................................................................................... 6
Prince and socialite who strived for international co-operation ................ 7
New regime in Afghanistan ........................................................................ 10
A divided opinion on Assange .................................................................... 13
A reminiscence of my childhood ............................................................... 15
Guantanamo Prison's future ...................................................................... 17
Julian Assange on suicide watch ................................................................ 19
Looking above petty Covid-19 squabbles .................................................. 22
India's army on the rampage ..................................................................... 24
Kashmir is bleeding .................................................................................... 27
Free Julian Assange campaign ................................................................... 30
World Peace and Prosperity awards ceremony ......................................... 32
Global campaign gearing up for Julian Assange's freedom ....................... 34
How long would the Kashmir dispute last? ............................................... 37
Jinnah: An incomparable political leader .................................................. 40
Is alcoholism a weakness, an evil or insanity? .......................................... 45
Pakistan's unholy alliance .......................................................................... 48
Will Guantanamo exist forever? ................................................................ 52
Trump devalues himself ............................................................................ 54
Iqbal lives beyond his death ...................................................................... 57
Terrorism redefined ................................................................................... 61
Journey into Europe (A film) ...................................................................... 65
Refugee crisis splits European Union ........................................................ 68
NATO's legacy of the refugee crisis ........................................................... 71
Nirbhaya (The Fearless) ............................................................................. 74
The Jeremy Corbyn phenomenon ............................................................. 77
Ethnic cleansing of Palestinians and British betrayal ................................ 79
War crimes but no criminal justice ............................................................ 83
Islamophobia leads to Muslim awakening ................................................ 86
Demonising Muslims is a recipe for 'radicalisation' .................................. 89

| | |
|---|---|
| Urdu: Third largest language in the world | 93 |
| Sworn enemy | 96 |
| What did I see in Lahore? | 98 |
| Rally for Moazzam Begg | 102 |
| Ukraine better off with Russia | 104 |
| Dr Abbas Khan: Murder most foul | 106 |
| Drones must be withdrawn | 109 |
| Osama bin Laden's assassination: An answer to an Iranian journalist's question | 111 |
| Thatcher the "Milk Snatcher" | 113 |
| Allama Shabbir Ahmed Bokhari: scholar, poet and educationist | 116 |
| Assange is an institution and must be saved | 119 |
| Assange's fate in the balance | 122 |
| Squeezing squash in Olympics arena | 124 |
| Prince Mohsin Ali Khan to mount peace offensive | 127 |
| Regime change made easy in Libya | 129 |
| Colour of racism then and now | 131 |
| Palestinian return | 134 |
| Ten years of folklore | 137 |
| Bin Laden's death linked with US seeking exit strategy | 141 |
| Brian Haw, a scourge of British politics | 145 |
| Obituary: Champion and chronicler of Pakistan in turbulent times | 147 |
| Samuel Martin Burke: Jurist who helped found Pakistan's Foreign Service | 150 |
| A diplomat par excellence | 154 |
| Whither Pakistan cricket? | 161 |
| Torture inquiry must be public | 164 |
| Afghan policy needs change | 167 |
| An error is not a mistake until corrected | 170 |
| The Chilcot farce | 172 |
| Brown wants Pakistan Army to fight his dirty war | 175 |
| Transforming Pakistan | 177 |
| Muslim Holocaust denial | 178 |
| Media coverage and the Mumbai attacks | 181 |
| Pakistan in a great political turmoil | 184 |
| Ex-convicted prisoners up to the same old tricks | 188 |
| Khuda Kay Liye: In the Name of God | 190 |
| High Sheriff of Greater London promotes multi-faith observance | 192 |
| Community leaders stress respect for faiths | 194 |

Palestinians appeal to the world to bring down apartheid wall ............... 195
March from London to Karachi ............................................................ 198
"Don't Attack Iran" ............................................................................. 201
Dr Moazzam Ali Alvi ........................................................................... 204
Blair's role in Iraq caused the bombings in London ............................. 208
Livingstone urges Londoners to shop at Palestinian Trade Fair ........... 210
A day in the life of Conway Hall .......................................................... 212
Book Review: *Islam Under Siege* ........................................................ 214
Is the clash of civilisations inevitable? ................................................ 217
Prince Mohsin's idea of solving the Kashmir problem .......................... 219
German stalwart values cosmopolitanism in Europe ........................... 220
Schimmel eulogised at German embassy in London ............................ 222
First Schimmel Memorial Seminar held in London .............................. 223
Hawks pounce on Iraq to redraw its map ............................................ 226
An Islamic scholar made in Germany .................................................. 230
Turkey at a crossroads after Iraq War ................................................. 233
Hyde Park rally exposes war of conquest not "Liberation" ................. 235
BBC One's 'Question Time' ................................................................. 237
Galloway explains his expulsion after thirty-six years ......................... 239
African Union to sort out the killer loan sharks ................................... 242
Multi-faith conference condemns State terrorism ............................... 244
War on terrorism is no way to end terrorism ...................................... 246
Congo exploited – right, left and centre .............................................. 248
Scholars see no quick fix of Kashmir dispute ....................................... 250
Old Ethiopia recalled .......................................................................... 252
Book Review: *Landmarks of the Pakistan Movement* ......................... 254
Bush needs to concentrate on causes of conflict ................................. 256
Beating about Bush ............................................................................ 260
Islam's contribution to Western civilisation ........................................ 262
Seminar calls for an end to feudalism ................................................. 264
Legal and political sides of the Lockerbie affair .................................. 266
Quaid-e-Azam Mohammad Ali Jinnah: His Personality and His Politics ............... 270
Reflecting on Pakistan's lost years ...................................................... 276
The legacy of Dr Kalim Siddiqui .......................................................... 278
Media in a trap ................................................................................... 283

# Preface

This book is not an autobiography, a novel, or an account of someone's life written by someone else. It is a short chronicle of the work of a journalist who wrote for international newspapers and magazines over three decades.

The idea first came from a number of my readers who suggested that I should write a book. But, instead of writing about myself, I decided to collate some of my published articles into a single volume.

I see this as a book of the future, that also reflects upon the past and the current affairs of the day. The articles and op-eds may provide an insight into how particular issues were treated at the time and their relevance today.

Arranged in chronological order, most of them were published in *TheNews*, London; in Fleet Street newspapers; and some in Canada and Africa. They comprise a broad range of subjects, including Afghanistan; Kashmir; Palestine; Guantanamo Bay prison; the journalist, Julian Assange; the Covid-19 pandemic; alcoholism; racism; drone bombings by the United States; Mr Jinnah, the founder of Pakistan; poet/philosopher Allama Mohammed Iqbal; torture in Iraq; book reviews; film reviews; obituaries; and some childhood memories of growing up in Pakistan.

I am deeply grateful to those readers who, from time to time, praised, criticised or kept me awake by sending their feedback, which I found exceedingly encouraging and inspiring. Thank you all!

**Nisar Ali Shah**

# Prince and socialite who strived for international co-operation

Obituary published in *The Times*, London, December 24, 2022

Prince Mohsin Ali Khan, who died in London on September 25, 2022, aged 93, was a familiar figure to the staff of Harrods. Not keen on eating alone, he had at least one daily meal – usually breakfast – in the Garden Terrace restaurant of the Knightsbridge department store in the course of his 70-odd years living in London. He liked his omelettes cooked a particular way, and the restaurant's chefs were given his favourite recipe.

Britain was a country that the Hyderabad prince made his home after partition in 1947. He arrived on his own at the age of 17. A devout Muslim, and financially comfortable, he made it his mission from the start to bring faiths together and to support human rights and Islamic issues. One of his biggest contributions was the founding of a Muslim, Jewish and Christian society that grew into what he called "One Nation of All Faiths" to promote dialogue among people of all religions.

The prince also forged a reputation as a London luminary and socialite, carving out a role as a roving international diplomat. He rubbed shoulders with British and foreign aristocracy and became known to the capital's ambassadors and high commissioners, in particular at the US and Saudi embassies. His name frequently appeared on the list of guests at ceremonies, functions, diplomatic receptions, memorial services, lunches at Admiralty House, discussions at Portcullis House and Requiem Masses at the Brompton Oratory.

A concise, articulate speaker with a wry sense of humour, Prince Mohsin was often invited to give talks, including for the European Atlantic Group, a think tank, on how to improve economic and political co-operation. He introduced the English-Speaking Union to several countries, including Denmark.

Prince Mohsin shunned worldly goods

The territorial conflict over Kashmir, in northern India, preoccupied the prince, and he organised discussions on India-Pakistan relations when he could. In 1994 and 1995 he represented the subcontinent at a world peace conference in South Korea, and back in London he formed a project to explore the possibility of a confederation of India, Pakistan, Bangladesh, Sri Lanka and Nepal.

In 2012 he helped to create the World Peace and Prosperity Foundation, recognising those who had given service to humanity with a popular annual awards dinner at the House of Lords. He received two honorary doctorates (one for humanities and the other for literature), several awards and the freedom of the City of London.

Prince Mohsin was born in 1930 in Khana Bagh palace in Hyderabad, Deccan, India and was descended from the Nizams, the rulers of Hyderabad. Brought up in the family's schools, where one of his teachers was the Arab-Indian poet Nawab Sir Nizamat Jung Bahadur, he was taught in the Sufi tradition in which worldly things are immaterial. To the end of his days he never learnt to drive, did not own a car and always rented the properties he lived in.

The violence of partition in Hyderabad horrified him, and while his siblings emigrated to the US, he travelled to Karachi and from there flew to Britain. Finding accommodation with a relative in East Finchley, he later rented in west and central London, including in Pont Street and Wilton Street, and ended up in Maida Vale, northwest London. He married a Swiss science lecturer, who survives him, and they have a son.

Mohsin was an elegant dresser, who had his three-piece suits tailor-made at Harrods. He was usually in a dark blue sherwani, with a colourful silk handkerchief in his breast pocket. He was energetic to the end; his last contribution was at an international conference held at Drapers' Hall in May 2022, where he gave a speech encouraging strategic, economic and geopolitical partnerships by promoting trade and investment in Africa and Asia.

# New regime in Afghanistan

Published in *TheNews*, London, August 21, 2021

As the invasion of Afghanistan was a stupendous war crime based on a deception – no Afghan was responsible for the September 11, 2001 incident – the United States and NATO countries are morally obliged to compensate for a million Afghan deaths, displaced persons, and considerable infrastructure in ruin.

There was no way the country could be liberated from the invaders, so the Taliban had agreed to a long-term strategy to get rid of the US and NATO armies even before the series of Doha conferences in Qatar took place last year.

The Taliban stayed ahead of the game during the negotiations with President Donald Trump's negotiating team, and their leaders outwitted the seasoned American politicians and senior advisers of the US administration at all levels. The Taliban's forward momentum has never been stronger.

The inspired and reinvigorated future generations will be the guardian of the newly named Islamic Emirate of Afghanistan. The world has to learn the name of the country and accept the reality of a new regime.

The West must have learnt a lesson after a desperate and hurried withdrawal and humiliating defeat.

The US may now listen to the best advice of refraining from such misadventures in the future in the interest of regional and international peace.

Afghanistan needs to be left alone. Let Afghans themselves take care of their own country's education, defence, economy and foreign policy.

It would seem futile shedding crocodile tears over Afghan 'women's education' and condemning the Taliban for fighting and liberating their country from foreign invaders after 20 years of brutal occupation and a spree of killing innocent civilians and establishing torture camps in Bagram.

Afghans have repeatedly stated that they are capable of running their own country, safeguarding the honour and safety of their women, children, men, young and old, the whole lot, and preserve their Islamic culture without subversive intervention from imperialistic warmongers.

These Afghan nationalists, one has to digest quickly, are the children of Mujahideen who bravely fought the Soviet Union's well-equipped military power and dragged it out of their fatherland during the eighties.

The then US President Ronald Reagan and the British prime minister were very fond of calling them Mujahideen and never called them terrorists.

In many of his speeches, Reagan declared that Islam was in danger and the brave Mujahideen were fighting to save it. If it was true then, never mind the hypocrisy, why is it not true now?

Can an American president or a British prime minister make such a statement today?

The present Mujahideen or Taliban, with exactly the same inherited mind-set, fundamentally Islamic in nature, are an offshoot of the same patrimony and are proud indigenous people of Afghanistan. Their track record suggests they have comprehensively defeated the two superpowers by dint of their bravery, faith, determination and resolve.

During their previous stint, the Taliban had made it abundantly clear in 1998 that there was no point for the decadent West to shed crocodile tears over women's education and freedom of speech. Instead, they countered their critics by saying to go and care for their own women who daily suffer in silence from domestic violence, rapes and sexual offences in their countries. They claimed the rape cases in the West were the highest and out of control.

Those random opinions, ideas and thoughts were expressed and documented 23 years ago and are kept alive today with more vigour. The Taliban's interpretation of the interpreters who worked for their foreign masters is "traitors".

Afghanistan is a diverse country with several factions and faiths like any other country on the planet. All Afghans culturally follow a strong belief that an attack on their country is a crusade against Islam, and nothing to do with nation-building as the US/UK often claim.

That belief adequately explains why the whole country was taken over in a matter of days without much resistance from the well-equipped, Western-trained army.

Both the Republican president Donald Trump and the Democrat Joe Biden belatedly realised that there was no military solution in Afghanistan even if the country remained occupied for another 20 years. The outcome would have been the same as now.

Using the divide and rule tactics, a tried and tested tool, the occupation forces bought hundreds of Afghans through financial inducement and other amoral means of bribery. Huge amount of money laundering which should have been a criminal offence did not apply here by the occupying forces.

Money, as the old cliché goes, is the root of all evils, and this proved true to form. Almighty dollars flowed like a river. Both the civil service and the army were corrupted by the alliance of 42 hostile nations who converted the country into a lawless land for 20 destructive years.

Those who helped the international coalition and became very rich overnight, many millionaires among them, now wanted to leave the homeland.

Ex-president Ashraf Ghani also fled with allegedly a bagful of dollars. His country's ambassador to Tajikistan disclosed that he had stolen 169 million dollars from the public funds, while the Russians alleged he had left in a helicopter with a stash of cash.

Mr Ghani, who is now in the United Arab Emirates, denied claims he fled the country with millions of dollars of state money. In a video he says: "I was forced to leave Afghanistan with one set of traditional clothes, a vest and the sandals I was wearing".

The word Taliban is a misnomer. The meaning of this word is simply "students". The West uses this word in a highly politicised terms as a terrorist group. The Taliban or Mujahideen regard themselves as freedom fighters and liberators of their homeland. Any country militarily occupied by aliens will act the same way.

Under the gaze of the victorious government in Kabul, television screens would be without the West's cultural encroachment. Any influence which may be likely to corrupt an impressionable youth will be excluded.

# A divided opinion on Assange

Published in *TheNews*, London, May 1, 2021

Hero or villain – this might give a clue as to how the world opinion is divided about the WikiLeaks founder/editor Julian Assange, who used digital technology to unleash an information war against governments, corporations and scandalous practices of the powerful elite.

A recent television documentary was a detailed chronicle of Assange's wretched existence for the past eleven years. Watching the film, one can sense that the official US line is still prosecuting him in the United States. The popular opinion indicates that he is neither a spy nor did he break any US laws. He is widely recognised as a courageous journalist who worked for the protection of human rights.

In quite a number of Zoom webinars, the hosts and the audience discussed and debated extensively his past, and widely shared the view that he is a researcher who diligently reported, explained and educated the voiceless public who are unable to hold the authorities to account for their cronyism and corruption.

The publication of those public interest files were carried in various leading newspapers, but he is scapegoated and blamed for all the wrong doings.

What irks the US side is that the WikiLeaks publisher exposed the war crimes committed in Iraq and Afghanistan. The relevant videos rapidly went viral.

The world would have never known about tortures in Guantanamo Bay detention centre, the Panama Papers, and secret prisons, without the disclosure by the WikiLeaks documents.

The extradition of Assange to the United States had been rejected by a judge at London's Central Criminal Court on January 7, who decided that Assange should not be extradited because of his fragile health. He faces 175 years of imprisonment for alleged espionage, if convicted.

This case, which has profoundly dangerous implications not only for Assange but also for the freedom of the press, would put other journalists at risk too, allowing the governments to decide what gets published around the world.

Assange's legal team believes the US appeal may not succeed in the higher court in view of the already blocked extradition. There is a possibility, then, that the Biden administration may decide to abandon the proceedings altogether.

Nothing much is known at the moment about the pending appeal. Scores of petitions, letters and emails have been sent to the US president.

The struggle to save Assange from extinction continues. Human rights activists around the world have been keeping up the pressure and spreading awareness of how press freedom in the twenty-first century is under attack.

Mr Jameel Jaffer, Director of the Knight First Amendment Institute at Columbia University, said: "There is near-universal agreement among human rights, civil liberties, and press freedom organisations that the case against Julian Assange poses a major threat to press freedom, not just here in the United States but around the world. The Justice Department should drop the appeal and dismiss the indictment".

The Press Freedom Group also urges President Biden to free Assange, and requests to dismiss the underlying indictment and undo Trump's war on journalism.

# A reminiscence of my childhood

Published in *TheNews*, London, January 24, 2021

Round about this time, in the early 1950s, I was learning to ride a bicycle in this area with much difficulty. I remember a cousin of mine taunted me:

"You will not learn to ride a cycle like this. Don't keep looking at the handle and don't hold it tight as if your life depends on it, look upwards and far ahead." I followed the advice.

After repeated attempts, I eventually mastered the 'art' and felt very proud. From then on, leafy Mall Road (renamed Sharah-e-Quaid-Azam) became like a village lane for me sans traffic.

I vividly remember the petrol filling station, motor car show rooms; a little further down, there used to be the well-known large tea house called the Lords, frequented by generations of journalists and politicians, but now closed. Because of the vicinity of many newspaper offices, the Lords tea house always seemed buzzing with people, chirping like birds.

Lahore in 1950: This photograph reminds me of my childhood

Farthest down the series of blocks, where you see a globe-like structure, these were the offices of Urdu *Daily Nawai-Waqt* newspaper. These offices are now shifted at the back of the building.

On the opposite side of the road, where the shopping plaza is now situated, there was the world-famous English newspaper, *Civil and Military Gazette*, once edited by Rudyard Kipling. I cut my teeth there briefly while still a young student at Dayal Singh College, before arriving in this country decades ago, yet I feel I came here yesterday.

One cannot bring back one's childhood; only a distant memory remains of carefree bygone days and a feeling of how life rapidly slips away from your grasp. It's yesterday once more; nostalgia returned all over me all of a sudden.

My younger brother Aizaz Ali Shah, former editor of *Sportslight*, sent me the above picture, Lahore in 1950, a few days ago, to uproot me, perhaps!

*My dear and respected Nisar Ali Shah Saheb,*

*I loved your article. I myself was a BSc student at Islamia College, Civil Lines, in the years 1958-1960 in Lahore and rode on a bicycle. I used to live very near to Lahore Railway Station. Those were great and good carefree days.*

*Lots and lots of prayers for you and your good family.*
*Engr. Dr Maqbool Ahmad Siddiqui*

# Guantanamo Prison's future

Published in *TheNews*, London, December 7, 2020

When President-elect Joseph Biden takes over power next month, he will inherit a number of domestic and international issues left over by his predecessor. Will he remember the Guantanamo Bay detention camp amid all that is trending in the world?

In his own country, the coronavirus is causing widespread devastation; more than quarter of a million people have already lost their lives, partly because of mismanagement of the whole situation by the previous regime. The brutal murder of George Floyd is still fresh in the minds of people, and this is not going to go away. Black Lives Matter has made it quite clear that the issue of racial discrimination in the United States remains at the top of the agenda. The new president will face a rising unemployment crisis which is currently 3.7 per cent.

Before he gets down to tackle the above problems, Biden will soon be petitioned, emailed, and lobbied by human rights organisations and individual campaigners for closing the notorious detention centre, which was established in 2001 by the George W. Bush administration at Guantanamo Bay naval base in Cuba to lock up 'terrorism' suspects.

It must be understood that most suspects were not captured on the battlefield; the US forces arrested no more than four percent of the detainees. Instead, US officials dropped leaflets over Afghanistan and Pakistan offering sizeable bounties for al-Qaeda fighters, the ones who were once regarded by the US as Mujahideen when they fought against the Soviet Union.

Many people fell for it and grabbed this rare financial inducement, and sold them for bounties to the United States. Former secretary of state Donald Rumsfeld, during the Bush era, invented a ridiculous phrase 'enemy combatants' for those suspects and deprived them of proving their innocence in the US courts. Instead, they were kept away on a foreign land in Cuba – a place outside the law – raising the possibility that most of the detainees were innocent and unlawfully imprisoned. The whole project is costing the American taxpayers millions of dollars a week.

During the past four years, the world media had been captivated by the antics of Trump and forgot or ignored the existence of Guantanamo, a location where the victims of torture, never charged or tried, are still awaiting justice and longing for freedom from their small cages to rejoin their families.

Abdul Latif Nasser, detainee 244, was promised his freedom by one administration, and then the next one decided to keep him locked up forever. The 40 prisoners who remain at Guantanamo are ageing and their health is increasingly deteriorating, making them particularly vulnerable to the current virus. Saifullah Paracha is 72 years old, has had two heart attacks, and suffers from coronary artery disease. There are numerous other such episodes.

Ex-president Barack Obama promised to shut down this place before he won the election. He is said to have tried, though not vigorously, in his first term of office, but failed in the face of Congress's objection and did not fulfil his promise. Biden was vice-president under Obama, therefore, he knows all about it. Now he will have full power, he can restore the tarnished reputation of his country by doing the right thing, and close down this mega prison and go down in history as a decent, thinking, president. This high-cost prison is an indefinite detention centre, a symbol of injustice, which has gained global notoriety for abuse and lawlessness where illegally held prisoners are denied the basic necessities. The United States must respect human rights and abide by the international laws.

# Julian Assange on suicide watch

Published in *TheNews*, London, August 12, 2020

The WikiLeaks founder/journalist Julian Assange's extradition trial is on September 7 in London.

He will defend his innocence of all accusations levelled against him by the United States.

Reportedly, he is fighting a living death in Belmarsh prison, east London, where, according to his lawyers, he is illegally held.

After appearing several times in various courts, he is denied bail and remains in his cell 23 hours a day and not receiving the medical care he desperately needs. He is suffering from a long-term lung condition.

If he is extradited to the US, he faces rest of his life in jail in the horrific conditions of a notorious US super max prison under special administrative measures.

The name of Julian Assange is becoming familiar. On November 22, 2019, a group of 60 doctors had written to the UK home secretary to express their serious concerns about the physical and mental health of Assange.

Mr Tim Dawson, former president of the National Union of Journalists said: "If Julian is sent from here to start a prison sentence in the US, then no journalist is safe. Unless journalists wake up to this threat and focus on the grievous harm that his successful prosecution represents, the ability of any of us to report will be seriously damaged".

On November 28, 2019, a strong Committee to Defend Assange, comprising human rights lawyers, academic researchers, prominent journalists and activists organised a heavily attended public meeting in St Pancras Church Hall, London, to debate the ways and means with which to legally make it possible for Assange's release. He has been in and out of prison for the past 10 years, completely cut off from the outside world.

He had been held for nine days in London's primeval wing of Wandsworth prison in solitary confinement. He was holed up in one small room in Ecuador Embassy for seven years. Having suffered mental torture for a long period of time, he is now on a suicide watch.

His admirers argue that he has done his time, even though he has done nothing wrong, so he should be released and given a safe passage to his homeland.

He was originally accused of disclosing classified diplomatic files, but now under President Donald Trump, the US administration has added a further 17 spurious indictments against him of espionage. He has repeatedly denied those allegations and says: "One of the best ways to achieve justice is to expose injustice".

Assange is not an American citizen and he was not working in the United States. The US government has no jurisdiction over him. If he is extradited, he faces ending his life in prison for exposing war crimes of the US and NATO armed forces in Iraq and Afghanistan. This is the crux of the matter. His supporters say that he is being accused not because he has done anything wrong but because of what he has done right.

The information made available by WikiLeaks has enabled people in most countries to hold powerful politicians to account.

The public around the world is beginning to understand what is really involved. It is not the man but the politics behind it.

Human rights activists argue that had he reported on China, Iran, and North Korea, the traditional rivals of the West's economic/political policies, no criminal allegations would have been brought against him. Moreover, the US would have hailed him as a hero, fighting for freedom of speech and human rights issues.

The whole idea of freedom of speech and holding the corrupt politicians to account are at stake. Disclosing information to the public should never be equated with espionage.

If journalists such as Assange are eliminated by hooks or by crooks, and would-be whistleblowers are threatened and intimidated, then what would be the meaning of investigative journalism?

The internationally renowned Australian journalist and film maker John Pilger met him in Belmarsh on November 28, the same day as the public meeting was held. In his speech the same evening, he reported, among other things, that Assange did not look a normal human being; exposing him for several years to severe forms of degrading treatment must have had a punishingly dehumanising effect on him.

The United Nations Special Rapporteur on Torture, Professor Nils Melzer, identified more than 50 serious irregularities with the case and has called for investigation.

The learned professor further elaborated that he had visited Assange in prison last year, along with two doctors, and then saw "all the symptoms of progressively severe forms of cruel, inhumane and degrading treatment, the cumulative effects of which can only be described as psychological torture". He expressed alarm, saying his life is now at risk.

Assange's character assassination and smearing of him by the mainstream media has been thorough, in line with the British and American policy objectives which aim at discouraging whistleblowers now or in the future, but making an example of him and punishing him hard may not serve the intended purpose.

Many people are reluctant to speak out about his persecution. The two most dedicated supporters, Craig Murray, the former British ambassador, and journalist John Pilger, have relentlessly protested over many years against his incarceration.

His well-wishers suggest that he should be nominated Nobel Peace Laureate for his services to journalism and freedom of speech.

He is an Australian citizen and holds an Australian passport. He could be transferred safely to his mother country and let Australia look after its own, but no extradition.

He has a wife and two children despairingly waiting for his release.

After his visit to Belmarsh prison on October 21, last year, Craig Murray wrote: "Everybody in that court yesterday saw that one of the greatest journalists and most important dissident of our times is being tortured to death by the state, before our eyes".

# Looking above petty Covid-19 squabbles

Published in *TheNews*, London, April 23, 2020

The entire world is grappling with pandemic war, trying to fight it out without the necessary tools. It was apparently patented in 2007 in the United States. This invisible killer, indiscriminate and uncontrollable in nature, threatens every individual, irrespective of race, colour, creed or religion. It cannot be connected to or with anything. It is just coronawireless, colourless, and callous.

China, where this virus first emerged, has successfully quelled the outbreak, lifted the lockdown from Wuhan City and then remarkably helped more than 90 countries, including Britain and Spain. Italy has expressed gratitude to China for lending a helping hand. Europe and the United States, with the highest death tolls, are still struggling with this undeclared war.

China has earned admiration for its discipline and competence the world over, while the US President Donald Trump, in his usual uncertain and devious way, politicised the issue as the 'Chinese virus' for his own forthcoming electioneering purposes. He didn't take the virus seriously at first, thinking that this will affect the country where it originated or some other countries, but not the US. He had no choice but to request his economic rival to supply millions of face masks and other medical equipment.

It is worth noting the World Health Organisation has warned that the 'virus should not be linked with any specific country or region', and praised China for its transparency. The world will need China's experience and contribution in fighting this deadly menace now and in the future.

This global crisis is not going to be over soon or easily. The blame game, started prematurely, will continue in earnest after the event. It is likely to be one-sided because some of the Western politicians, led by the US and its allies, would be ganging up on, and stigmatising, China.

The cause of the virus is still unclear and needs exploring further. Initially, we were told about the fish and live animal market in Wuhan city which may have caused the problem. Different camps are making a myriad of opposing claims about the origin. China blames the United States, and vice versa.

However, the global powers should realise that the entire planet stands on the same pedestal against this invisible enemy. This single rickety platform, on which the entirety of mankind has been forced to huddle on, provides a brilliant chance of uniting the nations of the world as one single unit, a task the United Nations has thus far failed to execute effectively.

All nations in the East and in the West together are busily battling to find an effective solution. After achieving the victory together, the pre-coronavirus problems will still remain to be tackled.

To enumerate them here briefly, the complete withdrawal of the US and NATO soldiers from Afghanistan; human rights of Palestinians and lifting the blockade of Gaza; Apartheid Israel's illegal settlements and demolition of Palestinian houses; atrocities in Occupied Kashmir, a flash point if ever there was one, where the struggle for freedom has been raging with greater intensity for more than 70 years; a decade long strife in Syria requires immediate attention; and last but by no means least, defeating racism, wherever it rears its ugly head.

Thousands of starving women, children and refugees, weakened by suffering from poverty, inequity, corruption and cruelty, will emerge much worse as a consequence of this cruel pandemic.

Once this crisis is over, the world will not be the same again; massive economic and political disruption will take place. People who lost their jobs, homes and livelihood, for no fault of their own, will find it difficult to rebuild their lives after the lockdowns are lifted and the planet gains its freedom.

An economic equilibrium and equitable distribution of global wealth to help the impoverished nations should be on the agenda, and assume urgency in order to attain any semblance of peace and prosperity on this shrinking globe.

Can coronavirus fortuitously unite the whole of humanity while all other institutions have dismally failed?

# India's army on the rampage

Published in *TheNews*, London, March 4, 2020

The siege of Kashmir is now more than seven months old and no one knows when it will be over. The earlier information had revealed in audio and video recordings that the Indian army was on the rampage. This is not new. Ever since the Narendra Modi government came to power, it has enacted a series of measures in order to make the country into an exclusively Hindu state. It has increased the number of soldiers and armed gangs of RSS volunteers permanently stationed in occupied Kashmir. This is new.

The army is encouraged to do whatever it likes in this disputed area. Emboldened, it has increased its atrocious crimes knowing well that the perpetrators would not be prosecuted. Kashmiris have already endured tortures, kidnappings, rapes and massacres for the past 72 years. No soldiers have ever been taken to court for their crimes.

Some physical changes may have taken place in the Valley under continued lockdown and curfew. No journalists, print or broadcast, are allowed into Kashmir to investigate the real effects on the population.

The entirety of occupied Kashmir today is described as a torture camp where people are not permitted to think for themselves and to decide what they wish to do with their lives.

The international community is aware of what is happening behind the scenes, but no one does anything practical beyond expressing "shock and horror". American and European countries, which pride themselves as the champions of human rights and democratic values, are disturbingly silent, and dare not warn India about the long term consequences of the reign of terror in this territory. An accidental war is likely to lead to nuclear confrontation.

The fallout will be felt beyond the Pakistan-India subcontinent, and the whole world would suffer in one way or the other. In the event of such an unpredictable occurrence we do not know what the world would look like. It is for this reason that the Kashmir dispute needs to be resolved as quickly as possible.

The fascist government of Modi, Indian media, the police and the army are working hand-in-hand to attain the Hindutva objective. Occupied Kashmir, under indefinite curfew since August 5, 2019, remains the largest jail on the planet. Internet and mobile phones remain closed. A complete communication blackout is in place. How are the people coping with the lack of food and medicine? Do the most vulnerable people have the stamina to survive?

In this day and age of globalisation, where manpower, financial resources, technology and mixed cultures of all religions are commonly shared and accepted, how can India refuse to face this reality and survive with a Hindus only ideology?

Cross-cultural society is regarded as an enormous asset for any modern country, but the "India for Hindus only" ideology is taking India thousands of years back. Millions of people from the Muslim minority are in danger of being ethnically cleansed by Hindutva design. It will be naïve to keep hoping that United Nations resolutions on Kashmir about a referendum will be implemented by India.

Successive Indian governments have rejected the offer to talk about the future of Kashmir, a majority Muslim area, for centuries. In all other cases of accession in 1947, India had accepted the religion of the majority of the people and the geographical contiguity of the state as the criteria for accession. According to those principles, Kashmir belonged to Pakistan. The future of Kashmir was not conclusively decided then.

Governor-General Lord Mountbatten wrote to the Maharaja at that time as follows:

> "Consistently with their policy that in the case of any state where the issue of accession has been the subject of dispute, the question of accession should be decided in accordance with the wishes of the people of the state. It is my Government's wish that as soon as law and order have been restored in Kashmir and her soil cleared of the invader, the question of the State's accession should be settled by a reference to the people."

The clearly defined principles of accession at the time of Partition, agreed by both India and Pakistan, and particularly the above historical statement, leave no doubt in anybody's mind as to how this dispute should be settled.

India keeps blinding the world by saying that Kashmir is an internal issue, which is wrong and a blatant lie.

# Kashmir is bleeding

Published in *TheNews*, London, February 10, 2020

Pakistan has repeatedly warned the international community that peace and stability in south Asia is threatened by the irresponsible actions of the Narendra Modi regime in India, its state-terrorism in occupied Jammu and Kashmir, and war mongering threats against Pakistan.

Indian soldiers are killing civilians on both sides of the Line of Control. This line is an artificial border between Pakistan and India. It was agreed to stop cross-border firings. There have been more than 2,000 ceasefire violations by Indian troops in the current year.

Although Pakistani forces have responded by targeting the Indian military posts, this cyclical routine goes on every day of the week.

Turkish President Recep Tayyip Erdogan described the Kashmir dispute as a "burning issue" in his speech to the United Nations General Assembly's 75th session last Tuesday, September 22, 2020.

The Indian army is committing gross human rights abuses and the world is not reacting to these continued atrocities.

Prime Minister Modi's fascist regime has transformed India into a truly racist country, inflicted a great number of deaths, and is causing fear among religious minorities in Delhi and elsewhere.

Politicians in Pakistan keep hoping that United Nations resolutions on Kashmir about a referendum will be honoured by India. Pakistan needs to think afresh and develop a new defence strategy about the speedy resolution of the problem, before it is too late and war does become a reality in the long run.

It needs to make it clear whether Kashmir is a territorial dispute or a religious one, or both. So, if the demography is changed and population ratio is altered by importing non-Muslims into Kashmir, Pakistan still has a legitimate claim of its contiguous territory. Without Jammu and Kashmir Pakistan will be greatly weakened in defence in the event of war with India.

India makes claims of being a democratic country, but the evidence is quite the opposite, and that evidence can be seen in the world's largest open prison on this planet, where India has usurped all democratic rights of its majority Muslim population and deprived them of medicines, food and other necessities of life, including cutting off communication with the outside world.

More than a year's curfew, imposed on August 5, 2019, plus coronavirus restrictions, must have done great damage to the physical, psychological and mental health of the Kashmiris.

What democracy in the world would deploy 800,000 fully armed soldiers to subdue, intimidate, arrest and torture its own people in their homes?

Would England, for instance, send a large occupying army to subdue the Scots or the Welsh if there is an independence movement, and deprive them of food, medicines and cut off their communication network? Simply not.

Time and time again it has been proven beyond doubt that Indian 'democracy' is a fraud. India has been misleading the world by saying that the territorial conflict with Pakistan is an internal matter. If so, why are the outside observers and media personnel not allowed into Kashmir to investigate the real situation?

Pakistan's moral support at diplomatic, political and humanitarian levels are not enough to resolve this menacing dispute. Something more tangible, practical and material rather than verbal is required now.

The United Nations Security Council, whose responsibility is the security of the oppressed people, has dismally failed in its duty to implement its own resolutions on this burning issue.

Crucially, the US has always supported dictatorships in Asia, Africa and Latin America because it is easy to handle its clients with less effort. In Narendra Modi, the West has fortuitously discovered an elected dictator who can get away with whatever he likes with the tacit support of the US, UK, EU and Apartheid-Israel. India is in good company.

The ongoing daily killings in occupied Jammu and Kashmir are reminiscent of the killing fields of Cambodia and Vietnam in the seventies, and of chillingly similar Srebrenica massacres in Bosnia Herzegovina between 1992 to 1995.

Atal Bihari Vajpayee, the late Indian prime minister, had once said at the height of tensions on the borders of the two countries that one billion Hindus are the second line of defence for the Indian army in the event of war with Pakistan.

Pakistan, on the other hand, cannot boast that one billion Muslims are behind the Pakistani army in the event of war with India.

Apart from Turkey, Malaysia and a few African countries which have condemned the Indian brutalisation of Kashmiris, Arab countries' response has been lukewarm for their co-religionists in the occupied Valley. The international community is focused only on the Covid-19 pandemic.

India is in the hands of extremist Hindu racists who love to promote hate against their fellow citizens. Muslims and other minorities are scared.

The Indian media faithfully toe the official line on Kashmir and have lost objectivity, and that is also part of the problem. This will lead to destruction and India will eventually suffer. It has already lost a secular status while its trigger-happy soldiers are committing war crimes and crimes against humanity.

Hindutva ideology of hate and racism has no place in the twenty-first century. Every developed country in the world today is multi-ethnic, multi-religious and multi-cultural, but the Indian politicians tend to go against the norm. Families of Kashmiri leaders who have been imprisoned indefinitely are demanding the release of their husbands, sisters and brothers. If justice is of any moral value today, a dialogue for a peaceful solution must start. Both Pakistan and India cannot afford a war, let alone nuclear warfare.

# Free Julian Assange campaign

Published in *TheNews*, London, December 23, 2019

In April, I wrote a column on this page about the global campaign to save journalist Julian Assange from being extradited to the United States. Since then, the campaign has intensified.

In early November, the International Federation of Journalists (IFJ), the world's largest organisation of journalists, pledged its support to the campaign at a meeting in the European Parliament in Brussels. The event heard testimonies and expert statements on the case, which speakers, including IFJ General Secretary Anthony Bellanger, said could have serious implications for the rights of journalists.

In his speech, Bellanger said: "The IFJ considers Julian's arrest an attack on press freedom, international law, and the right of asylum, only because he revealed the truth. The dissemination of information of public interest cannot be considered a crime".

On November 28, a strong Committee to Defend Julian Assange, comprising human rights lawyers, academic researchers, prominent journalists and human rights activists, organised a heavily attended public meeting in a church hall to discuss and debate the ways and means with which to legally make it possible for Julian's release from the maximum security Belmarsh prison in east London.

Assange has been in and out of prison for the past 10 years. He has suffered psychological torture, and now he is on a suicide watch. The WikiLeaks director is accused of disclosing diplomatic files. The United States has levelled a further 17 spurious indictments against him of espionage. He has repeatedly denied these allegations and says: "One of the best ways to achieve justice is to expose injustice".

His supporters claim that he is being charged not because he has done anything wrong, but because of what he has done right. Assange is not an American citizen and he was not working in the United States. The US government has no jurisdiction over him. If he is extradited, he faces 175 years in prison and torture for exposing war crimes of the US and NATO armed forces in Iraq and Afghanistan.

The information made available by WikiLeaks has enabled people in many countries to hold the powerful elite to account. The public around the world is only now beginning to understand what is really involved. It is not the person but the politics behind it. The whole idea of freedom of speech and holding the corrupt politicians to account is at stake. If journalists such as Assange are forced to be eliminated by hooks or by crooks, and any would-be whistleblowers are discouraged and intimidated, then what would be the meaning of investigative journalism?

The internationally renowned Australian journalist and film maker John Pilger met him in prison on November 28, the same day as the public meeting was held, and reported in the evening that Assange did not look normal.

A strong media propaganda demonising him and exposing him for several years to severe forms of degrading treatment must have had a punishingly dehumanising effect on him.

Assange has never been charged with any offence relating to events in Sweden. The United Nations Special Rapporteur on Torture, Professor Nils Melzer, identified more than 50 serious irregularities with the case and has called for investigation in Sweden and in the US. He said that he had visited him in prison on May 31 along with two doctors, and then saw "all the symptoms of progressively severe forms of cruel, inhumane and degrading treatment, the cumulative effects of which can only be described as psychological torture".

He expressed alarm, saying his life is now at risk. Julian's character assassination and smearing him by the mainstream media has been thorough, coinciding with the British and American foreign policy aims without the presence of whistleblowers now or in the future. Most people are afraid or reluctant to speak out about his treatment, but the two most dedicated supporters, among others, Craig Murray, the former British ambassador, and John Pilger, have relentlessly protested over many years against Assange's illegal incarceration.

# World Peace and Prosperity awards ceremony

Published in *TheNews*, London, November 10, 2019

The World Peace and Prosperity Foundation (WPPF) held an awards ceremony in the House of Lords for acknowledging exceptional services to humanity.

At the ripe age of 90, Prince Mohsin Ali Khan, an enthusiastic campaigner for holding interfaith seminars, and Lady Frances Stanton, former mayor of Hammersmith and Fulham, both organise every year this and other such events at a high level of standard and scrutiny.

On this occasion, the guests included international peace makers and like-minded doctors, lawyers, politicians, scientists and performers in the art and film industries.

Many travel every year from overseas, specifically for this annual dinner. Prince Ulrik Greve of Rosenborg of Denmark said he comes to London only for this clubby event. Several speakers spoke about the disequilibrium of world resources, and emphasised that there cannot be peace in the world without prosperity, and no prosperity can be achieved without peace. After the reception and dinner, there was a lively award ceremony to honour those who have spent their lifetime serving humanity and dedicated their careers to try to bring about change through humanitarian causes.

Among those who qualified for this coveted award was Sarah Wade, founder of charity Humanitas, who lived in Romania for 13 years and then took her charity to eastern Europe, Africa and Asia, delivering healthcare, education and providing medical aid to children of families in refugee camps.

Also present was Aina Khan OBE, an international lawyer and expert in Islamic and Asian law, who founded the Register Our Marriage law reform campaign and helped families to cope with the

Prince Mohsin Ali Khan addressing the audience

aftermath of unregistered marriages in Britain which leave them with no legal rights. The Government asked her to spread awareness of this "ticking time bomb".

Lord Shinkwin has used his position to champion disability equality issues in the House of Lords as well as in the media. He spent most of his career in the charity sector, such as Cancer Research UK and bereaved armed forces families. He was chosen for his distinct services and his charitable heart.

Caroline de Guitaut, a distinguished art historian and curator, was awarded for her long service to the arts and culture. She says that "art always rises above politics".

Two prime ministers of countries thousands of kilometres apart were recognised as the peace makers and respected world leaders in this field. Although they were not physically present when their names were announced, there was a rapturous applause and clapping.

The prime minister of Pakistan was honoured for preventing serious upheaval in challenging circumstances. He opened the Kartarpur Corridor, enabling people to enter without visa to visit the Sikh holy places in Pakistan. Prince Mohsin Ali Khan remarked that he hopes that Imran Khan shares his vision of forming a Common Market of regional countries such as Pakistan, India, Bangladesh, Sri Lanka and Nepal. The second prime minister to be honoured was Jacinda Ardern of New Zealand for her remarkable leadership ability.

# Global campaign gearing up for Julian Assange's freedom

Published in *TheNews*, London, July 26, 2019

A global campaign to prevent Julian Assange's likely extradition to the US is shaping up. In Ecuador, a five-day general strike raised the demand for the freedom of the founder of WikiLeaks.

The protesters demonstrated their solidarity with the stand that Assange has taken in his fight for his release. He was unceremoniously dragged out of the Ecuadorean Embassy in London in April, and taken to the Westminster Magistrates Court and then straight to Belmarsh high security prison, where he stays until his fate is decided by the British authorities.

This is the first major action in South America on behalf of Assange which shows the potential that exists for building a powerful movement by the masses around the world. Recently, in Melbourne, Australia, a rally was held in the city centre which strongly urged the Australian government to protect its citizen and to grant him safe passage back to his family in Australia.

In London, a campaign to defend Assange was also organised. A strong response was won from the transport workers at Tottenham bus depot. Further campaigns at other bus depots are scheduled over the next few weeks.

The founder of WikiLeaks is accused of raping two Swedish women. He could be sent there for trial. However, the Swedish prosecutors dropped the allegations in 2017, presumably because of weak evidence.

Assange insists that he is a victim of a smear campaign which is, to a high degree, politically motivated. He says: "I don't like to see the word rape next to my name; I have never had a sexual relationship with anyone without consent".

It is clear, though, whatever happens next, the United States would not give up on Assange easily. That is why the ordinary workers of the world are uniting when the journalists of the world are not. What does this tell us about modern day journalism?

Just to remind you, he was electronically tagged in a Norfolk mansion of his friend, where he lived under a strict curfew regime for almost a year. He had been held for nine days in London's ancient Victorian wing of Wandsworth prison in solitary confinement.

The lawyers who defended him in various courts over the past few years say that he is vilified by biased politicians for publishing classified files and videos related to war crimes of the US in Iraq and Afghanistan, and disclosing torture camps the US had been operating in many countries.

He has many trustworthy friends in Britain. His supporters believe that if he had focused on Iran, North Korea or China, no conspiratorial criminal allegation would have been brought against him by Sweden or any other country, and moreover, the US would have hailed him as a hero, fighting for freedom of speech and campaigning for fundamental human rights issues. He is portrayed as a dangerous whistleblower by his enemies on both sides of the Atlantic, but a highly respected and courageous editor-in-chief of WikiLeaks by his admirers.

Labour Party leader Jeremy Corbyn has warned that if Assange is extradited, he will not be treated justly, and will end up in jail for life. He said the British government should not place him in such an obvious danger.

John Pilger, the Australian journalist, film maker and author of many books about international current affairs on human rights issues, has urged that Corbyn should do more to resist Assange's extradition to America.

He is an Australian citizen and holds an Australian passport. He could be transferred to his mother country. The support and sympathy for Assange is mainly derived from the fact that he has suffered enough for the past decade. He has committed no crime in the United States. He has had to attend all sorts of court hearings in the United Kingdom, and has been subjected to jail sentences in high security prisons.

He was holed up in one small room in the Ecuadorean Embassy for seven years. His admirers argue that he has done his time even though he has done nothing wrong, and he should be released and given a safe passage to his homeland.

His well-wishers say that Assange should be nominated as a Nobel Peace Laureate for his human rights credentials and holding the powerful elite to account.

# How long would the Kashmir dispute last?

Published in *The News*, London, February 20, 2019

How long would the Kashmir dispute last is a question in the mind of millions. Kashmir is the longest running territorial dispute in the world, and the most dangerous flashpoint on the planet if it is not resolved by peaceful means.

Pakistan and India are laced with lethal nuclear arsenals; if used in anger or in an imminent defeat in a conventional war, there would be no trace of India, Pakistan and Kashmir, and other countries would also suffer.

The border killings, nevertheless, have continued with increasing intensity ever since the partition of India. More than half a million Indian soldiers are deployed around Kashmir, many of whom are guilty of torturing, burning, kidnapping, gang raping and brutalising the population of innocent Kashmiris.

The culprits are known to the Indian army, to the government, and the police, but the perpetrators are never caught and brought to justice. The hapless Kashmiris are increasingly determined to keep fighting an Indian colonial rule and demanding independence, just as India demanded independence from Britain.

Indian soldiers killed 49 Kashmiris and wounded more than 5,000 in the riots which followed the murder of Burhan Wani, a Kashmiri freedom fighter on July 8, 2016.

Since then, scores of women and children have been blinded by pellet gun wounds in demonstrations against the oppressive police forces, using all manner of military means. Yet, the Indian army chief had threatened to retaliate against Pakistan over the killing of a border guard and three policemen in Indian-occupied Kashmir last year. Prime Minister Imran Khan was quick to reply by saying the Pakistani nation would not tolerate any act of aggression. No one should misconstrue Pakistan's desire for peace as weakness. Pakistan would respond befitting a proud nation, he had warned. In the wake of the suicide attack on a military convoy on the Srinagar-Jammu highway, where 44 Indian troops died, Indian Prime Minister Narendra Modi threatened a crushing response against Pakistan. He believes that this attack was organised by Pakistan, which it denies.

So, incidents and dialogues like this, sometimes in sorrow but mostly in anger, do nothing to encourage the likelihood of peace in the region. Until this perennial problem is resolved, warmongering gestures could develop into a full scale war through an error of judgement by either side.

An unintended escalation or miscalculation about each other's intentions may lead to a pre-emptive strike and plunge the subcontinent into total destruction. No one would be a clear winner if a conventional flare-up broke out accidentally.

India is under the obligation of implementing the United Nations resolutions which stipulate that the Kashmiris will decide their own future by a referendum. India has defied those resolutions because the international community is silent on this issue.

The West is meekly on the side of India and not on the side of justice for the human rights of Kashmiris. President Donald Trump is quick to impose sanctions on Russia and Venezuela, but people are questioning, why not consider imposing sanctions on India for its oppression in occupied Kashmir? A desperate cry for release from the inherited Indian colonial rule is not being heard by the proponents of human rights everywhere else, but not here.

Moral and verbal support for the oppressed people is important indeed, but it is not enough. This does not compel India to come to the negotiating table. Something extracurricular, so to speak, has to be devised on an international level, involving some other influential nations.

Such an initiative at last has just begun to take shape in the form of holding an international conference in the British Parliament on February 4, where Foreign Minister Makhdoom Shah Mehmood Qureshi and High Commissioner Nafees Zakaria spoke and highlighted the issue, hitherto unknown to many participants. The European Union countries and America have no intention of tackling India for its tyranny for fear of losing a substantial market and trade. So, no outside organisations and countries are prepared to mediate.

The West in general and the US in particular want to have good relations with India, and ignore the human rights violations in that country. Some commentators and observers have suggested that propping up India against China is a foreign policy focus of America. The US may like to play the China/India game. The two Asian giants may be made to lock horns in the future in some geopolitical conflict of interest, or revival of their old border dispute, in order to restrict the Chinese commercial expansion in Africa and around the world.

Meanwhile, Kashmiris living overseas observe Kashmir Black Day every year; for them every day is a black day under an extremely brutal military occupation of their land.

Looking ahead, Kashmir remains a crucial issue to be sorted out sooner. Both Pakistan and India spend an awful lot of money and energy on procuring more and more weapons of mass destruction, instead of spending on health and education and alleviating abject poverty.

# Jinnah: An incomparable political leader

Published in *TheNews*, London, December 24, 2018

In commemoration of Quaid-e-Azam Mohammed Ali Jinnah's birth anniversary (December 25), this article explores some of the misconceptions about the man who put a new country on the world map.

To begin with, Independence Day in India is celebrated with pomp and ceremony every year, and, as usual, only two names connected with the freedom struggle dominate: Mohandas Karamchand Gandhi, and Jawaharlal Nehru. But Jinnah, the founder of Pakistan, is either mentioned in a passing reference as a separatist or some other derogatory remarks.

Jinnah experienced deep-rooted prejudice from both the British and the Hindu politicians throughout his life; their refusal to negotiate with him not only plunged the country into complete disarray but also led to an unjust and unequal partition of the subcontinent in a haphazard manner.

Among the history makers of modern times, Jinnah was/is the most misunderstood politician outside Pakistan. The reasons for this are several and are scarcely explained.

The first reason, very likely, is that the history of India's independence, partition, and Pakistan, has been dominated by Hindu writers, who lost no opportunity of indoctrinating a falsely perceived animosity towards their Muslim citizens.

Second, the British writers did not really write much about him because he stood up to them on equal footing during the freedom movement and the colonisers do not like that kind of attitude. So, they largely ignored him as a non-entity. Jinnah's status, nevertheless, remains as an incomparable political leader.

Third, Jinnah presented his forceful arguments with dignity, courage and impeccable manners. Lord Mountbatten, Britain's outgoing representative in India, found him more than his match; Jinnah's upright and transparent personality and a barrister's skilful, polite, and decidedly unambiguous stance bothered him most.

Jinnah was his own man, his greatness as a leader lies in the fact that at all times he presented himself as he really was, irrespective of how others may have wanted him to behave.

Ironically, Pakistanis themselves have not written sufficiently well about either Jinnah or Pakistan to redress the imbalance. So, the gap was filled by outsiders and foreigners with little sympathy for, or knowledge of, Jinnah's personality and his politics.

Pakistan and Jinnah are still universally misunderstood, even by Muslims, particularly in the Arab world. Moreover, his critics' dislike of him also emanates from a notion that he wanted to divide India to satisfy his own ego.

Jinnah and his supporters vigorously denied this, time and again. He was determined, though, to fight for the civil and political rights of Muslims within the union of India; his concentration on this point was unbreakable.

During his dealings with the Indian National Congress Party, he thought of himself as an Indian nationalist and a strong believer in Hindu-Muslim unity. His long membership and active participation in the Congress party testify to this.

After working within the Hindu-led Congress for many years, he became disillusioned with the machinations of Gandhi and was thoroughly disgusted with Nehru and other Hindu nationalists' undisguised bias.

The Hindus at no time showed fellow feeling towards their Muslim citizens. This made it difficult for Jinnah to maintain his faith in the possibility of a permanent amicable relationship between India's two major communities.

Jinnah's relations with the Congress lasted only long enough for him to discover its true nature, which he found incompatible with the aspirations of the Muslims who longed for their civil rights to be protected under constitutional and electoral guarantees.

Disillusioned and disappointed, Jinnah finally realised that the parting of the ways was unavoidable and made a clean break from his chosen party.

Crucially, Gandhi himself admitted that religion was the inspiration of his politics long before Jinnah started to demand a separate homeland for Muslims. Gandhi frankly declared in his autobiography in 1927:

> "I can say without the slightest hesitation, and yet in all humility, that those who say that religion has nothing to do with politics do not know what religion means."

In another book, Gandhi is quoted as saying:

> "If I seem to take part in politics, it is only because politics today encircles us like the coils of a snake from which one cannot get out no matter how one tries. I wish to wrestle with the snake. I am trying to introduce religion into politics".

Nehru, too, concedes that Gandhi introduced religion into politics. He says in his autobiography:

> "Gandhi ji, indeed, was continuously laying stress on the religious and spiritual side of the movement. His religion was not dogmatic, but it did mean a definitely religious outlook on life, and the whole movement was strongly influenced by this and took a revivalist character so far as the masses were concerned".

Jinnah, on the other hand, was convinced that Hindu-Muslim cooperation was a noble and achievable aim, provided the political and religious rights of the Muslims could be safeguarded.

A united India, free from tensions and social chaos, was Jinnah's original dream. An ideologically united, politically integrated, constitutionally secure India could not be achieved as Jinnah envisioned, because Gandhi and Nehru never reassured the Muslims that they would be safe in a Hindu-dominated country.

The final chance for India-united came in 1946, when the Cabinet Mission Plan, which included autonomy for Muslim majority areas, was accepted by Jinnah, but rejected out of hand by Nehru. Many leading politicians were disappointed when Nehru announced his rejection on All-India Radio from Allahabad.

If Gandhi and Nehru had had their way, the Muslims would have suffered permanent Hindu majority domination in the name of democracy.

Gandhi left no option for Jinnah but to demand a separate state. A Pakistan, albeit truncated, mutilated and moth-eaten, was the only option Jinnah could accept.

It is most unfair that Jinnah is often described by some Indian and British writers as arrogant and unfriendly. The loneliness of a long distance leader may have left Jinnah aloof, but many of his opponents have researched Jinnah's past to discover the sort of person he really was.

Their findings after meticulous appraisal belie that description. Even the television footage, shown in Britain two years ago on his birth anniversary on December 25, does not support that misleading idea of Jinnah.

On the contrary, he is shown smiling at Gandhi, receiving him respectfully at his Bombay residence with good grace.

Jinnah's character assassination may be based on the belief that if enough mud is thrown at him, some is bound to stick.

Had Jinnah been dealing with such Hindu leaders as Bal Gangadhar Tilak, who understood the fears of the Muslims, and an accord at the Lucknow Pact of 1916 between the Congress and the Muslim League, or Gopal Krishna Gokhale, another realist who got on well with Jinnah and understood Hindu-Muslim aspirations well, India would be one country today, and a more powerful and prosperous one perhaps.

It was after Gokhale's death in 1915, and Tilak's in 1920, that the political atmosphere radically changed. Had either or both lived a bit longer, and with Jinnah at the helm of Muslim affairs, not only would India have remained undivided but independence could have come much sooner.

In discussing the aspects of Gandhi's philosophy and political tactics, it is not to question his status as a venerated Hindu of modern times. It is needed to explain, though, that Gandhi was not a practical politician, and that he, and not Jinnah, was really responsible for wrecking the chances of Hindu-Muslim unity.

A lot of attention is focused on Gandhi's theory of non-violence. Jinnah's arguments were essentially non-violent too, but not much is noticed about this.

In fact, most cruel violent acts in the history of mankind were committed in India when more than a million civilians were mercilessly slaughtered under the very noses of Nehru and Gandhi. Millions more were displaced and dragged out of their ancestral homes and made refugees in their own country.

It is hard to ignore the duplicitous character of the Indian leaders' political thinking, particularly when Jinnah was made to look like a separatist leader. This sham was also promoted by the Hindu media barons who dominated India's press.

Evidently, some Hindu writers and politicians did not approve of Gandhi's politics either. For instance, Tilak is quoted as saying, "I have great respect and admiration for Gandhiji, but I do not like his politics. If he would retire to the Himalayas and give up politics, I would send him fresh flowers from Bombay every day because of my respect for him".

On May 9, 1933, a joint statement by Subhash Chandra Bose and Villabhai Patel declared: "We are clearly of the opinion that as a political leader Mahatma Gandhi has failed. The time has, therefore, come for radical reorganisation of the Congress on a new principle and with a new method. For bringing about this reorganisation a change of leadership is necessary".

Many events and decisions of that period may have been lost in the mist of time or blurred by subsequent developments in India and Pakistan, but the anecdotal, written, and historical evidence lead to only one conclusion – that both Gandhi and Nehru were not farsighted politicians, and that it was they, and not Jinnah, who shattered the unity of India.

# Is alcoholism a weakness, an evil or insanity?

### Published in *TheNews*, London, August 23, 2018

Many compulsive alcohol drinkers are seemingly lost in a hopeless state of mind and body. So the answer to the above question may not be expected from them.

Alcoholism kills more people in the UK than any other drug.

According to government statistics, one adult in 13 is dependent on drink. A staggering 33,000 people die each year due to alcohol related accidents or associated health problems.

The number of such deaths has risen consistently since the early nineties, more than doubling in the past 10 years. There were an estimated 917,000 violent, alcohol related incidents in 2011 and 2012. Almost all victims of violence reported that their attacker was affected by alcohol at the time.

Alcoholism is a factor in 30 per cent of suicides each year in Britain.

Forty-seven per cent of 14 to16 year olds have been involved in an accident or been injured as a result of drinking alcohol. Teenagers who drink regularly are seven times more likely to be in a car crash because of drinking, and eleven times more likely to suffer unintentional injuries.

Each year there are some 13,000 hospital admissions linked to young people's drinking, and some 15,000 sought specialist support for alcohol misuse.

Britain ranked third out of 35 countries on the proportion of young people being drunk in the past 28 days, and seventh on the proportion who reported binge drinking. The UK has one of the highest rates in the European Union of accident and emergency hospital admissions due to alcohol use by 15 to16 year olds *(Source: Department of Education).*

Those statistics are verified by Mr Kelly Burks, FRSA, Director of External Relations, Initiatives of Change, whose personal experiences with alcoholics for the past 16 years, including six years of going into Wandsworth prison to work with adult alcoholics, shed more light on the enormity of the problem. He met many drinkers caught in the cycle of relapse and re-offending.

He found some prisoners sober up in prison; many of them are never out of prison for long before drinking again and then committing further offences. Some of them had woken up in police cells covered in blood with no memory of what they did.

This cycle can go on for periods of up to 20 or 30 years. In the end they do not wish to be released from prison, because they can't face going through the cycle any longer.

For four years Mr Burks has been going into Feltham Young Offenders Institution, the largest facility of this type in Europe, where there are 800 young men between 14 and 21 years of age. He found out that about 70 per cent of the young men in Feltham have a serious problem with drinks or drugs. The boys are there for several reasons, including murder, rape, grievous bodily harm and so on. These are the ones who were caught; they are far outnumbered by those who are not. There is a charity called Spirit of Recovery, which helps young ones with drink and drug problems on a one to one basis. This charity informs them about recovery plans and what resources are available to them. Many are not out of prison for more than a few weeks or months before they are back inside because they cannot stop drinking. Many of them are extraordinary individuals, shaped by their environments and desperate for change. However, if they would like to change, there is a way.

Initiatives of Change is a mini think-tank, based in central London, whose principal thinking is singularly focused on what is right, not who is wrong. It puts people first, especially the vulnerable. Its main task is coordinating human security work with all communities and believes in healing history, and organises conferences on such topics as, for instance, Learning to Live in a Multicultural World, and Trust and Integrity in the Global Economy. Recently, it invited three young ex-prisoners, former alcoholics, now fully recovered, to share their experiences in and out of prison. Their stories were awe-inspiring on the way to overcome their powerlessness and shame and completely giving up drinking. Perhaps as a teaser or merely testing their resolve, a man from the audience stood up and asked these three young persons – a girl and two boys – if he offered them a glass of champagne would they accept it. All of them resentfully rejected the offer out of disgust. Certainly, there is suffering for the alcoholics, but between 15 and 20 people's lives around an alcoholic are deeply affected. There is recovery literature available to help families and friends of an alcoholic and also suggestions from Alcoholics Anonymous.

# Pakistan's unholy alliance

Published in *TheNews*, London, April 4, 2018

The US President Donald Trump is not really a Trump if he is not blunt in his political or diplomatic pronouncements. He has bluntly threatened loyalist Pakistan to either implement US policy of "war on terror " or its pocket money would be stopped, which, in fact, had been stopped many years earlier.

It is a similar threat to which the former military ruler General Pervez Musharraf was confronted with, when George W. Bush gave him a stark choice of either being with the terrorists or with the US in September 2001. Musharraf wisely chose the latter option.

Let us examine in more detail the relationship between Pakistan and the United States over seven decades.

Historically, the country had been plunged into various unholy military alliances with the United States. It had joined the South East Asia Treaty Organisation (Seato) in the early 1950s. The main purpose of that pact was containment of communist China in exchange for a few million dollars, and granting the US a military base in northern Pakistan.

The net result of accepting this bribery was that Pakistan sacrificed its independence of formulating a foreign policy of its own.

In 1955, Pakistan offered itself yet again in another pact with the US and joined the Central Treaty Organisation (Cento), also known as the Baghdad Pact (Iraq was a member, as was Turkey). The only aim of this alliance was to spy on the Soviet Union at the height of the Cold War.

Neither China nor the Soviet Union were ever threats to Pakistan. The country gained nothing out of those love affairs when Pakistan desperately needed the US help, and it made the Soviet Union unnecessarily hostile towards Pakistan.

In 1965 and 1971, Pakistan asked for assistance in its wars with India invoking Cento. The request was flatly rejected, and Pakistan was told in no uncertain terms that Cento was aimed at containing the Soviet Union, not India.

Pakistan withdrew from Cento in 1971, just after the diabolical disaster in East Pakistan, now Bangladesh.

Pakistan virtually surrendered its independence when the United States continued pursuing a covert policy of intelligence gathering of military establishments of the Soviet Union from Pakistan.

The most publicised incident occurred on May 1, 1960, when a CIA U-2 spy plane flew from a northern airbase on a reconnaissance mission over Soviet Union airspace. The plane was shot down by the Soviets and its pilot, Gary Powers, was captured alive, prosecuted in an open court, and imprisoned.

The pilot disclosed other details of previous spy planes which were routinely flown from the same airbase since 1957. Nikita Khrushchev, the leader of the Soviet Union, was extremely furious, and in his own characteristic style he warned President Ayub Khan that if another secret spy plane flew from there over Soviet territory he would wipe out Pakistan.

The relationship with the Soviet Union over that incident had become really bad because of the US' illegal activities from a compliant vassal state.

Pakistan lost a real opportunity of fostering friendship with the Soviet Union, its nearer neighbour than the far flung perfidious America. Pakistani leadership could not untangle itself from the stranglehold of the superficial alignments, devoid of any political benefit, whereas India remained non-aligned and exploited both superpowers for its own gain.

Pakistan could have fared even better had it not put all its eggs in one basket, for it has a geographically important location.

Looking back at the early part of its history Pakistan could not make its own foreign policy decisions.

Internally, the country failed to abolish feudalism. India, under Nehru, got rid of feudal lords immediately after the Partition. Japan too had done away with feudalism after the Second World War. As a result, Japan became the first tiger economy of the world.

Pakistan learnt nothing from those examples, and continued relying on the US dollar rather than developing the local resources which are in abundance. The main beneficiary of the US dollar was the army.

Sensing the uncertain leadership in Pakistan, the former US president George W. Bush blackmailed Pakistan with his false "war on terror" propaganda by threatening either you are with us or with the terrorists. Barack Obama had also followed in his predecessor's policies and increased drone bombings in northern Pakistan.

Today, the government of Pakistan is not bold enough to say: "Look, Mr Trump, you are committing crimes against our people, we have our Air Force, stop or we will shoot down your missile-laden drones". An RQ-170 Sentinel (unmanned aerial vehicle) was famously shot down by Pakistan's neighbour, Iran, in 2011. No known violation of the Iranian airspace has ever been reported since then.

Pakistan relies on Washington for its foreign policy in return for money. It is in fact a loan, not an outright gift, and must be repaid with high interest to the US money lenders.

Ironically, Pakistan spends this lovely money on goods such as fighter planes, from America, so the money eventually comes back to the US coffers for recycling.

The US favours India unconditionally over the disputed territory of Kashmir, and has not questioned Narendra Modi's government on why Indian soldiers brutally kill young and old civilians in occupied Kashmir practically every day.

Recently, the Pentagon has refused to sell F-18 aircraft to Pakistan. The bizarre reason given by a Senator was that these fighter planes could be used against India; so, that means the US can supply aircraft only if used against its own people.

After an alleged withdrawal from Afghanistan, the US bombardment continues. A so-called precision missile from a drone hit a hospital near the border "by mistake", killing 42 civilians, including doctors and nurses. Instances such as these cause hundreds of displaced persons fleeing to Pakistan or heading for Europe as refugees.

Many political parties in the country have denounced the unequal nature of the friendship with the US; they insist that this arrangement must be thoroughly re-examined.

Pakistan has been America's most loyal friend since birth, as I indicated above, and rendered help when needed. Pakistan provides facilities, for instance, for transportation of goods, logistic materials and weaponry from Karachi seaport to Afghanistan, a land-locked country, but the US has not reciprocated as a trustworthy friend; otherwise the lingering problem of the Kashmir dispute would have been sorted out by applying the same principle of self-determination as in the cases of South Sudan and East Timor. Pakistan needs real friends, not real masters.

Pakistan continues to suffer from self-inflicted woes which have corrupted national institutions, plus widespread fraud, bribery, nepotism, patronage, tax evasion by the filthily rich, manipulation of the judiciary, and Panama and Paradise papers.

Complaints made by the weaker segment of the society are hardly ever taken notice of by the authorities and the culprits are rarely punished.

Professor Francis Fukuyama, author of *The End of History* and one of the most celebrated intellectuals of our age, describes Pakistani democracy in these words:

> "If you take a country like Pakistan, which is the most dangerous place in the world right now, and you cut one level below the surface of these supposedly democratic institutions, what you see is this hierarchy of kinships, led by feudal lords that have serfs working on their territory. They run this country by patronage networks. That is why democracy has never worked well there, and so it's an extremely traditional country in that sense, one in which patronage and kinship are the story of politics".

Fukuyama had made an insightful observation about democracy in Pakistan.

Equally, he has studied many other countries' failure in implementing the government of the people who elected them.

Two-thirds of the world is governed undemocratically; the core values of democracy are not followed after the elections are over.

Professor Fukuyama has criticised many countries for pretending to be democratic; I wonder if he would be tempted to write another book titled *The End of Democracy.*

# Will Guantanamo exist forever?

### Published in *TheNews*, London, August 26, 2017

One is often reminded that the US president is the most powerful man in the world. Yet, former US president Barack Obama dismally failed to close down the notorious Guantanamo Bay detention centre. He repeatedly promised and desperately wanted to shut it down and take the credit for being an inspired human rights champion.

Had he succeeded in fulfilling his promise, his name would have gone down in the history of his country as a great leader. However, he was not powerful enough to persuade Congress to follow through with his vision.

This shows the powerlessness of a president, in this case Obama, who needed to fulfil his election pledge, but could not. So, the conflict in the power base in the US seems to suggest that a president is not quite omnipotent at home or abroad after all.

George W. Bush had opened this prison on January 11, 2002, and so far there has been no sign of its closure in the foreseeable future. Instead, Donald Trump, the current US president, has promised the opposite and stated that he will "load it with more bad dudes".

Will Guantanamo exist forever? The long-suffering inmates are getting old and infirm after 16 years of courageously enduring physical abuse and psychological mistreatment at various levels.

The scandal of Guantanamo, a blot on the US, which has frequently lectured the entire world about rights violations, shamelessly continues. Amid torture and the ins and outs of the darkest CIA secret prisons around the world, the inmates rely on the international community to do something to secure their release.

Sustained political campaigns have been mounted in Britain and have succeeded in securing the release of British detainees in Guantanamo, including Shaker Aamer. Since then, there has hardly been any mention in the press.

Both the broadcast and print media are preoccupied with Brexit and a difficult divorce from the European Union, which is a highly emotional political issue. Therefore, stories concerning the plight of victims of torture in Guantanamo do not qualify for any space in the mainstream media.

So far, nine detainees have died in custody. There are still 41 others languishing under extreme conditions. During the Bush administration, the number of prisoners released was 532, Obama released another 198. Many were tortured in secret prisons overseas before being transferred to Guantánamo. Only four percent were captured by US troops as terror suspects; others were sold to the US for a bounty. The inmates have not been charged with any offence, most were caught at the wrong time and at the wrong place.

The US argues that if these inmates are released, they would endanger the security of the US as an act of revenge, but 59 countries have accepted the detainees who have not posed even the slightest risk to the security of any country.

Trump wants to "make America great again". This sounds like a good idea, a very good idea indeed, but he will have to do some noble acts on his way to achieving that goal. The starting point could ideally be to close down this concentration camp by overriding objections from the Congress.

The second good deed that Trump could perform is to hand over the illegally-occupied Cuban territory on which the prison is based back to Cuba. By doing this, he will be able to kill two birds with one stone and simultaneously make America great again.

Half a billion dollars are paid every year by taxpayers to operate Guantanamo. If Trump is ready, willing, and serious about making America great again, he could do himself and his country a favour and save this huge amount and spend it on the needy and on improving health services.

# Trump devalues himself

Published in *TheNews*, London, July 5, 2017

President Donald Trump has now made it absolutely clear that he would indeed ban Muslims from seven predominantly Muslim countries: Syria, Iraq, Iran, Libya, Sudan, Yemen and Somalia. He will also impose a rigorous regime to make it more difficult to obtain a visa. The ban would apply to immigrants, tourists and refugees until he is able to understand the problem. How long he would take to understand the problem is not known. Trump had called for a total and complete shutdown of Muslims entering the United States during his presidential election campaign. True to his word, he is now about to fulfil that promise. He has never hidden his brand of racism from the public. Trump values are not likely to take him beyond a one term presidency. He has already devalued himself. This may be a blessing in disguise for Muslims. Brain drain from developing countries, mainly Muslim, will fortunately come to an end. These developing countries have been trying hard for years to stop the brightest and the best of their people emigrating to America and Europe.

The affected countries, on the other hand, could also reciprocate and stop Americans entering their countries. The slogan "Yankee go home" would suddenly become redundant for good measure.

After taking over the most powerful country, Trump supports torture of human beings. The United Nations has outlawed torture and has ordered that under no circumstances can an individual be allowed to be tortured. Instead of closing down Guantánamo Bay concentration camp, he intends "to load it up with some bad dudes".

After his inauguration, he asked the Central Intelligence Agency to find places outside the US for secret prisons. He also insists on introducing new torture techniques.

Muslims need not worry too much if Trump succeeds in getting them banned from entering the US; they would be mentally healthy in their own countries, and more importantly, safer from every day violence in American schools, colleges, universities, supermarkets, cinemas and crazy gun battles in streets between the police and the ordinary citizens.

Many US politicians are quick to lecture the world about freedom, human rights and democracy, but they cannot boast about being a peaceful or a civil society at peace with itself. Yes, you can earn a few dollars for your labour, but in an anxiety ridden sort of atmosphere.

In Britain, the BBC reported on 25 January that more than 40 people had been murdered and 228 shot and injured so far in 2017. This happened only at the beginning of the new year.

Most developing countries nowadays have higher education on top of their list. If adequate facilities are not available in their own countries and students wish to travel to study abroad for vocational or technical training, they might choose to look eastwards: Japan or China. A second tier option may be considered for Canada, Australia and Germany, avoiding the US altogether.

The continent of Africa as a whole and many Asian countries are quite rich, and possess enormous mineral resources ranging from gold, uranium, silver, diamond, zinc, copper, rubber and liquid gold – oil. The list is still longer.

However, a nation's greater capital is its people, comprising doctors, nurses, engineers, architects, legal practitioners, carpenters, builders and technology personnel who can enrich their own country rather than someone else's. One of the reasons why developing nations record an inadequately slow economic progress is the skilled workers disappearing abroad.

There has been a historical hostility between Islam and Christianity for more than 1,000 years, including the vicious crusade wars, before the United States even existed. This trend has continued unbroken to this day. For the past 60 years, and particularly since September 11, 2001, an uneasy peace exists between these two largely identical and yet different modes of civilisations.

The US has a stranglehold over Muslim countries' rulers. Is the US a dangerous friend to have? The US's erstwhile friendship with Saddam Hussein of Iraq and Colonel Muammar Gaddafi of Libya had eventually finished them off brutally, and destroyed the modern infrastructure of their beautiful, prosperous and progressive countries. Pakistan, a close ally of the US, succumbed to this "friendly" threat, and ever since has been loyally fighting a proxy war for the US for 14 years. So far, 64,000 Pakistani soldiers have lost their lives. The civilian deaths are far greater than that figure, the exact number is unaccountable as yet. There are about 52 Muslim countries which are not united, do not speak with one voice like the European nations do, and their corrupt rulers dare not protest against America's bombardment of defenceless people, such is the impotency of those in power.

Last December, the Philippine President Rodrigo Duterte became an instant hero to his countrymen when he declared: "Bye bye America". Three short and sharp words speak a high volume of political wisdom.

Can a Muslim 'leader' have the sense and the faith in his nation to emulate the Philippine leader?

# Iqbal lives beyond his death

Published in *TheNews*, London, April 17, 2017

Germany has won praise from the world, particularly from the developing world, ever since its acceptance of one and a half million refugees from Syria, Iraq, Afghanistan and North Africa.

The poet and philosopher Allama Mohammad Iqbal (79th death anniversary April 21) who had a deep fondness for Germany, would have been delighted to see his favourite country's extraordinary efforts of help in today's humiliating refugee crisis.

When Iqbal came as a young scholar to study and to research in 1905, Europe was quite a different place, and Germany bore no imperialistic colonisers tag against its name like Britain and France. He did his serious research, therefore, in Germany, and was inspired by its literature and scientific knowledge. He admired Nietzsche and Goethe. Many of his writings and poems indicate that the works of German philosophers had been a source of inspiration to him. Iqbal compares *Faust* author Goethe with Ghalib, the great poet of Urdu and Farsi, and also with the Iranian sage Maulana Jalaluddin Rumi. By bringing Rumi and Goethe together, Iqbal had played an

Allama Mohammad Iqbal

unparalleled role in drawing the East closer to the West and vice versa.

Iqbal himself tells us in *Payam-e-Mashriq* of his preoccupations with German civilisation and thought. He read Shakespeare, but Goethe won a place in his heart.

Iqbal wrote in Urdu, Farsi, German and English flawlessly. His deep knowledge of all those languages and their literatures is unrivalled to this day. No surprises then that he gained recognition as a poet-philosopher of the East and was equally admired in the Western literary circles.

He taught Arabic at London University for many months during his sojourn in London. He created a name for himself that enables him to live beyond his death.

Iqbal travelled widely and stayed in Europe from 1905 to 1908. Germany, a highly efficient and meticulously disciplined country, impressed him. His admiration for that country never left him.

After he arrived back in Lahore (then India), he continued his association with Germany and frequently wrote to Miss Emma Wegenast, his German language tutor in Heidelberg. The correspondence with her is not only fascinating philosophically, but it has also contributed to the cultural link between Pakistan and Germany. Miss Wegenast had graciously given those letters as a present in the early Sixties, shortly before her death, to the Pakistan-German Forum.

On receiving the news that Fräulein Wegenast's father had died, Iqbal sent a thought-provoking message of condolence to her as follows:

*Dear Miss Wegenast,*

*I am extremely sorry to hear the sad news of your father's death, and though my letter must reach you a good many days after this sad event, neither time nor distance can make my sympathy with you in your bereavement any the less warm. The news has pained me very much indeed, and I pray that Almighty God may be pleased to shower his choicest blessings on the venerable old man, and to give you strength to endure your sorrow. Such events, though, do happen in everybody's life, and we must meet our troubles like those who left us their lives to imitate. I remember the time when I read Goethe's poems with you, and I hope you also remember those happy days when we were so near to each other, so much so that I spiritually share in your sorrow. I wish I had been in Germany to convey my sympathy to you personally. May God be with you.*

*Yours ever,*
*Mohammad Iqbal*

There are 23 letters and two postcards. Iqbal's letters, like his poems, are an absolutely compelling read. Here are a few brief excerpts:

"Never shall I forget the days I spent at Heidelberg when you taught me Goethe's Faust and helped me in many ways. Those were happy days indeed."

"It is impossible for me to forget your beautiful country where I have learned so much."

"My stay in Heidelberg is nothing now but a beautiful dream. How I'd wish I could repeat it."

"I am very fond of Germany, it has had a great influence on my ideals, and I shall never forget my stay in that country."

"I'd wish I could see you once more at Heidelberg or Heilbronn whence we shall together make a pilgrimage to the sacred grave of the great master Goethe."

"My body is here, my thoughts are in Germany."

"The other day I was reading Heine, Kant, and I thought of the happy days when we read the poets together."

"Germany was a kind of second home to my spirit. I learned much and I thought much in that country. The home of Goethe has found a permanent place in my heart."

The letters also reveal a unique piece of information – the addresses at which Iqbal stayed in London in 1908, and again in 1931 and 1932 when he attended the Round Table Conferences:

49 Elsham Road in Kensington in 1908;
113A St James's Court, Buckingham Gate in 1931;
Queen Anne's Mansion, St James' Park in 1932.

The house where Iqbal stayed in 1908 is a stone's throw from where Quaid-e-Azam Mohammed Ali Jinnah, the founder of Pakistan, lived as a young law student in 1895. The vicinity of the neighbourhood of the two greatest sons of Pakistan is interesting.

The Greater London Blue Plaque Scheme, which welcomes suggestions from private individuals and organisations alike, should be requested to put a commemorative blue plaque at one of these addresses.

I have visited all three places. The third one seems to have been demolished or rebuilt. The second one, which in those days may have been an apartment block, is now converted into a modern hotel. The first one, in Kensington, is the only one where a plaque could be installed.

The Pakistan High Commission should take an interest in initiating the proposal of installing a plaque to remember an internationally renowned historic figure. Germany honoured the poet-philosopher by naming a street called Iqbal-Ufer on the bank of the River Neckar in Heidelberg. There is also another large commemorative plaque outside the house where Iqbal lived, which reads:

Mohammad Iqbal 1877-1938 National Philosopher, Poet and Spiritual Father of Pakistan lived here in the year 1907

# Terrorism redefined

Published in *TheNews*, London, August 9, 2016

Terrorism is not an exclusive trait of Muslims. Terrorist acts are perpetrated by Jews, Hindus, Buddhists and Christians alike, and in all continents.

Take the prime example of massacres of the Palestinians by the racist Israelis. The whole population in the occupied Palestine has been terrorised for the past 70 years; kidnappings and brutal murders are committed frequently by the so-called 'only democracy' in the Middle East.

Two years ago the Israeli military slaughtered 2,200 Gazans, and 553 children in their beds. The massive onslaught with weapons of mass destruction continued for 51 days and no Western government condemned the killings.

Gaza is now flattened by Israeli bombings and no re-building material is allowed in, because of the Israeli sea, air, and land blockade.

No politicians worth their salt, with the exception of Jeremy Corbyn, dare call the genocidal crimes committed by apartheid-Israel as Jewish terrorism. Take another identical example of mass murders: the Indian army is engaged in killing, gang-raping, kidnapping, torturing, and arbitrary arrests of innocent women and children. People disappear overnight without trace in Occupied Kashmir, which is surrounded by more than half a million soldiers.

This Indian state terrorism is never condemned as Hindu terrorism by the West for fear of trade and investment reasons with numerically the 'largest democracy' in the world.

Indian soldiers killed 49 Kashmiris and wounded more than 5,000 in the riot which followed the murder of Burhan Wani, a popular Kashmiri separatist leader on July 8.

Pankaj Mishra, a well-respected Indian author and journalist, describes the tragic condition of Kashmir thus:

"With more than 80,000 people dead in an anti-India insurgency, the killing fields of Kashmir dwarf those of Palestine. In addition to the everyday regime of arbitrary arrests, curfews, raids, and check-points, enforced by nearly 700,000 Indian soldiers, the valley's four million Muslims are exposed to extra judicial execution, rape and torture, with such barbaric variations as live electric wires inserted into penises."

In one of her many articles on Kashmir, another world-renowned author and journalist Arundhati Roy depicted the condition in which Kashmiri youths were "raised in a playground of army camps, check-points, and bunkers, with screams from torture chambers for a sound track".

The news of brutalities in disputed Kashmir is daily reported around the world, but the Indian government's terrorism is ignored by the European Union and the United States.

One seldom reads about the radicalised Hindu terrorists or Jewish terrorists because the West is selective in choosing as to what is terrorism and what is not. If it is committed by a lone wolf with a Muslim sounding name, it is terrorism, no problem there, and all Muslims (1.5 billion) are demonised; it makes no difference where they happen to reside or however far they may be from the scene of the crime.

If the perpetrators of terrorism are Jews or Hindus it is not terrorism, and the word terrorist is non-existent in the dictionary and becomes irrelevant. The US and its NATO allies are focused on the wrongdoings of "Islamic terrorists" only.

The meaningless term, "Islamic radicalisation" is used as a political jargon which has absolutely nothing to do with Islam; this may produce an adverse effect to the not yet radicalised.

Using phrases such as war on terror, Muslim terrorists, Islamic extremists, Islamic militants, Islamic fundamentalists, and a few more hate-ridden slogans in order to smooth the public opinion, and then embarking on innumerable expeditions of revenge attacks in the Middle East, will not solve the security problem of the West – it will increase the size of the problem.

After the recent British and French bombardment of Iraq and Syria, *Daesh* or Islamic State followers have gained a large number of sympathisers in Afghanistan, Pakistan and Bangladesh. Some Uzbek and Tajik fighters also threw their full support behind this organisation.

If the West sticks to its misguided agenda based on 'Islamic terrorists', and keeps repeating it, then that will only help more and more radicalisation and create an ugly atmosphere of fear among the already integrated Muslim population in Europe.

The issue is not religious, it is political. The attacks in European cities have nothing to do with the teachings of Islam. Without an iota of doubt, it is a tit for tat job, revenge against revenge, terror against terror, a battle between the oppressed of the world and the oppressors, the so-called Western democracies.

The neo-cons, aided and abetted by the compliant media, are playing a dangerous game blaming Muslims for everything while turning a blind eye in the more serious cases of Israeli and Indian terrorist crimes.

There is a passionate debate going on in the Arab and other ethnic minorities' press and broadcasting media about the recent attacks in Paris and Brussels, and how the ultra right-wing parties in France and Netherlands are whipping up hostility against migrants settled in Europe as law abiding citizens since the end of Europe's colonialism in Asia and Africa.

After the Nice incident, France's president Francois Hollande responded by saying that he vowed to show "real force and military action in Syria and Iraq". Similarly, Boris Johnson, the Foreign Secretary of Britain, has also pledged to take further and tougher action against those countries.

Evgeny Lebedev, the owner of the London *Evening Standard,* in his column on July 18 urged Obama, Mrs Theresa May, German Chancellor Angela Merkel and others to wage an "urgent war against the true menace of Islamic fundamentalism". He admits: "However distasteful I find it to agree with the Front National's Marine Le Pen, she is right to state that the war against Islamic fundamentalism has not yet started. It is time, urgently, to declare it".

Wars in Afghanistan, Iraq, Syria, and Libya have given birth to *Daesh,* which never existed before the invasion and destruction of the infrastructure of those countries by the NATO and the US military forces. More wars and violence will strengthen *Daesh,* not weaken it. You can kill a man but not an idea.

The politicians and commentators I mentioned above are naïve if they think that full scale war against "Islamic fundamentalism" would win them security in their respective countries. In any case, how do you wage a total war against a dedicated suicide bomber? Would you fight with a dead man?

It would be impossible for any country to deal with this type of guerrilla warfare and protect citizens in crowded cities and beaches.

So, what is the answer? *Daesh* is addressing the NATO nations: "If you continue bombing and mercilessly killing our people in Syria, Iraq, Libya, Somalia, Afghanistan and Pakistan using drones and airstrikes, we will retaliate. We have no other means of combating your combined armies. Stop killing our brothers and sisters in Muslim countries, and we will stop killing your brothers and sisters in your towns and cities".

In the light of the above frequently heard statements, the inference is that major cities in Europe will continue to be targeted in the future.

One way, perhaps the only way, of preventing that cyclical terror/counter-terror could be to apply a bit of psychology, and take Islam and Muslim anything out of the equation, and completing a process of final withdrawal of American and NATO armies from the Middle East.

# Journey into Europe (A film)

Published in *TheNews*, London, July 9, 2016

Let us take leave from the monotonous reference to the referendum and Brexit, and remain on the European continent in history. *Journey into Europe* is a full length film, written, scripted, directed, and produced by the world-renowned Islamic scholar, anthropologist, and former Pakistan's High Commissioner in Britain.

No stranger to the filmmaking business and despite his diplomatic and academic background, Professor Akbar Ahmad has already a film to his name, that of the founder of Pakistan, Mohammed All Jinnah. He has done an enormous service to the Muslim world by painstakingly researching and visually-recording the golden era of the Muslim architecture, culture, and social structure in Europe, including the mighty Turkish Ottoman Empire.

The documentary is not only about the past. It shows graphically the state we are in today. It deals with, for instance, the problem of

Professor Akbar S. Ahmad

Islamophobia, colonialism, terrorism, violent extremism in all religions' communities, widespread racism, immigration, and the refugee crisis.

You will watch presidents, prime ministers, archbishops, chief rabbis, heads of right-wing parties, discussing and debating Islam's place in Europe. It may be interesting to see the Danish editor, who published the anti-Islam cartoons, being interviewed by Akbar Ahmed, who explained to the publisher why the cartoons were deeply offensive to the Muslims around the globe and why similar work cannot be treated as a so-called freedom of speech pretence.

Rowan Williams, the former archbishop of Canterbury, was full of praise and commented: "It is hard to exaggerate the importance of this work". Many would come round to believe that this work, which took two years to complete, may help remove some, if not most, of the misunderstandings which are deliberately created by the subversive one-sided Western media manipulations. The movie takes you to all over Europe and Britain, and explores Islam in European history and civilisation which evolved over seven centuries.

Its DNA is in the present day Europe. Prof Ahmed wrote many books, the most recent among them were *Journey into Islam* and *Journey into America,* published by Brookings Institution Press. Not content with writing books, Akbar Ahmad has produced not entirely a blockbuster but a stronger educational tool. The likes of Donald Trump, the presidential hopeful who has declared that Muslims should not be allowed in the US, would be irked to learn, if he watches the film, the cultural, political and social changes Muslims have made for centuries in his ancestral home before there was such a thing as the United States.

I obtained a copy of the DVD from the professor. I have shown it to individuals as well as to some audiences. It needs to be shown to the wider world. The video is not available to the public at the moment, so, I asked the professor if it could be linked in on the Internet. His answer was that as for putting it online, his team was at the moment attempting to get it shown on television, and for it to be shown it can't have already been posted online. Online distribution will come after it is shown. YouTube is also a likely outlet, and producing thousands of copies may not be cost-effective.

Another way of publicising it can be showing it in schools, colleges and universities in the US and UK. It is important that the 27 European Union countries have access to view this documentary. It may lessen the fear of Muslim refugees, who are forced to leave their war-torn homes to seek asylum in Europe.

The perennial problem of the Jewish and Arab conflict in the occupied Palestinian lands is not covered in the film and remains a constant source of hatred on both sides, thus causing unnecessary West versus Muslim hostility. If this problem could be tackled by world powers, the world would be at peace with itself.

It took two years to make this movie, during which time Akbar and his team travelled to almost all parts of Europe, particularly wherever the Muslim population had settled since the end of the Second World War.

The earliest part of the Muslim rule in Europe ended in 1492 after 700 years of peace, progress and security for human beings. It was an era when Jews, Christians and Muslims intermingled and lived peacefully side by side under the benign Muslim rule in Spain, which the Spanish recall as Convencia, living together.

The second spell ended in 1924, six years after the First World War. After that, European countries, mainly Britain, France, Belgium and Holland, took control of the Muslim lands in Asia and Africa under distasteful colonialism, and this relates to another chapter in the film.

Professor Akbar Ahmad now holds the chair of Ibn Khaldun at the American University in Washington, DC. He was on a film-screening tour of Europe in May when the film was shown at the School of Oriental and African Studies (SOAS). Among the attendees were the current High Commissioner of Pakistan in Britain, Syed Ibne Abbas, and surprisingly the former retired teacher of Akbar Ahmad. He told the audience that Akbar had already written a book while a student, long before his PhD thesis.

# Refugee crisis splits European Union

Published in *TheNews*, London, March 15, 2016

European Union countries are shifting the responsibility of dealing with the refugee crisis on to Turkey, which is already overburdened by two and a half million refugees who were forced to flee after their houses were bombarded in the war torn areas.

After the EU foreign ministers' talks in Brussels, Turkey was being cajoled to stop the inflow of refugees to European shores in exchange for about three billion euros and keeping the asylum seekers at bay.

Surprisingly, Turkey was also told that its chances of joining the EU may be closer if it helps prevent the destitute refugees entering northern Europe.

Turkey's deputy ambassador to Britain, Cem Isik, has said that only a negligible sum of money has arrived. Turkey's accession to the EU is not guaranteed, it is only a promise. All 28 countries in the EU will have to agree on this step, which seems an unlikely prospect in the near future. Two major countries, France and Britain, have already criticised Turkey for not abiding by the "European values", whatever that may mean.

Division and distrust among the European nations is not new either, but opinions on this issue are splintered. The outcome of all this ongoing wrangling may be the eventual break-up of the Union.

Also, the British dilemma on the forthcoming referendum on June 23, whether to leave or remain in the EU, poses altogether a new situation. How this seemingly economic and partially political organisation would look after the referendum without entailing some newer issues is not foreseen.

Whatever the outcome, the refugee crisis is not going to go away. Several media reports suggest that a bribery of three billion euro and a tricky notion of joining the European Union does not appeal to the

Turkish people. Some have called it an act of political expediency, others a potentially dodgy deal.

Some media pundits are sceptical about handing over money to Turkey, which, they say, may not be able or willing to stop refugees drifting towards Europe.

Turkey has a proud record and traditions of willingly accepting refugees from all over the world, without questions being asked about religion, ethnicity or language, including thousands of persecuted Jews who fled from Spain after the Spanish Inquisition.

As a Muslim country it was a remarkable gesture towards Jews, at a time when no country was under obligation to admit refugees as it is today under the United Nations Convention 21, of 1951.

Angela Merkel of Germany must have studied the European history and apparently emulated the Turkish leaders' open door policy for the present-day asylum seekers.

Germany, in fact, has won the hearts and minds of Muslims everywhere; its generosity of spirit by taking in one and a half million mainly Muslims is widely appreciated throughout the world.

Migration is a live issue, much talked about every day. What are the central and eastern European responses to this crisis? Closing of borders is one, reluctance and outright refusal to accept refugees of Muslim religion and culture is another. There is no readiness to share the burden among the eastern European nations such as the Czech Republic, Hungary, staunchly Roman Catholic Poland, Slovakia, Macedonia, and wait – Serbia.

However, asylum seekers would not be happy in those countries; a few were accepted in Poland but they left for Germany or Scandinavia.

There is no denying the fact that NATO countries created the Syria, Iraq, Libya, and Afghanistan refugee problem during the past 14 years, and now they want to escape their collective guilt and responsibility of dealing with this crisis.

Even President Obama, whose country is not without blame either, has strongly criticised Prime Minister David Cameron and the former French president for their involvement in Libya's political and economic destruction.

After conspiring to topple the legitimate leader of Libya, Muammar Gaddafi, and his assassination, the country is plunged into a horrible mess, causing millions of displaced persons who lost their homes and livelihood.

This is only one part of the story. The relatively recent advent of Russian intervention on behalf of the Syrian President Bashar al-Assad has complicated the ever growing unresolved conflicts in the region.

The influx of refugees will continue, unless the US, Russian, Syrian and NATO air strikes of Iraq and Syria are completely halted and displaced persons rehabilitated.

Russia has had enough, and its president Mr Putin has announced a partial withdrawal of its army and air force; some military equipment and personnel will remain in Syria.

If the West can follow the Russian example, peace is achievable in this region.

Solving the ten million displaced persons' rehabilitation will continue to exercise the mind for many years.

# NATO's legacy of the refugee crisis

Published in *TheNews*, London, October 28, 2015

Germany has won the admiration of the world by welcoming refugees from the Middle East, with no German and belonging to a different culture and religion. So far an estimated million migrants have arrived in the country. Other European countries, including the UK, have not shown that open-heartedness. While the British public is willing to accept refugee families and has shown a welcoming attitude, the government has not extended that feeling of common humanity. Hundreds of thousands had marched recently, carrying placards boldly announcing "Refugees are Welcome Here".

The prime minister has set a very low figure of 20,000 refugees by the end of 2020, compared with Germany's offer of a million plus. So, these refugees, therefore, would remain in the newly created shanty towns in Calais in France, until the British government decides to take some of them in to share the burden.

After monitoring for months, the United Nations High Commissioner for Refugees has said that 130,000 of the most vulnerable refugees should be immediately resettled. Former foreign secretary David Miliband, whose father and grandfather fled from Belgium in similar circumstances during the Second World War, has pleaded with the government to take its head out of sand and facilitate more refugees to enter Britain. In his article in the *Evening Standard* on September 4, he pointed out that only 216 Syrians have been given refugee status in Britain this year. "That figure needs to move to tens of thousands", he advised.

It came to light last week that 84 Church of England Bishops wrote to David Cameron asking him to take in more refugees. In an interview with the BBC Radio 4 on October 18, David Walker, Bishop of Manchester, suggested that the government can easily absorb

10,000 refugees this year and 10,000 next year, and 50,000 by the end of next parliament.

The NATO nations are collectively guilty of creating the refugee crisis in the first place, by destroying the economy and infrastructure of Iraq, Libya, Syria and Afghanistan. It is this region where the entire families have been uprooted and forced to leave their ancestral homes, which had been turned into ashes after years of uninterrupted wars and destruction by European armies.

These unfortunate people have no choice but to leave or die for lack of food, sanitation, medicine, health care, clothing and shelter. Some politicians have wrongly dubbed asylum seekers as "economic migrants", while Germany alone had resettled 46,000 out of 54,000 in a short period of time. Other developed economies, for example Canada, Australia and the US, are also capable of helping without straining their resources.

The real problem is that many countries are not prepared to accept Muslims, and tend to selectively pick and choose Syrian Christian refugees. Some countries have come up with their own excuses. For instance, the Prime Minister of the Czech Republic had announced in a nice diplomatic fashion that because there were no mosques in his country no Muslims can be admitted. In Poland, several right wing parties similarly are campaigning against the "Muslim invasion". Their argument is that if Poland allows in some Muslims, they are likely to multiply and eventually will take over Poland.

The above attitudes go against the grain of the United Nations Convention relating to the Status of Refugees. The Convention's Article 1 describes a refugee as someone who is unable or unwilling to return to their country of origin for fear of being persecuted for reasons of race, religion, nationality, membership of a particular social group, or political opinion. The Convention further stipulates that subject to specific exceptions, refugees should not be penalised for their illegal entry or stay.

Human rights laws also reinforce the principle that the Convention be applied without discrimination and oblige states to comply with the provisions of the 1951 Convention to all persons covered by the refugee definition, and that seeking of asylum can require refugees to breach immigration rules. In view of the protection of refugees and the requirement for their humane treatment, it is important that those provisions of the Convention be strictly adhered to by the European Union countries.

It seems the lessons have not been learnt. The US and NATO are already bombing in Iraq and Syria, causing a new movement of people fleeing towards Europe. After the invasion and occupation of Iraq in 2003, the West's reputation has been irreparably damaged. If a culture of bombings is maintained, not only would that result in more deaths, but also more refugees.

The fact is that there are several religious and political factions in the Middle East, and each has its own individual agendum; alliances and loyalties change overnight. No factual reports emerge from that area, so no one knows exactly what is happening there. The Russian and the American administrations are as much confused as the public at large.

Syrian President Bashar al-Assad is identified by all and sundry as an enemy of his own people. His regime is evidently responsible for nearly half a million dead and injured. Many towns and villages and thousands of homes are seen completely flattened since 2011. Four million people have fled their country and are now merely existing in tents in Turkey, Jordan and Lebanon. Their plight is such that they have lost fear of being sunk in shaky, unseaworthy boats in hostile oceans, as long as they can get away from war zones in their own countries.

Disengagement of military intervention from this volatile area could bring about a semblance of stability, but that would be a part solution. All too often civilians bear the brunt of any assault. In any case, there is no military solution.

The NATO countries are mainly, but not exclusively, responsible for creating the refugee crisis, and if they want to stop the flow of refugees, they must stop air bombardments and start accepting refugees in accordance with the United Nations regulations in relation to the status of refugees. It is a moral crisis, it will not go away by magic.

# Nirbhaya (The Fearless)

Published in *Confluence Magazine,* August, 2015, and *TheNews,* London, August 21, 2015

Sir Edmund Hillary, the mountaineer, was once asked why he climbed mountains. He answered: "Because they are there". If a question is put to a serial rapist why he raped women, he may emulate by saying because they are there.

Man-woman and man-mountain relationships have always been tricky. An assault on a mountain does no harm; assaulting a woman does irreparable damage or death. The most horrible cruelty and death in recent rape crime history occurred on December 16, 2012.

Jyoti Singh Pandey, 23, boarded a bus in Delhi with her male friend going home after a cinema outing. She was set upon by six men already on the bus, who brutally gang-raped her. Her friend, Awindra Pratap Pandey, was badly beaten, gagged and knocked unconscious with a long, sharp metal bar. While half dead, she and her friend were thrown out of the moving bus. The whole world was shocked and condemned this horrible crime in the most condemnable terms.

For weeks, her name was not revealed because India does not permit a rape victim's name to be published. Her parents agreed to publish her name. Until then, reporters called her Nirbhaya, which means the fearless one. This gender-based crime was widely reported globally and the world has not fully recovered from the shock of this intense brutality, perpetrated by six rapists against this unfortunate physiotherapist. She died from her intestinal internal injuries in a Singapore hospital after two weeks in an intensive care unit.

This story was retold on the stage at the South Bank Centre, London, from 21 to 24 May to packed audiences. It was a completely sold-out show for all four days.

We were shown how the metal rod was used in this extreme sexual violence. The audience was stunned in disbelief to watch this powerful simulated rape scene, the struggle, and the cries of the actress. Some people were moved to tears.

The popularity of this stage play, produced by Yaël Farber, was such that this could have continued for months or years, but the Indian performers were on a short tour under the yearly festival called Alchemy. I saw the show on May 22.

The tragic death of Jyoti broke the culture of silence on rape crimes with an astonishingly loud bang that cannot be ignored.

Encouraged by the worldwide media support, five women participated in this reality theatre and narrated their experiences of being raped when younger.

Ms Neel said that she was forced into marriage at 12 years old, she did not love him and was a reluctant partner. Her husband attacked her when she was 14. He demanded a dowry (an amount of money brought by a bride on marriage), but her family could not provide one. He wanted to sell her. When she refused, he threw acid in her face and fled with their five-month-old son. She spent six months bandaged up, and could not move. She is horribly defaced.

Another woman told the audience that she was raped by a stranger in her own flat. She was confronted with an intruder waving a knife and threatening to kill her. She said she struggled but was overpowered and was raped at knife point. She suffers from psychological scars. The rapist was never caught.

The third woman told her experience of being raped by a close relative when still a young girl. Her nightmare is not over. She told the audience that she is regularly groped in New Delhi crowded buses where people travel virtually on top of each other.

The other two women had shared their harrowing accounts in a straightforward manner without fear or inhibitions of being similarly abused.

Police figures indicate a rape reported on average every 18 hours, and rape cases rapidly rose between 2007 to 2011. Nirbhaya's case was the only conviction among the 706 cases filed in New Delhi in 2012. Delhi has the highest number of rape crimes among India's major cities. A rape is committed every 27 minutes in India. Rapes occur in all countries, but Delhi has earned a name for itself as a rape capital of the world.

Nirbhaya is the live stage play. The BBC has also made a documentary, *Daughter of India,* about this tragic event, which was shown here on March 4. The government of India has banned it from being shown, fearing the reaction and subsequent chaotic demonstrations by women's rights campaigners who are more active now than ever before.

Farber's idea of staging this play illustrates graphically that rape in caste-ridden and male-dominated India is widespread, and nothing much is done about this plague.

Those who missed this extraordinarily colourful event, with installations, posters and big audiovisual TV screens all over the Royal Festival Hall, will have to wait until next year.

# The Jeremy Corbyn phenomenon

Published in *TheNews*, London, August 18, 2015

Britain is rejoicing in Jeremy Corbyn's success in keeping the Blairites at arm's length. His supporters are confident that he will make an excellent leader, not only of his party but also of the country. The nation is fed up with the warmongers, war criminals and spin doctors, and needs a new direction which can restore Britain's reputation as a just, caring, and truly democratic country. Corbyn is the only candidate capable of bringing about that change with his more enlightened, progressive and fresh ideas.

Tony Blair's irrational and illogical statement that the election of Corbyn will be the annihilation of the Labour party, is as good as his series of blatant lies about the Iraq war before the invasion in 2003. That conflict, still not resolved, resulted in the brutal massacre of two million Iraqis on one hand, and hundreds of British soldiers' lives lost on the other. Blair does not claim this time how many minutes Corbyn would take to annihilate the Labour party. Is it going to be 45 minutes or less?

The ex-prime minister, a spent force, and a total failure as Middle East peace envoy, can fool some of the people some of the time, as

Jeremy Corbyn: An extraordinary orator with clarity of thought

the saying goes, but not all the people all the time. There is a limit to what people can take in.

So, why is Blair undermining the democratic process and denigrating Corbyn? Is he frightened by the likes of Jeremy or any future leftist government to press prosecution of Blair's war crimes at the International Criminal Court in Netherlands?

Corbyn's appeal to the vast majority is that he is anti-wars, anti-austerity, and anti-Trident. He supports the trade union movement for workers' prosperity, collective bargaining and right to strike, and believes that new anti-trade union laws are counter-productive. He has always encouraged the underdog and strongly supports the Palestinian cause. He is a staunch supporter of nuclear disarmament. He says he will oppose any new wars abroad and thus save billions of pounds for spending on higher education, the National Health Service, raising the national minimum wage level, and poverty alleviation. If those are his most frequently declared policies for the future, then there is little room to argue against them. Jeremy's known opponents, Blair and his former spin doctor Alastair Campbell ,are yesterday's men who together ruled Britain two general elections ago. Since their sudden interference, Jeremy's popularity has considerably increased over other candidates, according to the latest poll projection. Liz Kendall, another leadership candidate, has conceded that Jeremy is doing really well.

An extraordinary orator with clarity of thought, he is quite capable of challenging the Tories. Under Blair and Brown, the so-called New Labour followed right-wing Thatcherite policies and was indistinguishable from the Conservative Party. Under Corbyn, leadership the Labour Party would have a different feel to it, and would rapidly regain at last its original principles and ethos which were abandoned by the Blair and Brown regimes.

While his rivals in this campaign criticise him on economy and taxation, Corbyn is not reciprocating in the finger pointing game. Corbyn phenomenon is such, as his supporters claim on hustings, that he will win this battle quietly with his hands down. It is mystifying why Blair is conspiring to undermine mild-mannered Jeremy's chances of becoming leader of the Labour Party and a great prime minister in 2020.

# Ethnic cleansing of Palestinians and British betrayal

Published in *TheNews*, London, July 31, 2015

It was Lord Balfour who ignited Zionism. A 67-word letter from the British Foreign Secretary Lord Balfour to Lord Rothschild plunged the Middle East in a horrible conflict between the original Arab inhabitants of Palestine and the incoming immigrant Jews from all parts of Europe.

The letter, dated November 2, 1917, typed on paper without the government's letterhead or logo, was intended to pass on to the Zionist Federation through Lord Rothschild.

This came to be known as the Balfour declaration, which may give an authoritative ring to it. If this were to be written and sent today it would simply be called an email.

Jews were not much liked in Poland, Hungry, the Soviet Union, Britain, France and Ukraine. Europe, in fact, was edgy and discriminated against them, and clearly wanted to get rid of the Jews from its midst. So, the Jews of Europe, but not American Jews, were actively seeking a homeland of their own around about that period.

Balfour's statement came handy as if a divine word, and was fully exploited by the Zionists in their favour to the detriment of the Palestinians. It declares that Jews were to have a homeland in Palestine, but also provided the safeguard for the non-Jewish communities' rights. Legitimate rights of the Palestinians, a condition in the document, were not protected at any stage and totally ignored.

The declaration proclaims as follows:

"His Majesty's Government view with favour the establishment in Palestine of a national home for the Jewish people and will use their best endeavours to facilitate the achievement of this object, it being clearly understood that nothing shall be done which may prejudice the civil and religious rights of existing non-Jewish communities in Palestine or their rights and political status enjoyed by Jews in any other country".

The part of the letter where it says that Palestinians' rights will be safeguarded was never publicised over many decades, and it is now beginning to come to light in the wake of Balfour centenary year; it was deliberately kept from the public attention by the media bosses, who were then, as now, in control.

Balfour himself was not a Jew. He may not have liked them, but he was persistently lobbied by the Zionist leaders. His thought that Arabs and Jews could live side by side in Palestine, which was then populated by 95 per cent Arabs, and respecting each other's civilian and religious rights, proved to be a line in the sand.

One hundred years of ethnic cleansing of Palestinians has made it more difficult for the Palestine diaspora to return to their ancestral homes, because of drastic geographical changes. A systematic erasing from the ground of more than 400 towns and villages and expelling the remaining inhabitants paved the way for apartheid-Israel to construct a new infrastructure of road works, checkpoints and settlements. This altered the appearance of the whole area beyond recognition.

Apartheid-Israel has followed exactly the same pattern as that of the European settlers, who first invaded and occupied North America and then methodically wiped out the entire indigenous population and destroyed an ancient but excellent civilisation.

Israel replicates the Australian example of eliminating the original aboriginal inhabitants by the European colonisers a century and a half ago, and destroyed their well-established culture in the name of progress without giving them a choice of determining their own future.

To commemorate one hundred years of the Balfour declaration this month, numerous seminars and street demonstrations by Palestinians and human rights groups across the United Kingdom and Ireland have taken place, demanding recognition of a Palestinian State in what is now illegally occupied territory.

Before the final Balfour document was signed, Jewish leaders in London were consulted, but Palestinians were not. So the seed of conflict was sowed from the very beginning.

All Jews are not Zionists and all Zionists are not Jews. Many Jews, incidentally, opposed the establishment of a Jewish homeland in Palestine. Those who supported the Zionist project were a tiny minority within the Jewish community at that time.

One of the most prominent critics of the Balfour declaration was Sir Edwin Montagu, the Secretary of State for India and the only Jewish member of the Cabinet. Montagu argued that he reflected the views of at least half the Jewish community in Britain who opposed Zionism, and regarded Chaim Weizmann as a "religious fanatic".

Every British Foreign Secretary worth his or her salt must have read this declaration, because Palestine has always been hot front page news for the past 70 years. The British government has not only not honoured its commitment, it has instead blindly supported Israel's illegal and immoral actions.

The successive British governments have failed to respond to their responsibility of implementing the letter and spirit of the declaration, which amounts to a clear breach of promise and a betrayal.

As the political landscape of the Middle East recurrently changes and the Arab/Jewish problem in the region becomes more complex, it seems there is no one or two states solution in Palestine.

However, many prominent Israelis had sent a message this month calling for the British government to recognise the State of Palestine, stating that both the Israeli and the Palestinian people have equal rights to two states – Israel and Palestine – living side by side along the 1967 borders, in peace and stability.

The 23 signatories from the Policy Working Group, led by their Chair, retired Ambassador, Ilan Baruch, have asked to correct the historic wrong and implement the original Balfour Declaration. The full message and the list of signatories can be found on the Balfour Project website.

The Palestine Solidarity Campaign took the entire front page of *The Guardian* on November 2, asking the Foreign Secretary Boris Johnson and the Government to begin holding Israel to account under international law. The 58 high profile signatories are demanding the government apologise for failing to take action to prevent Israel's continuing occupation of the West Bank, East Jerusalem and Gaza since 1967.

A new pro-Palestine organisation called Balfour Project organised a conference in Central Hall Westminster, on October 31, under the banner of "Britain's Broken Promise, Time for a New Approach".

This seminar was ticketed, more than 1,200 people participated and the tickets were sold out rapidly, according to the organisers.

This and other organisations are doing their best to discover as if by magic wand or Solomon wisdom to bring this Arab and Jew clash in Palestine to an agreed peaceful end.

However, whatever the future holds there is a little chance of a solution soon, unless the West's policy towards Israel changes.

A starting point could be to immediately recognise the State of Palestine and to bring about an end to the siege of Gaza.

# War crimes but no criminal justice

Published in *TheNews*, London, July 15, 2015

The people who started illegal wars in Afghanistan and Iraq are liable to be prosecuted. The United Nations Security Council Resolution 1386 on Afghanistan was forced by George W. Bush through a combination of threats, coercion, blackmail (either you are with us or else), and the false accusation that Taliban were responsible for the attack on the Twin Towers in New York and the Pentagon in Washington on September 11, 2001.

There was no evidence then and there is no evidence now of that charge. No Afghan was ever involved in this incident.

The resolution was adopted on December 20, 2001, and the United States' invasion started two months earlier on October 7, 2001. So, the invasion, occupation, and destruction of that country was totally illegal, uncalled for and criminal.

October 7 is not remembered as much as September 11 of that year. It is now permanently earmarked as a tragic day in the Islamic calendar.

The UN authorised only an International Security Assistance Force (ISAF), which was established for an initial period of six months "to give the Afghan people freedom from oppression and terror". Thus, the term "war on terror" gained a political currency, largely aided and abetted by the Anglo-American media. Ask an Afghan, man or woman, if they have ever received that assistance for which this resolution was passed.

Demonstrably angry, Bush started revenge killing in retaliation of September 11. Having killed millions in Afghanistan and Iraq his inflated ego could not be satisfied, and once he tasted the blood, Bush, with a healthy appetite for violence and torture against his so-called "enemy combatants", opened a concentration camp at Guantánamo Bay, a Cuban territory, where hundreds of suspects are held without charge and routinely tortured, according to the lawyers who visited that camp.

The war in Afghanistan is in its twelfth year. This war of aggression, a crime under the UN Charter, should have been stopped a long time ago, after the infrastructure of the country had been so cruelly destroyed.

The United Nations, as its name suggests, is not in the business of starting wars, it was originally designed to stop wars and unite nations. Why then is there no UN resolution to stop this illegal war? The impotency of this organisation is glaring.

The US used highly sophisticated weapons of mass destruction and caused more than 100,000 Afghan deaths in the first month alone; villages and towns around Kabul and Tora Bora had been completely wiped out. Osama bin Laden, for whom this incredibly barbaric bombardment was launched, was nowhere to be found.

According to Population Policy Research, more than two million Afghans have lost their lives for no fault of their own through an incessant surge of cluster-bombings and cowardly drone missiles. The superpower dismally failed to impose its will on the proud and fiercely independent indigenous population.

The US has, in effect, scored an own goal by evidently turning practically most Afghans into Taliban supporters in one way or another. The history has shown that Afghans, of whatever political persuasion, hate foreign occupation of their land. You only have to look at the "green on blue" deaths in recent days, when American and NATO soldiers are being chased and killed by local policemen. It is a revenge killing in reverse and it is likely to increase.

Newly re-elected president Barack Obama has a better opportunity to withdraw his army from Afghanistan now than in 2014. The majority of the American masses, like the rest of the world, do not want this war to continue any longer. To justify his existence in office he could announce in his inauguration speech next January that the Guantánamo torture camp is closing down and the Afghanistan war will end sooner. Is he a brave man or is he a brave orator?

It is well known that the Iraq war, too, was illegal because the UN never sanctioned war against Iraq. Hans Blix, the chief weapons inspector, was due to report to the UN Secretary General Kofi Annan two weeks before the invasion, in which he was to confirm that

Saddam Hussein had no weapons of mass destruction. The US administration never allowed this fortnightly report to be heard by the Security Council. Bush was impatient and was criminally ill-advised by the powerful pro-Israel lobby to attack Iraq as quickly as possible, and he obediently obliged.

A few movements and individuals, supported by international lawyers and human rights activists, want to take ex-president George W. Bush and former British prime minister Anthony Blair to the International Criminal Court at The Hague to face war crimes allegations.

The appearance of Bush and Blair together, shoulder to shoulder in the dock, would be a welcome sight for Iraqis and Afghans who lost their loved ones through invasion and occupation of their countries. What a stark difference it will make from the usually African dictators being arrested and brought to stand trial. No European settlers, incidentally, from South Africa or Rhodesia (now Zimbabwe), have ever been taken to the ICC for their crimes over many decades. It is as black and white as that.

Now the world is going through a dangerous patch and the Middle East is on fire. Internecine violence in Syria and Iraq may engulf other countries into conflagration.

The politicians in the UK, US and Israel are playing a waiting game. If the West again miscalculates the cultural, political, religious and regional sensitivities and try to interfere militarily, you might have a prospect of a third world war at your hands.

The most effective way to prevent more imperialistic wars in the future is to round up the existing war criminals in the political and military establishments in the West with dozens of their partners in crime, and bring them to criminal justice. Nuremberg, where is thy spirit?

# Islamophobia leads to Muslim awakening

Published in *TheNews*, London, July 8, 2015

The recent killings in Tunisia, by all accounts, seem a direct result of the intervention by Britain and the United States in Iraq, where already more than two million people had been slaughtered and four million made refugees after the 2003 invasion and occupation. As a result, Iraq is burning, the cradle of civilisation is bleeding – an utter chaos and confusion.

The current Anglo-American airstrikes in that country are the main reason for the recent violent attacks in Paris and in Tunisia, the hallmarks of a revenge cycle.

It is often said that foreign interventions and occupations of Muslim lands give rise to Islamophobia, and in turn, Islamophobia leads to "radicalisation" among the better informed and educated young men and women than their parents.

The first and second generation immigrant parents' docility is utterly detested by the new Muslim awakening, also known somehow as the Arab Spring.

The older generation, nevertheless, is deeply worried about the constant barrage of media manipulation that spares no time in demonising the entire Muslim communities. A dangerous form of McCarthyism (a witch-hunt against communists in the US in the 1950s) is being re-imposed under the guise of "security": replace Communists for Muslims here.

A terrorist is always a Muslim, and never described as such of any other religion's members who commit even worse terrorist crimes.

Many instances can be quoted, but only a few recent examples come to mind: Dylan Roof, who massacred nine worshipers in a church in Charleston, South Carolina, was not called "terrorist", "extremist" or his religion invoked.

An English soldier went to Iraq to fight against the Islamic State, stayed there for five months and came back last week with no fear of being arrested or called terrorist or Christian extremist.

Another much-quoted example is that of the British Jews who are frequently recruited for the Israeli army to fight against the Palestinians in Gaza and the West Bank. The number of volunteers had increased last year during the latest Israeli attack on Gaza. The returnees were not called terrorists or Jewish extremists. They don't get detained at airports, arrested, or questioned about their activities in Palestine/Israel.

Quite the opposite method is strictly applied when the British Muslim citizens return from Iraq or Syria after a humanitarian help mission. The double standards are too obvious and the Muslim communities take note of this duplicitous policy. This kind of openly discriminatory behaviour is found to be leading to radicalisation.

Many people now refer to crusade wars, which were fought more than a thousand years ago. One would have thought those wars were over and done with, a relic of the past, but the reality is that after a respite of a millennium, the conflict has taken a different shape in its intensity in modern times.

The destruction in Iraq by the combined armies of European nations and America has shown that the crusade is rearing its ugly head under the banner of democracy, replacing Christianity.

The West hardly ever uses the word Christianity or Christian soldiers these days. Instead, it uses "war on terror" to make it look as if it has nothing to do with Christianity.

When George W. Bush used the word crusade in his very first speech after September 11, 2001, and before the invasion of Afghanistan, he was told he dropped a big political clanger. The clever counsels immediately prevailed and the president was advised against using this word ever again, in case the entire Muslim world is united and provoked.

Tony Blair, however, was sufficiently radicalised, and joined the president shoulder to shoulder to invade Iraq on a false pretence that Saddam Hussein had weapons of mass destruction and was capable of blowing up Britain in 45 minutes. Because British foreign policy is inextricably intertwined with the US foreign policy, Blair and Bush wars effectively created radicalised British-born Muslims.

So, it looks as though the struggle between Islamophobia and so-called radicalisation, whatever that means, is likely to continue indefinitely. Prime Minister David Cameron describes it a generational struggle against "extremist ideology". Is it Cameron's definition of Islam?

To add insult to injury, print and broadcast media tend to focus on Islamic issues in a negative narrative and create fear of the Muslims as if they belong to an alien planet.

The home secretary is introducing new laws under the Counter-terrorism and Security Act 2015, which will adversely affect a largely law-abiding and peaceful populace. The majority of persons affected by the new powers would be Muslims, who are wrongly perceived as rejecting British values because of their religious or political opinions.

Those laws already exist in the Prevent programme. Where there is a danger of the new laws being unscrupulously applied to criminalise Muslim citizens for expressing strong opinions or opposition to government policy, democracy is rendered as a meaningless slogan. One wonders how democracy will look here in future. One way of preventing violence is to widen the range of opinions that can be freely expressed, not restrict them.

Most worrying is the possibility that freedom of speech and dissent, the two British values, would be lost for ever under this dubious, confusing and counter-productive counter-terrorism legislation.

Not everything is lost yet; the West is capable of finding a new, more productive, rather than destructive, non-aggressive role in complex Middle East politics. This can only be done from a moral high ground. Airstrikes and bombings of weaker countries are not the solution and will not stop terrorism, it will help increase it globally.

The world has experienced death and destruction in Afghanistan, Iraq and Syria throughout the past 14 years. More wars must not be contemplated. The rules of imperialistic games have to come to an end to make the world safer, away from both terrorism, and warmongers.

# Demonising Muslims is a recipe for 'radicalisation'

Published on the *Stop the War Coalition* website, July 7, 2015

Prime Minister David Cameron's latest political agenda will not go down well among the Muslim community. He attacks British Muslims at home and abroad for violence in the Middle East, instead of blaming the legacy of 14 years of death and destruction in Afghanistan, Iraq and his direct role of intervention and bombings in Libya's complete destruction and elimination of a good friend of Britain, Muammar Gaddafi. Now Syria is next to be attacked.

There is no gainsaying that foreign invasions and occupations of Muslim countries give rise to Islamophobia, and in turn Islamophobia leads to "radicalisation" among the better educated young men and women.

Like technology, the political language is fast changing. Take radicalisation, for instance – what does it mean? One dictionary describes it as radical political and social reform. Surely a noble and positive idea of change for the better; nothing wrong with radicalisation here. If one is radicalised by prison reform, or welfare reform, of which a great deal is being said at the moment in the government's five year plan, it is a positive thing. But this word, like "war on terror", is badly corrupted in the negative sense by politicians and is highly politicised.

Another word we have been used to hearing every day of the week is "terrorist" or "terrorism". A terrorist is always a Muslim and never described as such if others commit similar crimes and worse. The media deliberately avoid calling them terrorists and their religion is never mentioned.

Obviously, Muslims take note of this duplicitous policy. This openly discriminatory behaviour is also found to be leading to radicalisation.

It looks as if the conflict between the demonisation of Muslims and so-called radicalisation, whatever that means, is likely to continue indefinitely. Cameron describes it a generational struggle against "extremist ideology". Using such obscure phrases doesn't help. He should explain to the public what he means by that term.

A liberal section of the population is deeply worried about the constant barrage of media manipulation of portraying Muslim citizens as wicked. It reminds us of McCarthyism in the United States, when the communists were targeted, suppressed and persecuted in the 1950s.

Many people now refer to crusade wars, which were fought more than a thousand years ago. One would have thought those wars were over and done with, a relic of the past, but the reality is that after a respite of a millennium, the conflict has taken a different shape in its intensity in modern times.

The destruction in Iraq by the combined armies of European nations and America had clearly shown that the crusade is rearing its ugly head, under the banner this time of "democracy", replacing Christianity.

The West hardly ever uses the word Christianity or Christian soldiers these days. Instead, it uses "war on terror" to make it look as if it has nothing to do with Christianity.

When George W. Bush used the word crusade in his very first speech after September 11, 2001, and before the invasion of Afghanistan, he was told that he dropped a big political clanger. The clever counsels immediately prevailed and the president was advised against using this word again, in case the entire Muslim world gets united and provoked.

Tony Blair, however, was sufficiently radicalised, and joined the president shoulder to shoulder to invade Iraq on a false pretence that Saddam Hussein had weapons of mass destruction and was capable of blowing up Britain in 45 minutes. Since British foreign policy is inextricably intertwined with the US foreign policy, Blair and Bush wars created radicalised British-born Muslims.

Cameron and Home Secretary Mrs May may have good intentions of preventing terror, and it is understandable, but the root causes of radicalisation are bombings and the destruction of Muslim countries one by one.

Print and broadcast media tend to focus on issues in a negative narrative and create fear of Muslims, who, as the propaganda implies, do not integrate in the society.

That is absolutely wrong. The Muslim community has been an integral part and parcel of the British society for more than half a century.

In his speech on Monday, Cameron blamed the "Muslims not integrated sufficiently". It is not strictly true. Here we go again, we have another word, "integration", which has lost its meaning and is used as a tool to attack the already integrated Muslim population. Even technology cannot keep pace with the wordage revolution.

Muslims are as much integrated as other ethnic minority communities in a multi-cultural Britain. The majority of them have no intention, understandably, of frequenting pubs, striptease clubs and all-night dancing places. So they are not seen as sufficiently integrated, to borrow Mr Cameron's phrase.

The fact is that Muslims are largely integrated into the political and economic life of Great Britain. These, incidentally, include doctors, teachers, university professors, lawyers, solicitors, barristers, accountants, QCs, members of parliament, businessmen, engineers, councillors, political pundits, cabinet ministers, novelists, writers, historians, film makers, television and radio presenters, mayors, train and Tube and bus drivers, journalists and editors.

The list is endless, but in short, Muslims are integrated in all strata of society and make an enormous contribution to the well-being of their adopted country. Being the largest ethnic minority, it plays a crucial role in running the British essential services. Why upset the applecart by creating such an ill-conceived and ludicrous new law as crime of non-violent extremism? Cameron uses phrases such as "Islamist ideology". Islamic ideology makes perfect sense, but what is Islamist ideology? There is no such thing as Islamist in Islam. It is a politically motivated slogan and it carries no meaning.

The home secretary would be introducing new laws under the Counter-terrorism and Security Act 2015, which will adversely affect largely law-abiding and peaceful populace. The majority of persons affected would be Muslims who are wrongly perceived as rejecting British values because of their religious or political opinions.

Strong laws already exist in the Prevent programme. There is a danger of the new laws being unscrupulously applied to criminalise innocent citizens for expressing strong opinions or opposition to Government's foreign wars and bombings of other nations.

One wonders how democracy will look in this country in the future if these intimidatory laws are enacted. One way of preventing terror violence is to widen the range of opinions that can be freely expressed, not restrict them. Most worrying is the thought that freedom of speech and dissent, the two highly regarded values, would be lost forever. Under this dubious legislation, people would not be allowed independent thinking and critical writing without being labelled as "non-violent extremists". Consequently, that will have quite an opposite effect: a recipe for radicalisation.

Exploring a more productive rather than destructive role in complex Middle East politics should be the aim. Sheer military assault could not achieve peace, as we have seen horrendous death and destruction in Afghanistan, Iraq, Libya and Syria throughout the past 14 years.

Further bombings in Iraq and Syria would result in a lot of civilians killed. That would be brushed aside as collateral damage. It is not clear what the prime minister is hoping to achieve and how long the bombings will continue.

The rules of imperialistic games have to come to an end. There is no military solution to the political problem. The region needs to be made safe from both terrorists' attacks and warmongers' airstrikes, but not at the cost of yet another million dead.

# Urdu: Third largest language in the world

Published in *TheNews*, London, April 8, 2015

Urdu is spoken throughout the world, not only in India and Pakistan. It is ranked as the third largest language behind Chinese and English. The development of the language dates back from the fourteenth century. The word 'Ordu' is Turkish for horde, and is spelt this way. It is not known when in history it was changed to 'Urdu'. Perhaps it was an understanding between the Turks and the Indians. The connection with Turkey is explained by historians with the invading Turkish soldiers and their presence in India. The gradual evolvement of this new means of communication system with altogether different local languages and customs followed later.

From 1837, Urdu was the official and court language of India, replacing Farsi, which belonged to the bygone Mughal Empire. The British administrators, civil servants and army officers were required to learn Urdu during the empire days.

Written in Arabic script, this universal language is spoken and understood by more than a billion, the combined population of India, Pakistan, Bangladesh, although it is called Hindi in India merely for political reasons, presumably because it is deemed to be associated with the legacy or successor Muslim cultural heritage.

Urdu vocabulary mainly comes from Farsi and Arabic, but because of Hindu and Muslim inter-mixed culture in pre-Pakistan India, many Hindi words and verbs are derived from Sanskrit, an ancient language hardly spoken anywhere.

So, Urdu/Hindi, in unison, became one single language, also known as Hindustani. As a lingua franca, it is used in all parts of India. Urdu is the national language of 185 million Pakistanis.

Spread across other continents through emigration, for instance, to Australia and Africa, Urdu is now spoken in many parts of the Middle East, South Africa, Uganda, Kenya, Tanzania, Malawi and

Australasia. In most northern Europe and Scandinavian countries there are thousands of Urdu speakers with their numerous daily and weekly newspapers and magazines, and inevitably along with Urdu television channels, using the latest technology.

Farther afield in the Caribbean, where Indians had settled three hundred years ago, Urdu is spoken not only by Asians, but also many locals who picked up this widely recognised communication tool for engaging businesses and social interaction.

Mohammed Ali Jinnah, Nehru, who loved Urdu poetry, and Gandhi, made their speeches in Urdu while fighting for independence on hustings and on radio broadcasts throughout the subcontinent. They used this common language most effectively for a common cause. So, Urdu proved to be a useful mass communications instrument for the politicians to express their views and to impress the wider public.

Moreover, the Bombay film industry throughout the ages has revolved round Urdu films in which songs are written and sung in Urdu, making it possible to export, which gave rise to its expansion around the world. The public is enchanted with them on both sides of the border and beyond.

If the filmmakers had chosen Tamil, Telugu, Gurmukhi or Gujarati, for instance, the industry would not have made such an enormous impact as to rival even Hollywood, and would certainly not have lasted that long. Bollywood owes its popularity to Urdu.

India and Pakistan produced innumerable Urdu poets and scholars over the centuries who contributed exceedingly towards civilisation, and popularised the rich content of the language. Song writers and singers, male and female, delightfully played their part in keeping the language appealing, alive and kicking.

According to UNESCO, both countries print hundreds of books in Urdu every year, and these are far more in number than the ones produced in regional or Middle Eastern countries.

Urdu books in prose as well as in poetry are written and published from all continents locally, wherever the south Asians have settled. Similar books are found in almost all high street libraries in the United Kingdom. It looks like Urdu is going to retain its number three status in linguistic and spoken word.

Urdu is being neglected in India. Some ultra-nationalist parties such as the RSS and the BJP have labelled Urdu as an exclusively

Muslim language. That is absolutely wrong. Armed with Urdu you can travel in any region from one end of the country to the other, without difficulty in communicating or the religion bit coming into it.

In the heyday of the British Empire, Lord Macaulay, the arch-imperialist if ever there was one, recognised the charm, beauty and richness of the language, but at the same time feared the social, cultural and political influence of Urdu. He wanted to abolish it from schools, colleges and madrasas and replace it with only English. Had he succeeded in his design, Urdu would have been extinct today just like Latin and Sanskrit.

# Sworn enemy

Published in *TheNews*, London, May 30, 2014

Nawaz Sharif invited the then Indian prime minister Manmohan Singh to attend his swearing-in ceremony. Mr Singh, being a more superior politician than his counterpart, completely ignored the invitation and did not bother to travel to Islamabad. It was partly because of the opposition from many quarters of the Indian population, and partly because of soldiers being killed on both sides of the border in the high altitude of the Himalayas. Mr Singh could have come to Pakistan at that time for a peace mission. Both prime ministers once belonged to the same pre-partition Punjab and speak the same language, and an understanding could have been developed for future relations between the two countries.

Sharif, on the other hand, ignored his own people's feelings of reciprocating that snub and travelled to Delhi. The Pakistani army also seems unhappy about a Pakistani prime minister's unprecedented attendance of sharing a platform with an enemy country, particularly if there was no mutual political agenda.

Although most regional leaders attended the inauguration ceremony, it is noteworthy that Bangladesh, which was created with the help of India, was not represented by its prime minister.

Sharif's presence in Delhi may be seen as boosting the legitimacy of an ultra right-wing conservative Hindu nationalist whose past record towards Muslims in India amounts to fascist policies towards minorities.

The United States had banned Narendra Modi from coming to America; Britain had done likewise. Now he has been elected as a leader of a large country the world will have to look at him again in the light of his new capacity as prime minister, and deal with him according to international diplomatic norm.

It is hard to predict what mode of Modi foreign policy will shape into, but the Bharatiya Janata Party (BJP) has repeatedly declared a tougher stance on Pakistan. It is early days to speculate whether that position would change with the advent of the new regime.

Hindu terrorists have been killing Muslims by the thousands for many decades. More than 2,000 perished and many were burnt alive by Modi's fascist gangsters in 2002.

More recently, horrible anti-Muslim killings took place in Muzaffarnagar in Uttar Pradesh, where a large number of Muslims were killed. Others were forced to flee, and then their houses were ransacked, looted, and burned.

The so-called largest democracy in the world is guilty of killing civilians, political opponents, Christians, Muslims, Dalits, Mizos, Asamees and other minorities in the south. These minorities are up in arms against the Indian political system.

On other such issues, India needs to withdraw its half a million soldiers from Kashmir and solve the problem by implementing the United Nations resolution which says to let the Kashmiris decide their own future.

RSS (Rashtriya Swayasevek Sangh), meaning national volunteers organisation, and BJP together advocate "India for the Hindus" ideology, which can have a disastrous consequences for India if this Hindutva rage is not kept under wraps.

Modi in his new leadership role can control his Hindu fundamentalist violent criminals, if he wants to, and reassure India's Muslims. He should be seen to be protecting the human rights of the minorities.

On the back of his landslide victory he has a choice of turning the country into a peaceful, socially cohesive and less riotous place, or letting it drift into chaos, division and sectarianism.

He has promised to turn the economy around, which is a good thing for the country, but first social peace is more important than money in your pocket.

# What did I see in Lahore?

Published in *TheNews*, London, April 6, 2014

What did I see in Lahore this time round on my 24th visit to Pakistan?

Squalor, respiratory diseases, abject poverty, heaps of rubbish dumped everywhere, beggars, almost all elderly or women with a small baby on their shoulders, children as young as ten years old repairing old cars and motor cycles, with blackened garb and faces, seemingly dipped into oil, dust and grease, a sight that is bound to upset anyone. The government of Pakistan ought to tackle this child labour problem with the help of UNICEF.

On a rainy day most of the roads become flooded, and gutters clog up because of a desperate lack of a workable sewerage system.

Pollution, caused by car fumes, dust, and poor air quality, has reached a dangerous proportion. As a result, the number of asthma patients is on the increase. According to several medical reports, breathing difficulty, respiratory congestion and heart ailment among the young and the old alike are a common complaint.

Traffic jams have peaked to a bursting point, although the roads have been widened in the recent past. I see large piles of refuse and waste material, including non-recyclable smelly rubbish thrown in the streets and open spaces, producing nauseating stench. Places such as these are undoubtedly the home of the killer denghe mosquito.

People complain about dishonest and morally depraved officials in many government departments, including the judiciary and the police. I do not know whether they are depraved because they are deprived, or if they are deprived because they are depraved. However, no one, it seems, is prosecuted for abuses, so it becomes a normal way of life.

When the Punjab Assembly is in session, there is a chaos on the roads and misery for the public. From the busy junction of Charring Cross to Governor House and beyond, all approach roads are closed for days on end, causing a great deal of hardship for the workers who travel on buses. Adding insult to injury, the new chief justice was in the high court and again roads were blocked around the buildings for one man's safety at the cost of thousands of man-hours loss.

There are two five star hotels on Mall Road, Pearl Continental, and Avari; both look like fortresses in battle. Armed police are permanently stationed for security reasons, obscuring the façade of those beautifully refurbished hotels. I did not see any European or American during my stay.

I see the Lakshmi building, in the heart of Lahore, in McLeod Road, which has been demolished and erased to the ground, leaving the frontage as a grade one listed landmark. Lakshmi's statuette at the top had already been removed many years ago.

I see Quaid-e-Azam Mohammed Ali Jinnah and Allama Mohammed Iqbal's photos displayed in public places and shops, but they are only names and an average citizen is not fully aware of who those men were, what they did and more importantly what they said.

I find no television programme worth watching, there are too many commercial breaks. Those advertisements' cliché content and unintelligible language (a mixture of Urdu/English/Punjabi) are more often than not ridiculous and their repetitiveness sickening. If you switch from one channel to another that makes no difference either, because other channels have the same copycat identical format. The only relief may come from a sudden electricity cut off.

Dozens of television stations have sprung up, a lucrative business and a nice little earner if you can get one. The so-called anchors make a hell of a lot of money from messing about all day; most of them seem to have a little knowledge of the subject under debate, but they are experts par excellence in propelling their own political agenda, a tried and tested trait, good enough to suit their masters who employ them. None of these journalists prima facie can be regarded impartial and they show the least journalistic professionalism; they are supported by political parties or big businesses with large bundles of bucks as an irresistible temptation.

The majority of the invited guests on television shows are either semi-literate or sick as a parrot and stick to a stubborn point of view of their own, without a slightest hint of flexibility or a desire to learn.

Objective political reporting is missing in the entire media. There is party political reporting, though from a singular, self-centred point of view, designed to give a twisted and distorted slant to the events rather than to inform and to educate. Truthfulness is not a habit of media types in Pakistan. Most, if not all, have a price tag depending on their range of influence and ability to play ball. Most journalists are nouveau riche through a dishonest system and unethical practices.

In a so-called democracy, the poor, the down-trodden, the underclass, and poverty stricken are alienated by the very rich and ruling Mafia. These poor souls are left alone to have to fend for themselves.

On the other hand, some areas of Lahore such as the cantonment look like an implant from Europe. This area is quite different from the rest of the city in all aspects of living: its efficiency, excessively wealthy residents, peaceful green surroundings and luxurious life style. Retired and active army officers with their private golf clubs live here.

What else did I see in Lahore? The fire gutted the famous bookshop Ferozsons recently, and a small front door section has survived intact and some books are on sale. I was told the fire was caused by a short circuit. Another source said the insurance company is disputing this.

Lahore is expanding in area and population like other cities in the developing world. It might end up as a concrete jungle in ten years or so. At the moment the highest building in Lahore is the State Bank of Pakistan on the Mall. Thousands of people are migrating to Lahore from other parts of Punjab for work and residence. Newer and more innovative resources are needed to govern this ever changing city.

If you wanted to see the magical glory of peaceful surroundings of Lahore, you should have been born at least 50 years ago, when you could cross roads carefree without bothering to look right or left. If you want to see that now you needn't have been born.

Pointing out the social evils and unjust and unhygienic conditions prevailing in the city today does not mean that all is lost.

Lahore is an ancient, historical, architecturally rich large city and expanding. It was the capital of the Mugul Empire most of the time of its reign, along with Delhi in the second place.

It contains Jehangir's Muqbara, Empress Noor Jehan's Mausoleum, vast Baadshahi Mosque, Lahore Fort and Sheesh Mahal,

Lahore Zoo, Lahore Railway Station, Shalimar Gardens, Wazir Khan Mosque, Chauburji Gate, the beautifully maintained Fatima Jinnah Gardens, Lahore Museum and behind it the ancient Baara Daree, the magnificent Government College building, Allama Iqbal's resting place, more recently Minaar-e-Pakistan, and numerous other ancient structures which I may have missed.

# Rally for Moazzam Begg

Published in *TheNews*, London, March 3, 2014

On a bitterly cold and windy day, more than a thousand protesters gathered outside the Home Office in Marsham Street, central London yesterday (March 02, 2014) to express their anger and disappointment about the arrest of a man globally known and respected as a human rights campaigner.

Moazzam Begg was arrested a week ago and is charged with "Syria related terrorism". After a sustained campaign in Britain by the Stop the War Coalition and others for his release, he was finally sent back from Guantanamo Bay concentration camp to his home in Birmingham eight years ago without a blemish on his character.

Speakers after speakers, Muslims and non-Muslims, spoke very highly of him and expressed their annoyance and frustration.

Victoria Brittain, a writer, journalist and a scholar, said she knows Moazzam very well. She found three striking qualities in him: integrity, bravery and compassion. She said "he is the bravest man she ever came across. He has gone through a hell of a lot of abuse in his life. He is an innocent man, he is not a terrorist".

Kate Hudson, director of Campaign for Nuclear Disarmament, said "Moazzam has been accused of Syria related terrorism, what does that mean? He is not and has never been a terrorist or a threat to this country. He has nothing to do with terrorism. The government is trying to intimidate those who wish to help the refugees and brutalised starving Syrians".

A common theme among the speakers was that the government's wrong policies of demonising the Muslim community will result in polarisation with far reaching repercussions.

Most speakers agreed that the government is worried about what Moazzam knows about the illegal activities of the secret services and International Renditions. This is the only reason, they claimed, why Mr Begg is stitched up.

Ismael Patel, a Muslim scholar, deplored the arrest of Begg and asked the government not to incite religious hatred by picking up innocent Muslims. He demanded stop and search of Muslims must end. Moazzam is regarded a hero among Muslims around the world, he is most definitely not a terrorist and not an advocate of terrorism, he emphasised. Moazzam has been quite open about his travelling abroad for investigating cases of victims of injustice.

He worked hard and established an organisation called CagePrisoners, now changed its name to Cage, to help those whose human rights are being violated in several countries.

At one stage of the rally, every man, woman and child shouted loudly "Moazzam Begg", "Moazzam Begg" at the top of their voices to show solidarity and support for Moazzam.

People who made passionate speeches and pledged their support for Moazzam Begg are Anas Altikriti, Taji Mustafa, Shaykh Haitham al-Haddad, Hamza Tzortzis, Susan Bryant, Azad Ali, Abdullah Andalusia, Ismael Patel, Victoria Brittain, Dawah Man, Kate Hudson, Cerie Bullivant, Adnan Siddiqui and Asim Qurashi.

# Ukraine better off with Russia

Published in *TheNews*, London, February 25, 2014

Ukraine is the second largest country of Europe with enormous mineral resources and a considerable technological knowhow. This is not the only reason why this country is important. It is because there is a political tussle going on between Russia and the United States/European Union to keep this land on their side.

It is in the larger interest of the whole world to avoid the current situation in Ukraine to flare up. Therefore, it must not be allowed to be broken up.

The US and the EU would like Ukraine to join the North Atlantic Treaty Organisation (NATO). Millions of people around the world hold the view that NATO is an organisation that should have been abolished after the collapse of the Soviet Union as Warsaw Pact was also abandoned.

Although there is no love lost between the Ukrainians and the Russians, because of their uneasy historic past, the fact is that they cannot afford to separate themselves from each other in the present day of economic and political climate.

The EU and the US cannot be Ukraine's best friends in view of the fact that their democratically-elected president was toppled by the US intelligence services with the help of cash offering to his political opponents. Any deeper association with the EU may mean that the country would be under pressure to join the military alliance and obliged to contribute its share of soldiers to fight and be killed in the dirty imperialistic wars abroad for absolutely no benefit to Ukraine.

Russia is still in a superpower league and would not tolerate a NATO country in its backyard, supported by the US and, therefore, there would be an uneasy peace between the neighbours when one is permanently in a different political and economic camp.

This reminds me of an identical situation of mistrust, also a legacy of the past, which exists today in the Indo-Pakistan subcontinent, although closer in many ways, far apart in thought and ideology. The Western media, including the BBC and CNN, present news about Ukraine in their own typical fashion and political bias. Look at this issue beyond the headlines.

The American foreign policy objective of regime change is well-known; this has been adequately demonstrated in, for example, Iraq, Afghanistan, Libya and Sudan to name a few in recent history. The West is well practised in the art of regime change methods.

Ukraine has been destabilised by first demonising its legitimate president, now deposed, and then supporting anti-government demonstrations in Independence Square in the capital Kiev. Thus, the seed of division has been sown as it was in Iraq against Saddam Hussein a few years ago. This region as a whole is now in crisis, thanks to foreign interference. The political chaos created in Ukraine is also the result of foreign intervention. The ultimate aim is to build NATO military bases in Ukraine bordering Russia, with command and control in the hands of the NATO commanders.

A recent leaked conversation between the US Assistant Secretary of State Victoria Noland and US ambassador to Ukraine Geoffrey Pyatt revealed that they discussed which of Ukraine's opposition leaders they would like to see in government.

The secret plan is to see the break-up of the Russian Federation, that is the goal. The Ukrainians will be better off by keeping their country independent from the United States, NATO and European Union's entrapment.

# Dr Abbas Khan: Murder most foul

Published in *TheNews*, London, January 16, 2014

George Galloway, the Respect MP, has described the death of Dr Abbas Khan in a Syrian prison as "murder most foul". Michael Mansfield, QC, human rights lawyer, said Dr Khan's death appeared to be "a clear case of murder and eventually this case will have to go to the International Criminal Court in the Netherlands".

The Foreign Office minister Hugh Robertson says Syrian authorities have "in effect murdered him".

The mother of Dr Khan burst into tears when she said in anger: "The national security intelligence of Syria have killed him. They are murderers". She is surprised the Syrian regime "cannot differentiate between a humanitarian aid worker and a terrorist; it was his profession to give life, not to take life. He can't kill an ant, even".

Prime Minister David Cameron has said that "Abbas's death is a sickening and appalling tragedy and it is right that the Syrian regime should answer for it". In a letter to the mother of Dr Khan, he wrote that he will continue to press for those responsible to be held to account. By all accounts, observations and analyses, it looks a case of a murder pure and simple. The Syrians claim that he was found hanged in his cell.

This young man from Streatham, south London, was a fully trained and hard-working surgeon who served his country and communities with a deep sense of dedication and duty. He would not have gone there to treat injured children had he not had these exceptional qualities. He arrived in Turkey, where he treated in an open makeshift field hospital beneath a tent for a few weeks. His intention was not to go to Syria, but he was requested to cross over to tend badly injured children in Aleppo where the government had ignored their responsibility to look after them. The war-torn, lawless border area between the two countries is porous. In spite of his credentials as a doctor he was arrested, and because there are no diplomatic relations between Britain and Syria, no embassies in each other's country, no immediate representations could be made.

According to George Galloway, who also lives in Streatham, Dr Khan was elated as soon as he heard that he was going to be released and was to be reunited with his wife and two children. Galloway was to fly to Lebanon on that fateful Friday to fetch Dr Khan back home to London, as previously agreed with the Syrian foreign ministry.

There is no earthly reason why Dr Khan should kill himself. In the absence of knowing the height of the cell in which it was possible to hang oneself, some sort of witness or photographic evidence, it is hard to believe the Syrian side of the story. Furthermore, the timing of his death, just before his release and coming home, is also puzzling.

The Foreign Office knew about Dr Khan's plight during the entire period of his detention because the family remained in touch with them throughout, but they took only lukewarm interest which was absolutely no help to the worrying family. It was left for his mother to run around from pillar to post. She travelled to Damascus and singlehandedly discovered where his son was imprisoned. She succeeded in getting her son transferred from a military torture cell to a civilian prison. The world came to know about him after his death.

He had disclosed to his family that his captors enjoyed torturing him for their sheer pleasure. His mother saw him reduced in weight to alarmingly several stones. That also leads one to believe that a rogue element within the Syrian security service has killed him in order to hide its atrocities and tortures, of which Dr Khan was recipient. He was the man who knew too much.

The coroner's report will be made public next month. Whatever the outcome of the inquest, a young British doctor, in the prime of his profession, has all of a sudden mysteriously died in custody in Syria. Aged 32, he had a full life ahead of him, but both his life and work have been cruelly cut off.

In any investigation, the first and the crucial question to ask is why he was held in prison for such a long period of time as 13 months without charge or deportation. The circumstantial evidence is overwhelming in favour of a political murder rather than a far-fetched idea of a suicide, it is an inescapable conclusion that this was indeed a murder most foul. Kill the man to kill the evidence may have prompted the Syrians to kill an innocent man.

# Drones must be withdrawn

Published in the *Iranian News Agency*, December 7, 2013

It is no longer a secret that both the Pakistani government and the army are complicit in ignoring the slaughter of their own citizens, mainly women and children, by the American guided missiles. A hard-line Taliban as a small group of ideologues and the moderate element in it are angrier than ever before, because several of their men have been killed from missiles fired from unmanned aircraft miles into the sky.

Hundreds of drones have killed thousands of Pakistanis during the past few years. The ratio between the civilian deaths and the so-called extremists is one to 1,000 on average. Life is that cheap in that country.

That would be extremely intolerable for any self-respecting nation in the world, but the Pakistani politicians and the army keep mum about this new type of invasion of their country.

Since 2011, when the Iranian air force shot down an unmanned aircraft flying freely in its air space, the US has not been known to have ventured again with a similar vehicle in Iran. It is presumably because of the financial loss: one such weapon of mass destruction costs $25m-$30m. If a couple of Reapers are shot down in Pakistan, President Obama, who seems very keen in this business, will be forced to think twice before sending more. While the Iranians took a bold step, the Pakistani air force seems to be impotent to safeguard its territorial integrity against illegal and deadly raids.

The Obama administration takes pride in killing the movers and shakers of the future architects of peace in Pakistan and Afghanistan.

Twelve years of non-stop violence has achieved nothing. The Americans have finally, but belatedly, realised that they have been a total failure in Afghanistan, morally defeated, and forced to pack up and leave: reminiscent of their previous misadventures and debacle in Korea and Vietnam.

On other international issues, Obama has been faithfully following the Bush/Cheney/Rumsfeld/Wolfowitz agenda, concerning the Israel/Palestine crisis since he came to power. He has not closed down Guantanamo concentration camp as he promised before he became president. Many Americans and interested foreigners now believe that that was only a ploy to entice people to vote for him, which may not amount to an election fraud in the normal sense of the word, but it certainly amounts to a betrayal.

During his presidency, there has been an intensification of bombings in Yemen, Somalia and increasingly in Pakistan. The Western alliance is collectively guilty of inhumane and cowardly acts, and yet safely away from the scene of the crimes without accountability. No North American and NATO war criminals have ever been caught and brought to justice.

It is well known that the US has 183 military bases dotted around the world in 110 countries, including five in Pakistan and more than 16 in Afghanistan. It has radar, high-tech communications systems and, crucially, intelligence satellites which should be more than enough to watch over this planet from above. Not content with that, the US alone has eight submarines patrolling 24 hours a day, and several of the most sophisticated aircraft carriers in all the oceans.

In other words, the US has already conquered the world between hot and cold wars, so why is the US and its NATO partners in crime killing the poor people in Afghanistan and Pakistan on a regular basis under the cloak of "the war on terror"?

The Americans go to great lengths to fight with anybody anywhere; they put men on the moon and explored outer space, but to their disappointment they found nobody there to fight with. No 'Star Wars', then?

So, the US has now turned its attention towards the South China Sea, an already peaceful and progressive region of the world. What is the point in opening a new front?

Indiscriminate killing of civilians has to stop. Calling a halt to further interventions in foreign lands has to be the starting point. You cannot fight terrorism with terrorism, anyway.

# Osama bin Laden's assassination: An answer to an Iranian journalist's question

Published in *TheNews*, London, and in the *IRNA* (Iranian News Agency), October 18, 2013

The circumstances of Osama bin Laden's assassination have not been clear. Many people globally were and still are of the opinion that he was killed in the first phase of George W. Bush's carpet bombings of Kabul and Tora Bora, towards the end of 2001, before the Taliban offered to hand him over to a neutral country, Turkey, but Mr Bush, a very angry man at that time, rejected the offer.

A few, highly technologically manipulative fake videos of him have surfaced since then. We have had quite a number of contradictory and conflicting reports and analyses concerning his life and death in the media, which confuse the whole world.

You can safely ask whether the invading troops really killed Osama bin Laden on that fateful Sunday or if they have killed an Osama lookalike.

Since no hard evidence has been shown by the US, such as a photograph or video clip, the world would remain sceptical about the circumstances of his death.

Barack Obama and his security team must be naïve to think that what they say about Osama bin Laden would be believed without serious questions being raised.

The question is also being asked: How many times does bin Laden have to be killed?

It looks as if it is the beginning of withdrawal of American and NATO forces after their total failure in Afghanistan. This occasion can be used as a face saving formula for the Obama administration to declare the "mission accomplished".

We are entering a very dangerous neo-imperialistic phase when several non-European countries, Iran, Syria, Libya, Somalia and Yemen, seem unsafe from being droned from the skies.

Coming back to your original itemised questions, which I have not answered in that order, my initial reaction of the faked bin Laden death was that Obama needed to get out of Afghanistan, as he, like his predecessors, realises, though belatedly, that the US can never win the hearts and minds battle in Afghanistan. This war will end as the Vietnam War ended: humiliation for a superpower.

The American president wants to show to the Americans that he is ending the war after having got rid of the most wanted man by the US. What a triumph for him to go into next presidential election with a 'victory' behind him. I hope this answers your question.

# Thatcher the "Milk Snatcher"

Published in *TheNews*, London, April 11, 2013

Was Margaret Thatcher a heroine, or a "wicked" woman as the Respect MP George Galloway describes her?

It may depend on which side of the political spectrum you are on. Arthur Scargill's National Union of Mineworkers, and 6,000 sacked print workers on Rupert Murdoch's four newspapers, will agree with Galloway.

Mrs Thatcher was brutal with the trade unions of all kinds. In 1984, she closed down coal mines in the north of England, Wales and Scotland, making thousands of miners redundant and destroyed their livelihood and traumatised their families. The lifestyle and the camaraderie among the miners which existed for more than 100 years had gone all of a sudden. Every week, there were reports in trade journals of health problems, heart attacks, divorces, forced separations, break-up of marriages and premature deaths among those who remained unemployed for years and lost all they ever had. Some committed suicide, others migrated to such distant places as Australia, Canada and the US.

Ironically, to rub salt in wounds, she started importing coal from Poland and Australia, which was more profitable than the coal mining industry here.

The Unite union leader has described Thatcherism as an "evil creed". That is one of Mrs Thatcher's legacies.

Another legacy: banning Gerry Adams and Martin McGuinness, the IRA leaders, from appearing on radio and television programmes. They were not to be seen or heard. This dictatorial edict did not win her friends here or abroad, certainly not in the Irish Republic. No democratic country would take such a step. This may be put down to her lack of experience in international and intercommunal affairs when she took over.

It was round about the same time she declared that the country was being swarmed by Asians, when in fact the figure for the fresh intake of immigrants was the lowest in a decade. She became very unpopular among Asians who thought they were being made scapegoats.

She had a spat with the former leader and Prime Minister Edward Heath, who she beat in a Tory leadership election. Mr Heath, her erstwhile boss, never spoke to her again.

She got away with many things that a male prime minister would not have got away with, without being labelled as a dictator and worse. Being a woman of charm with a feminine touch which she used wonderfully well, she escaped that title, but even her admirers would admit that her style of management was dictatorial.

As a grocer's daughter she learnt the value of money and savings from the very beginning. One of the savings she made in her role as Education Secretary in 1974 was to abolish free milk in primary schools because it was a "waste of money". She made instant enemies among parents and children alike, who still remember her as "Thatcher the milk snatcher". She saved more money in the wrong places by closing down dozens of hospitals, clinics, and completely shut down industrial plants and establishments in the north and south of the country. Her privatisation of gas, electricity, water, and British Telecom, led to rising unemployment and did not help the country; only the rich had become richer and the poor poorer.

Those are her most damaging legacies from which the country is still suffering. Yet, she found enough money to spend on a nuclear arsenal.

She claimed that "there is no such thing as society". The dangerous implication of that notorious saying is everyone for themselves; make money, however you can, you are an individual on your own, develop a greed and grab culture without regard to other fellow human beings. That selfish political philosophy, unlikely to be taken seriously, leads to an unknown disaster and amounts to an economic anarchy. No institutions can work without a society. Law Society, High Court, Supreme Court, residential homes, media organisations, city institutions would become redundant. The only national institution then can be called Margaret Thatcher.

It is no secret that some of her own cabinet colleagues profoundly disagreed with many of her obviously divisive policies on the poll tax, milk for children, and a verbal war with the French over Europe. She imposed her will on those issues all the same.

For the sake of one media mogul, Rupert Murdoch, a foreigner, who sacked 6,000 print workers overnight in January 1986, ensuing a year-long Wapping dispute, resulting in regular pitched battles with the horse-mounted police outside the plant, Thatcher unwaveringly supported him to the hilt in order to crush the unions in Fleet Street.

That is another of her legacies of which no one can be proud. She vigorously opposed sanctions against the oppressive South Africa apartheid regime. It is safe to say, therefore, that people did not matter in her tenure of office, but profits and money for the rich did.

Her pursuit of unpopular policies was sidelined after the Falklands War with Argentina in 1982. As the lady luck would have it, that single event propelled her into a category of wartime prime ministers. Without the Falklands War credentials, she would have served only one term in office.

# Allama Shabbir Ahmed Bokhari: scholar, poet and educationist

Published in *TheNews*, London, December 7, 2012

Allama Shabbir Ahmed Bokhari, who died last week in Lahore, was a scholar, poet and an educationist of a higher calibre. He excelled in both Urdu and English literatures. Fluent in verbal and written prose and poetry in Farsi, he was the first Pakistani who translated Lord Macaulay's notorious treatise into Urdu.

Macaulay proposed that Arabic, Farsi, Urdu and Sanskrit (Hindi) should be gradually eased out from educational institutions in British India and replaced with only English; he wanted the supremacy of the English language in the subcontinent. He could not read, write, or speak a word of any of those languages. Mr Bokhari has done a favour by writing extensively about Macaulay and exposing his real imperialistic instincts in easily understood Urdu.

Born in a small farming village called Choonyan near Lahore on July 1, 1918 in a traditionally educated family, he graduated from S.E. University in Bahawalpur where higher education was free for Muslim students at that time. Subsequently, he post-graduated from Aligarh Muslim University with distinction.

It was this place where he acquired knowledge by hard work and which opened his mind, widened his horizon and changed his outlook on education and particularly the system of education.

As a young student, he happened to meet the visiting luminaries there, such as Allama Mohammed Iqbal, Quaid-e-Azam (then plain Mr Jinnah) and another great Muslim leader Mohammed Ali Johar.

He launched a quarterly high-brow literary magazine, *Tafakkur* (which roughly means

Thoughts) and continued editing it for several years.

He made valuable contributions in education while an adviser to the various departments in the Punjab education ministry where he

*Bokhari: An ardent advocate for building libraries and laboratories*

worked. He campaigned and worked hard to change the arcane colonial education system.

He opposed nudity, half-naked dancing girls, and sexually explicit low-level shows on television, which were made for merely commercial gain at the cost of corrupting the nation's morals.

In an open letter to the then Prime Minister Benazir Bhutto, he suggested to ban the vulgar TV programmes with sexual overtones which corrupted the impressionable youth. He argued that most crimes outside the box were directly related to the soap operas on the screens. He was against the import of Western culture into Pakistan; by doing so, he said, Pakistan could not remain the land of the pure as the word "Pakistan" implies, but, on the other hand, he wholeheartedly admired the Western improvisation and ever improving research in medical science and other technologies from which the humankind benefited.

The fact that he died at the ripe old age of 94 may have some explanation of longevity in modern times, not least his own.

Whenever he visited Europe and the US, he was disappointed to see violence and vulgarity in television channels and newspapers. He did not want this to be emulated by Pakistanis.

As an educationist he was an ardent advocate for building libraries and laboratories which Pakistan badly needed and lacked behind all south-east Asian countries. He wanted to see a developed culture of learning in the country through free education, for which he devoted much of his time and in which he partially succeeded.

When I visited him last April in Lahore I found him pretty sharp in his thinking in retirement. Visibly weakened in gait, but mentally agile, he relished in a lively discussion with his close friend and neighbour Professor Mazhar Ali Adeeb about international affairs of which he seemed remarkably well informed.

He is survived by his elder son, Professor Ashraf, who is currently Controller of Examinations at the Government College University Lahore and the younger son Arshad, who lives in England. His wife and another son Amjad, a retired Major, predeceased him.

# Assange is an institution and must be saved

Published in *TheNews*, London, September 2, 2012

Julian Assange is not only a brave man, he is an institution and must be saved from the dirty tricks of the international intelligence conspiracy against him.

He is not charged with any crime by the Swedish authorities who wish to question him about the rape stories told to them by the two women in Stockholm. It sounds more like a honeytrap than actually a pre-setup.

The media's attitude to portray the editor-in-chief of WikiLeaks as a criminal is deplorable. He must not be allowed to be extradited to Sweden on hearsay, as he could be sent to the United States to be locked up indefinitely for disclosing the war crimes of the US and NATO armies in Iraq and Afghanistan.

The original European arrest warrant system was intended mainly in cases of terrorism or murder, but Assange is neither a terrorist nor a murderer; he is a global icon and the whole world respects him as a hero. In the eyes of the arrogant and the powerful he is an enemy combatant.

Both Britain and Sweden have refused to give a pledge that he would not be handed over to the US after he has dealt with the Swedish courts, whenever it happens. Here lies the crux of the whole issue. Why cannot assurances be given if this is only a matter of sexual assault allegations?

Sweden's past record shows that it handed over two Egyptians to the Central Intelligence Agency (CIA), which passed them on to the Mubarak regime, which tortured them. Mr Assange must not be allowed to be kicked around like a football.

The media also have not explained properly the real issue. Instead, many sensational and emotional words such as rape, sexual assault, faulty or leaking condoms and high-tech terrorist are used in sexed-up stories that sell newspapers. This kind of reporting is not only discriminatory but can also influence the outcome of the whole affair.

Rape is a short four-letter loaded word which easily fits in a small space of a headline, but it is also an emotive word and people, particularly women, react to this emotionally, even though without proof of any concrete evidence or conviction.

To illustrate a point for instance, if a referendum is held in Britain in which a single, simple question is asked – whether Assange is guilty of rape – the likely outcome may well be a 51-49 ratio against him, because of what the public read and watch.

On the other hand, if the press shows a change of heart and fairness in its reporting, the result of the survey could be reversed in his favour by far a bigger margin. The point about this is the whole thing is being played out by the editors.

Most of the right-wing media are toeing the line taken by the Foreign Secretary William Hague, who declared in the House of Commons that Assange will not get a safe passage out of the country. Even some of the so-called lefty papers are at best lukewarm and at worse semidetached.

Many aspects of this scandalised episode are hidden from the public. For instance, we do not know about the two women involved, how reliable they are, or what motivated them to bring lurid details of their bedrooms into the public domain, a long time after the event.

It is known the women have not formally accused the WikiLeaks founder of rape. They had initially requested him to take an HIV test in Sweden.

The public fears that America's enemy number one after the late Osama bin Laden may eventually end up like Bradley Manning, a US soldier who passed secret files to WikiLeaks and who has been locked up for the past two and a half years without trial. Some reports suggest that he has been tortured in prison. If a US soldier is meted out such a punishment, what chance an Australian citizen, accused of treason, can expect from a US administration is worth pondering.

Thankfully, the British Government now seems to have realised that gunboat diplomacy is no longer an option, as it used to be under the archaic empire era of colonialism, only after President Rafael Correa of Ecuador had warned Britain that storming his embassy to arrest Assange will be suicidal.

Britain has footprints around the world, and by setting a precedent of invading a foreign legation in London in contravention of the 1961 Vienna Convention would certainly backfire on Britain. Is it worth taking a risk?

Assange denies allegations against him and says these are politically motivated. He is prepared to be questioned by the Swedish prosecutors in the Swedish embassy in London, or in the Ecuadorean embassy, where he has been granted political asylum by Ecuador. The alternative does not seem promising; it reminds us of a similar incident in 1956, when the Soviet Union invaded Hungary to crush anti-Soviet uprising. The prime minister Imre Nagy sought political asylum in the Yugoslav embassy in Budapest.

In spite of a written safe passage by his successor, Imre Nagy was arrested by the Soviets as he was leaving the Yugoslav embassy and subsequently executed, "as a lesson for other leaders in communist countries".

Well-wishers of Assange would hope that the WikiLeaks leader is not made a scapegoat to teach others a lesson, and the US will desist from following the Soviet path and leave Assange alone.

# Assange's fate in the balance

Published in *TheNews*, London, June 17, 2012

The fate of Julian Assange, who faces extradition on a European arrest warrant to Sweden, hangs in the balance.

The founder of WikiLeaks is accused of rape by two Swedish women. He was represented in the High Court in London which has yet to decide on this case. The Appeal Court, consisting of Lord Justice Thomas and Mr Justice Ouseley, has reserved judgment on whether Assange be extradited to Sweden to face sex offence allegations.

After protracted intense arguments by both the prosecution and the defence, lasting for two days (July 12 and 13), Lord Justice Thomas said that there would be another hearing to hand down the judgment. "We will take time to consider the numerous arguments and authorities", he declared.

It could be at least three weeks before the judgment is revealed.

Led by Ben Emmerson, QC, Assange's legal team is confident that its client could be saved from being sent to Sweden.

The court heard that the incident such as this would not constitute as rape in the United Kingdom, in view of the consensual nature and willing participation of the two women who changed their mind afterwards to charge Assange of alleged sexual misconduct.

At a previous hearing at Belmarsh on January 11, the main thrust of the defence argument was that if Mr Assange is sent to Sweden on unreliable and hearsay evidence, he could be extradited from there to the United States where he is seen as disclosing thousands of secret US diplomatic documents. The right-wing media and politicians have already campaigned against WikiLeaks to be declared as a terrorist organisation. Now electronically tagged in a Norfolk mansion, he had been held for nine days in London's Wandsworth prison in solitary confinement.

Julian Assange coming out of the High Court in London

At this appeal court hearing, on the other hand, the argument mainly, but not exclusively, centred on the lurid bedroom accounts of the sexual behaviour in a single bed of both partners, involving condoms and unprotected sex to which the women say they did not consent. Some of the details cannot be printed here.

Mr Assange insists that he is a victim of a smear campaign and the case is politically motivated. His lawyers say that he is vilified by most of the media for publishing classified documents relating to the wars in Iraq and Afghanistan. He is portrayed as a dangerous whistleblower by his enemies in the US, but highly respected as a courageous editor of WikiLeaks by his supporters around the world.

The court heard that the real issue is not of rape, but possibly of failing to use a leak-proof condom; his lawyers forcefully argued that this did not constitute as rape. The women's complaint is that it wasn't protected sex, to which they did not consent and they were forced into it.

Whichever way this case is settled, implied sexual criminality or not, it appears that the US and its army would not give up on Assange easily; his well-wishers argue that Assange should be nominated as a Nobel Peace Laureate, instead of awarding such an accolade to warmongers in Washington.

# Squeezing squash in Olympics arena

Published in *TheNews*, London, April 4, 2012

The International Squash Rackets Federation had floated an idea of making squash an Olympics sport. The International Olympics Committee has not yet taken a decision, but there is a likelihood that at some stage in the near future this game could be included. Triathlon and Taekwondo were the two new additions to the Sydney Olympics in 2000. Tiger Woods is trying to get golf as an Olympic sport.

Pakistan dominated squash for the best part of 50 years at the highest level. This supremacy has rapidly slipped away from its grasp, and it has lost its glory as being the most competitive nation to the least competitive within a few years since its most famous squash heroes Jahangir Khan and Jansher Khan retired.

The country has not won any major international squash tournament at home or abroad since then, and for the foreseeable future it seems unlikely that the role would be reversed, or the lost glory of the golden era of Hashim Khan, Azam Khan, Roshan Khan, Torsam Khan and the two hugely talented Mohibullah Khans be regained. What has gone wrong?

If Pakistan's world rankings do not improve considerably sooner rather than later, Pakistan would be better off by not participating in squash at a higher international level unless it rigorously overhauls its training, discipline, funding, selection, and sponsorship issues.

Squash is the fastest ball game bar none. Having acquired the taste, more nations have partaken in the recent past, making squash a truly global sport. The advent of squash in the Olympics arena would certainly spur the country for properly preparing the squads for the international competitions.

A few suggestions have been put forward by sports commentators which have not been taken up for discussion or for implementation. Here are a few more:

Sport psychology has to come into play to start with. The coaches in each sport must be fully trained in modern psychological techniques of training before undertaking their charges. They need to be able to instil in players a new confidence and a culture of winning habits.

Competitiveness with a "killer instinct" is the key to an international success. Australians are the best practitioners of this trait, which, evidently, they have developed in an art form, and are reckoned to be the toughest opponents in any international competition. Their sport psychologists can easily qualify for gold medals in their own sphere of expertise.

The youngsters and first-time participants must be taught how to play under pressure. Winning is the name of the game. There is no room for on and off days.

In addition, the sportspersons should be given ample time for training and financial support before, during, and more importantly, after the events, so that in their turn they could pass on their valuable knowledge and experience in a national spirit to the next batch of aspirants.

A sport supremo in the shape of a dedicated minister needs to be appointed, whose 100 per cent attention is focused on only sporting activities rather than on politics.

Thus, a national coaching and training system can be made to work, instead of importing foreign nationals who may or may not have the real interest of the nation at heart.

Meanwhile, there is an uneasy atmosphere prevailing at the cricket establishment after a disappointing performance in cricket for the past couple of years. The management and selectors have a lot of questions to answer. Besides, three test cricketers, M. Asif, M. Aamer and S. Butt, were convicted in a London crown court for corruption and match fixing and were jailed. One of them is released after serving his time. The other two are currently in prison in England. This shameful episode greatly damaged the reputation of Pakistan as a fair sporting nation.

As leaders of the world in hockey for the best part of half a century, Pakistan seems to have lost faith in itself and needs to revive its former brilliance in this game too. Pakistan were pathetically seventh in hockey in the Beijing Olympics, winning only two and failing to reach the quarter finals. The hockey team will again be participating in London's Olympics, starting on July 27 this year, where, with a bit of luck, it is expected to do well. More needs to be done to solve the coaching and fitness problems. A well-thought-out initiative will have to be taken if Pakistan cares to restore its pride in sport. Gone are the days when Pakistan willy-nilly lifted a squash, cricket or hockey trophy at the drop of a hat.

Olympic games are said to be a rich man's play-things, but it is not strictly true. There are about 300 events to be participated in, every four years. Some games do not require an investment of vast amounts of money and these equally attract top medals. Pakistan can afford to take part in at least 40 to 50 such events to enhance its position in medals pursuit.

Apart from weightlifting, boxing, and wrestling, the country could do more to include swimming, rowing, pole vault, hammer throwing, long jumping, high jumping, archery, javelin, cycling, volleyball, handball, badminton, table tennis, shooting, and many more inexpensive ones.

These games could be sponsored by a nation of 186 million. The private sector for its own commercial benefit could chip in without fear of making a dent in its profits.

Many smaller and poorer countries than Pakistan, such as Jamaica and Lithuania, do very well at Olympics, thank you, by winning gold and silver medals. Before Pakistanis can achieve that sort of success, they will have to learn how to get at those emblems.

# Prince Mohsin Ali Khan to mount peace offensive

Published in *TheNews*, London, January 13, 2012

Prince Mohsin Ali Khan is to travel this month to Pakistan, India, Bangladesh and Sri Lanka to explore the possibility of forming a confederation of these countries. Disclosing his plans at a Royal Over-Seas League dinner last Thursday, attended, among others, by Prince's Trust Director of Diversity, Mr Mike Waldron, he said he will have high level talks with government officials and cabinet ministers in those countries. The four Asian neighbours have been breathing down each other's neck for a long time.

Although having several things in common, paradoxically, these nations have much more pronounced diversity in culture, religion, political ideas and self-interest. He says that a politically coherent policy for the Indo-Pak subcontinent needs to be devised which will stick. The prince is confident that he will float the idea anyway.

His Royal Highness seems to have taken the Swiss Roll approach in international affairs. This means that when the whole task looks daunting, you decide to do a small but discrete part of it. You keep doing this until you have made enough 'holes' in the task for it to look more manageable. The difficult assignment the prince has taken upon himself is a starting point towards making a hole in the whole arduous task.

The Europeans share contiguous geographical borders, have a cultural and religious affinity, also identify themselves with one another and apparently seem to enjoy being all Europeans. In Asia, there are no such similarities or comparisons. In 1967, Charles de Gaulle, the then president of France, had opined that there was no political reality in Asia. He was right then and would have been right now. The idea of forming a European type of union of nations seems a bit remote at the moment, but the prince insists that this can be achieved.

A direct descendent of the late Nizam of Hyderabad, a Muslim majority state in India the size of France, the prince is usually seen in a dark blue sherwani (a fully buttoned up tunic from knee-cap to neck-line) with a colourful silk handkerchief protruding from his left-hand upper pocket. This is an unmistakable trademark and an instant recognition of a dress culture of the former Muslim rulers of India. As an ideologue, his geopolitical ideas may well have a strong popular appeal, but while he has invested much thought and effort in giving his theory a logical twist and knows how to win friends and influence people in Sri Lanka, India, Pakistan, and Bangladesh, the noble Nawab might find, if he has not already found out, that to persuade politicians is another matter.

# Regime change made easy in Libya

Published in *TheNews*, London, October 28, 2011

Many people, including Libyans, question as to who will most benefit from the NATO-led 'liberation' of Libya.

The *Wall Street Journal* answered that question in its weekend editorial which implies that the US, the British, and the French companies would expect exclusive oil contracts from the new regime.

The paper said: "President Obama, who led from behind, Britain's David Cameron and France's Nicolas Sarkozy deserve credit for the overthrow of Gadhafi, who was a global menace".

In an interview, Qaddafi had dismissed his Western partners by saying that he will give all the country's oil contracts to Russia, China and India and the West is to be forgotten.

The West was not happy about this, and was not accidentally involved in the pro or anti-Qaddafi conflict among Libyans, it carefully orchestrated by pretending that its aim of intervention was to save civilian lives. Evidently, more civilians were killed by NATO's bombing than previously known.

So, Sarkozy-appointed National Transitional Council, the West's pro-Israel politicians and the ultra-terrorist organisation called NATO, had all played a vital role in not only regime change but also murdering a leader of a sovereign country.

American Secretary of State Hilary Clinton was in Tripoli a couple of days before the execution of Qaddafi for talks with the leader of the National Transitional Council. She was interviewed on CBS News on October 21. The reporter asked if Qaddafi's death had anything to do with her surprise visit to show support for the Libyans. She replied: "I am sure it did". She joked and burst into a noisy laughter with a twinkle in her eye, and said: "We came, we saw, he died". Mrs Clinton may be forgiven for such childish remarks because she is after all a product of the extreme violent culture of her country.

Laughter may be the best medicine, but did she know that one should never rejoice in somebody's death, not even at the death of a rival?

So she can also joke and laugh at millions of people killed by her country over the past 60 years, starting from Hiroshima, Nagasaki, Korea, Vietnam, Cambodia, Granada, Panama, Iraq, Afghanistan, Pakistan, Libya, Somalia, Yemen, and the Gulf War.

The infrastructure of the most prosperous country in Africa has been horribly destroyed by NATO's stealth fighters, drones, and missile attacks. Aero-drones, refuelling tankers and satellites had menacingly hovered over Libya. After the devastation and destruction, Libya has to be rebuilt where a lot of work is created. Many companies seem to be jumping with joy. New British defence secretary Philip Hammond told the BBC that he "now expects business executives to move to Libya and to secure lucrative reconstruction work."

Muammar Qaddafi had lately steered clear of the mainstream Arab politics of Saudi Arabia, Egypt and Jordan. He was respected by most of the non-Muslim countries on the African continent because of his Pan-African stance. He had a dream of united Africa as one unit.

The new leader of National Transitional Council is an unknown quantity, much the same way as the young Colonel Qaddafi was when he overthrew King Idris in 1969. He may find it difficult to unite his nation in a torn society from the remnants of pro-Qaddafi tribes. The seed of conflict is already sown and it takes a hell of a long time to reconcile the factions.

Whatever the future holds, the brutal murder of Qaddafi will constantly remind the Libyans of their tragic history in years to come. It is reminiscent of King Faisal of Iraq and his prime minister, Nuri Es Said, whose bodies were dragged with much blood through the streets of Baghdad when the military staged a coup against the monarchy in 1958.

# Colour of racism then and now

Published in *TheNews*, London, December 21, 2011

References to Muslims in newspapers and TV channels as extremists, terrorists, and radicals are a dangerous phenomenon in British media today. This should concern all political parties and think-tanks. Although a majority of descendants of immigrants are content with how they are treated and enjoy living in the United Kingdom, there is an unpleasant element which loses no opportunity to stir up trouble, citing terrorists or terrorism.

From the middle of the last century to the end, there was a huge outcry against black or 'coloured' people taking jobs and housing. The 'rooms to let' notices stated: "No Irish, no coloureds, no dogs". The old guard which had seen the British Empire in its dying days in action, and also fought in the Second World War, had not lost its superiority and desire to rule the world again. The rapid decolonisation movements in Africa and Asia had dampened their last remaining wish.

Among those who were staunchly against immigration from the new Commonwealth countries were Sir Cyril Osborne and Enoch Powell, both Tory members of parliament. Osborne, whose views, like Powell's, were regarded as extreme even by the Conservative Party, died on August 31, 1969, to the distress of the racist National Front, which was hyperactive in those days, but to the relief of not quite settled immigrants, who had no idea of what was in store for them in the near future.

Following in the footsteps of Osborne's fierce opposition against blacks in the country and the peril that it may entail, Powell came up with even fiercer and more persuasive arguments for stopping immigration of any kind, and suggested that those already here to be sent back to their country of origin.

The most effective and influential speech ever heard about immigration in the UK came from Enoch Powell in April 1968 with his infamous prediction of "rivers of blood" flowing in the streets between the blacks and the locals. He argued that the newly arrived workers from non-European countries would greatly devalue and damage the cultural landscape of the green and pleasant land of Britain. The country was then slightly tinged with black and brown. In December that year, newspapers published cartoons satirising Powell's speeches. One caricaturist's caption read: "I am dreaming of a white Christmas", obviously intended for him. Curiously, it was then a colourful era in a darksome political climate.

Soon after the speech ended, many immigrants were racially set upon, abused, spat on, seriously injured with grievous bodily harm, and deaths were reported. Some did not turn up for work for fear of being attacked. Butchers from London's Smithfield Market and dockers from east London's Isle of Dogs came out in a big demonstration, shouting "Enoch, Enoch" in support of his ideas of racial purity and demanding that all immigrants be immediately sent back home. It was truly a frightening and anxious time, because the semblance of any peace and harmony suddenly disappeared.

Mr Rees Mogg (now Lord), the editor of *The Times*, argued in a powerful editorial roundly condemning the Powell diatribe which was widely quoted in all newspapers here and overseas. The then Prime Minister Edward Heath, a liberal-minded Tory, sacked Powell from his Cabinet for making such ferociously racial attacks in a sensitive immigrant area (Wolverhampton), and causing incitement to racial hatred and a breach of the peace.

Today, several popular newspapers, particularly the right-wing tabloids, seem to adopt yet another provocative hyperbole, fearing 'Islamification of Britain', which, in essence, is another subtle form of disguised racism; an antidote to multiculturalism. This kind of far-fetched idea may serve as a temporary and short term gain for an increase in circulation of the papers, but the intelligent public is likely to reject that calculated misinformation.

From some of these harmful Islamification of Britain stories, one gets the impression that every Englishman in future will be forced to put a cloth cap on his head and rush towards a nearby mosque for prayers. Every woman would cover her head with a scarf or veil. Alcohol will be banned, all pubs will be closed down because there would be no purpose for them. Striptease clubs would be disbanded.

Prostitutes would be stoned to death. Lap-dancing girls would be given 20 lashes each with a Libyan or Egyptian whip. Capital punishment will be restored. Murderers, thieves, rapists, robbers, and spot-fixers of cricket matches would not be imprisoned, but hanged or executed by a firing squad, or their heads will be cleanly sliced off with a sharp Arabian sword. Semi-naked women will automatically disappear from television screens and magazines. A section of the houses of parliament would be converted into a new grand mosque and an Islamic Education Centre would replace it.

The new constitution will be devised whereby the prime minister by law would have to be a practising Muslim. The monarchy will be retained for the time being until a new head of the calibre of an Ayatollah Khomeini or a Salahuddin is found, and only then would the monarchy be abolished. Lesbians and homosexuals will have a choice to reform themselves or be deported to the remotest parts of the globe with no right to return to their former abodes.

By the time the Islamification of Britain is fully flourished, there should be no problem of social cohesion or integration.

I am no expert on Islam nor studied the subject deeply, but the impossible scenario above may conjure up an Islamification of Britain idea of a few tabloid journos with which they scare the public. The media always play a powerful role in moulding the opinion of ordinary people. If scare-mongering goes on for long and people fall into the trap, then there is a real danger that the old time racist politics of Powell and Osborne will return with a vengeance and the victims this time would be exclusively innocent young British Muslims and their families.

# Palestinian return

Published in *TheNews*, London, September 29, 2011

The President of the Palestinian Authority has applied for a full membership status of the United Nations to keep the Palestine cause at the forefront of Middle Eastern politics.

As the Arab revolutionary forces are hard at work to change the political climate in the region, it seems important that the Palestinian Spring should not be left behind. Justice for Palestine springs from the same source.

To be recognised by the United Nations, if Mahmoud Abbas's bid is successful, does not mean that Palestine will be free any time soon or that apartheid-Israel would vacate the forcibly occupied land. It means that by joining the world organisation the Palestinians will have a unique voice of their own, and a workable trade and diplomatic relationship with other nations with whom they will come into diplomatic contacts. It will boost their morale and give them fresher confidence as a nation and a united liberation front.

Of course it will present a major psychological blow to the Israelis, who have been trying to wipe out the name of Palestine from the map.

The Israelis feel very uncomfortable when they hear the word Palestine, let alone the Palestine Solidarity Campaign, which is made up of many different nationalities.

Thousands of houses, schools, buildings, streets, mosques, villages, and any other traces of Palestinian presence and ownership have been systematically demolished over 60 years to make room for newer settlers from Europe, America and the former Soviet Union countries.

The names of roads and areas have been renamed and dramatically changed in such a way that they no longer can be recognised as once Palestinian country. Snatch and grab is still continuing unabated.

Orthodox Jews outside the British Parliament protesting against Apartheid-Israel's illegal occupation of Palestine

Christian and Muslim holy places are controlled by imported alien Jewish squatters. Mahmoud Abbas's move is a reminder to the world that it has a moral obligation to help recover the occupied land of the Palestinians. Some politicians have threatened to cut off US aid to the Palestinian Authority if it continues pursuing independence and statehood.

This could be a blessing in disguise, and should inspire the Palestinians rather than worry them. There are thousands of other sources where the assistance can readily come from. Palestinians desperately need professional military training like any other nation. They long for their own air force, navy, regular army, tanks and other means of self-defence. The US is not going to provide that. So, here is a chance to get rid of the American so-called aid, once for ever, and look somewhere else.

The threat from the US and its Zionist lobby is ever present. The most powerful president on this planet is helpless on the Palestine issue; he cannot do the right thing. He cannot take a moral judgment according to his conscience, such is the pressure from apartheid-Israel. He is looking the other way with an eye on the next presidential election, when the Jewish votes and donors are important. President Obama and his Democratic Party must realise that they may alienate African-American votes along with a large Muslim electorate.

Meanwhile, Turkey has belatedly found out what the Israeli entity is all about when nine Turkish human rights activists were cold-bloodedly slaughtered on the flotilla carrying food and medicines for Palestinian hospitals.

Diplomatic relations, irretrievably strained, are unlikely to be the same again, even if restored.

The Israeli embassy, some call it a Mossad spy-den in Cairo, was invaded by Egypt's new politically awakened youth who are demanding de-recognition of Israel and opening the Rafah border between Gaza and Egypt. All of these developments indicate that the Middle East is rapidly changing. Israel's position in the world is weakening and indefensible.

The thundering applause and standing ovation you have seen on your television screen after the speech of Abbas at the UN General Assembly is a clear proof of the popularity of the liberation of Palestine, if the proof was ever needed. Only two countries out of 189, Israel and the US, did not applaud.

Most political observers believe if the momentum is maintained and the Arab countries and Palestinians do not miss the opportunity, then there is a possibility of achieving a Palestinian State.

The Security Council of the UN is a relic of 1945 when there were far fewer nations than they are today. Most of the world then was under the yoke of colonialism. The Security Council today is a joke. It is an old imperialist tool of the West to suppress human rights of the Palestinians and others. It is abused to promote colonial wars of which the veto-flashing US is the main culprit. There is an urgent need for a complete reform of the 21st century United Nations. Abolishing the unjust power of veto of the five permanent members is absolutely essential.

# Ten years of folklore

Published in *TheNews*, London, September 10, 2011

Ten years have elapsed since September 11, 2001, and the truth about the attacks in New York and Washington has not been revealed yet, in spite of various investigations. Many conspiracy theories have been propounded over the years with no conclusive proof beyond a shadow of the doubt. The official line of the US has always been that it was the work of al-Qaeda. Some day, the whole truth will come out.

The Guantanamo concentration camp, which Barack Obama promised to close down before he became president, is still operating in the same inhumane way as it ever was. Mistakes that had been committed by George W. Bush are being repeated by Obama. This year another batch of thousands of Afghans and Pakistanis, and now the Libyans, have been killed by NATO drone bombings. Relations between the West and the Muslim world are at a very low ebb, if not deteriorated. Nothing is altered to change the course of history. No lessons have been learnt and hardly anything has been achieved in order to bring about peace to the world during the past decade.

Afghanistan had the worst fate by bearing the brunt of the wrath of a panicky George W. Bush at the time. More than a million innocent civilians, who had nothing to do with 9/11, perished through a persistent barrage of carpet bombings of Kabul and the surrounding areas. The full might of US and NATO Air Forces had gone berserk. Yet, no one in the West even mentions these horrible atrocities and crimes against humanity. The daily media keep telling us repeatedly of 2,800 dead on that day in America, but completely ignore the millions of Iraqis and Afghans who were killed and further millions made refugees in their own countries. Not a single Afghan was involved in the 9/11 attacks. Having tasted the blood, this kind of extreme violence, torture, and renditions were replicated in Iraq a couple of years later in 2003. The racist media, bypassing all the norms of modern journalism, have turned 9/11 into a thriving industry. It has become folklore.

The West has only one narrative and one line of thought, and that is al-Qaeda, which the alliance wants to finish off. There is no such thing as al-Qaeda as an organised institution; it has no hierarchical setup or kinship, no headquarters, no offices, no desktop computers, filing cabinets, or a command and control structure. Al-Qaeda is a delusional mythology permeated by the West to justify its wars of terror and occupation of one kind or another. The US used the misleading phrase "war on terror", but this worn-out term has outlived its purpose and has lost its novelty, and is no longer fit for political objectives. Currently, al-Qaeda has become fashionable, replacing war on terror which does not arouse emotions any more. One hopes that al-Qaeda's sell by date is shorter than ten years.

If, say for argument's sake, there is such a thing as al-Qaeda, then it lives in the hearts and minds of millions of people across the globe. That means the West can never fight against this in perpetuity, even though it has a superior surveillance technology, fire power, and secret services. You can kill a man but you cannot kill an idea. The battle that needs to be won, in all conflicts, is that of the hearts and minds. So, where do we go from here after a decade of devastation and destruction?

It looks like a clash of civilisations for better or for worse, but there is a hope and a way out of it. The Islamic and Western civilisations are now really intermingled in the twenty first century, identical in many of their shared core values. It will be hard to think that there can be a clear-cut victory for one or the other. However, the room for compromise and negotiations is wide open. For the next ten years or so, the aim ought to be to devise fresh ideas of common humanity to end these unnecessary and unwinnable imperialistic wars. All wars end on a negotiating table.

The alternative is the Afghan war will end as the Vietnam War ended: humiliation for a superpower. The British, who previously fought and lost two major wars in Afghanistan, had learnt that the empire could not occupy that country. Similarly, another superpower, the Soviet Union, had found to its terrible cost that this proud land could not be subdued.

The US and NATO armies have no choice but to leave Afghanistan to the Afghans, whether they call themselves Taliban or not, to sort out their own problems without imposing a foreign political ideology which is unacceptable to them. Twenty-first century proxy colonialism has no place in this world.

Many young people, in the meantime, have been arrested and put behind bars on mere suspicion of terrorism, without any charges. They might be guilty of one thing, and that is they do not tolerate their fatherland to be invaded and occupied by foreigners.

Britain and the US have recently passed draconian laws, such as control orders and tagging of young Muslims on a flimsiest intelligence rumour. A number of counter-terrorism laws have been instituted, but these have dismally failed to achieve anything and are counter-productive. Mr Robert Lambert, the former Metropolitan Police chief, said in an interview this week on BBC Radio 4 that these counter-terrorism laws are, "dangerous, damaging, demeaning, and demonise the whole Muslim community".

In dozens of seminars and symposia that I have attended, selected politicians, professors, and experts on Middle East and Afghanistan come up with a pile of heavy paperwork consisting of two to three thousand words of speeches which they enthusiastically read to the audience, where the rhetoric from the beginning to the end of their dissertation is invariably the same old variant that only al-Qaeda is responsible for terrorism in the world. They dare not speak about the daily atrocities, humiliation, and abuse suffered by the Palestinians in the West Bank and other parts of occupied Palestine. Everybody seems too afraid to criticise apartheid-Israel's war crimes. The International Criminal Court at The Hague has summoned a few African and Serbian war criminals, but Israeli war criminals are immune from being prosecuted, are above the law and remain untouchable.

I have yet to hear from these orators what terrorism is. How do you define terrorism? What is the difference between drone bombings from afar in the sky and killing wholesale civilians in Afghanistan, Pakistan and Libya, and the odd individuals who commit suicide and murder worshippers in mosques? Both forms of terrorism are cowardly operated. Both kinds of terrorism must be equally condemned.

This week a new four-day investigation (Sept 8-11) to find out the truth about 9/11 is taking place in Toronto, Canada, sponsored by the International Centre for 9/11 Studies. The organisers announced:

> "The credibility of the official investigation into the events of September 11, 2001, carried out by the US Government between 2003 and 2005, has been questioned by millions of citizens in the United States and abroad, including victim family members, expert witnesses and international legal experts."

# Bin Laden's death linked with US seeking exit strategy

Published in *TheNews*, London, July 6, 2011

After the raid on the compound in Abbotabad where Osama bin Laden was supposed to have been killed by the US special forces, the *Wall Street Journal* wrote an aggressive editorial on May 6, warning Pakistan in no uncertain terms: "Stop the double game and join us, or we'll do the job ourselves and with other friends, such as the Indians if need be".

It is a similar threat with which the former president General Pervez Musharraf was confronted with almost ten years ago, when President George W. Bush gave him a stark choice: "You are either with us or against us". The leader writer further warns, again in unambiguous style, that "if any Pakistani official helped bin Laden, America would need to consider it a hostile act".

Pakistan on its part has also warned the US in equally strong language and accused the US of violating Pakistan's sovereignty. The prime minister of Pakistan had declared in the national assembly that his country had the right to retaliate with full force against any future incursions. The public opinion in the country is highly volatile and uncompromising towards both the US and the Pakistani army and the air force which failed to intercept the two invading helicopters.

Impervious to the sensitivities of the Pakistani public, Mr Obama on his recent visit to London also dropped a clanger by contradicting himself, by saying on one hand that he respects the sovereignty of Pakistan, but, on the other, he would not hesitate to repeat Abbotabad type of raids if necessary. This has not gone down well in Pakistan. Both sides accuse each other of playing a double game.

So, by the look of it, the love affair between Pakistan and America seems to have reached a difficult juncture.

In the meantime, business as usual, the US, unfettered, has picked up the thread where it left off and has quietly launched drone bombings on Pakistani sites since the Abbotabad operation.

Whatever the outcome of the dispute between the two uneasy partners, scepticism about bin Laden's assassination has grown with the US refusing to publish photographs or a video of the attack. Conflicting accounts have been put out by the White House.

Also, the circumstances of the killing have not been clear, mainly because the Pakistani side has not explained much to go by.

Many people believe that bin Laden was killed in the carpet bombings of Kabul and Tora Bora at the end of 2001. The Taliban around that period had offered to negotiate with the US to hand him over to a neutral country, but the US president at that time rejected the offer. Had he accepted, the history of that region would have been dramatically different today.

You can safely ask whether the invading troops killed the real Osama bin Laden on that fateful Sunday night, or have they killed an Osama look-alike, since absolutely no hard evidence has been shown by the US, who only told us that the Navy Seals had killed him and dumped his body in the sea.

Obama and his security team must be naïve if they think that what they say about Osama would be believed without serious questions raised. How many times does bin Laden have to be killed, one wonders.

My initial reaction of the faked bin Laden death was that Obama needed to get out of Afghanistan, as he, like his predecessor, realised, though belatedly, that the US can never win the hearts and minds battle in Afghanistan.

This war will end as Vietnam War ended: humiliation for a superpower. The American president wishes to show to the Americans that he might end the war after having got rid of 'the most wanted man by the US'. What a triumph for him to go into next presidential election with a victory behind him. After a total failure in Afghanistan/Pakistan for a decade, he is likely to use this occasion as an exit strategy and declare the 'mission accomplished'.

There is a suspicion that the raid was planned with a Pakistani element involved at a highest level, such as a mole in the army. This cannot be proved beyond doubt, but it is strange that such an incursion could be carried out without an insider help. Was the air space around an important military town of Abbotabad not protected? What was the Pakistan Air Force, with all its sophisticated state of the art fighter aircraft, doing on that night? Did the American secret services, so accustomed to operating in Pakistan, recruit somebody from within the Inter-Services Intelligence unit or the army? All of a sudden Pakistanis find themselves unprotected in their own land and are angrily asking these tricky questions.

There is a short history lesson if someone wants to learn. War in Algeria started with a simple slogan 'Algeria for the Algerians' in the 1950s. Later on, this developed into a full-scale war of independence from France. The colonisers had to leave after the Algerians put up a massively bloody war for almost a decade and inflicted unbearable damage on the French economy and military. When Charles de Gaulle assumed power as president of France, he had the courage to withdraw his half a million soldiers fighting a losing battle against the determined Algerians. De Gaulle's status had been greatly enhanced in the world as a result of his courageous act and to save the honour of his country by his foresightedness. Obama also has a choice to leave Afghanistan for the Afghans, and enhance his position as a statesman.

There is another example of greatness: Obama's compatriot Mohammed Ali the boxer refused to go to Vietnam to kill the Vietnamese, who he said had done no harm to him or attacked his country. He was not being disloyal, but by not betraying his moral judgment he, in fact, enhanced his status and honour in his country and worldwide. To this day, Ali maintains a loving relationship and a status of a hero with his public and the successive administrations.

The late British Prime Minister Harold Wilson defied the US when he was asked to send troops to Vietnam. The Americans had used such terminology as 'flushing out Vietcong terrorists'. The terrorist is a powerfully loaded emotive word which is enough for the US political establishments to fool around with their population. Wilson understood this and did not betray his principle by getting involved in a pointless war, and still had the so-called special relationship in tact with America.

David Cameron and Co. also have an equal chance of following those examples I gave above, and show similar statesmanship and save the honour of Great Britain, and what is more, a safer Britain. The Government should dissociate itself from the policy of blindly supporting American aggression in Afghanistan and Pakistan. It is pointless to continue the war which seems to have no end and which by all accounts cannot be won.

Individuals and nations lose their honour and status when they betray their own principles. The US has lost its respect in the world because the democratic freedom, rule of law, human rights, and fair play it propagates and aspires to are denied to other weaker states by dint of its military might. That power does not have to be decisive to hold those aspirations.

Fair enough, 9/11 happened and there is no denying that a lot of damage had occurred. Who was responsible for that damage? Are those responsible being punished? The answer is emphatically 'No'. Instead, thousands upon thousands of Afghans, mostly children and women, have been brutally bombed and killed compared with the number that died on September 11, 2001. What kind of a revenge is this, one could ask. Enough is enough. How many more Afghans and the Pakistanis have to be killed before the US and the NATO high command would be satisfied?

# Brian Haw, a scourge of British politics

Published in *TheNews*, London, June 28, 2011

Even the right-wing media could not ignore the news of the death of Brian Haw, who died of cancer, aged 62. Almost all national newspapers carried his picture with detailed stories of his existence on this planet for cruelly a short time.

A Londoner to the teeth, peace activist Haw, a persistent campaigner for stop the imperialist wars, was a great inspiration for peace seeking people of the world.

His presence in Parliament Square for 24 hours a day in all sorts of harsh weather conditions was reassuring for those inspired by his political thought and courage. He was regarded a visionary by his followers and had become a universal face of moral courage and endurance.

He fiercely opposed the Blair and Bush atrocities in Iraq and Afghanistan and had greatly influenced people here and abroad. The tourists used to surround his small tent with their movie and still cameras most afternoons and evenings and chat with him.

Although his followers would continue the battle, Brian is irreplaceable. He spent ten years in his tiny tent outside the houses of parliament protesting against the ongoing wars in which his country was deeply involved.

He successfully fought several court battles. On many occasions he was violently arrested, injured, and imprisoned, but always came back to the same spot. He argued against make-shift, ad hoc laws to eject him from the square. He turned the place into a shrine as a saint, a sadhu or a guru. Young and old came to meet him on a regular basis. With his personal popularity among the public on a high, he could have easily become a member of parliament if he had chosen to do so, but he utterly detested the very people inside with whom he would have had to work, if elected.

He reserved his colourful language for those politicians such as Blair and Bush, who he thought were criminals, extremists, mad, bad, and greedy to start these wars. Politicians of a lesser breed and blind followers of warmongers were regarded as rats and cockroaches. The mayor of London, who had been trying to remove him from the square where Haw had pitched his tent, must be relieved. But not for long, because the supporters of Haw have pledged to carry forward the banner of his political philosophy of stopping further imperialist and colonial wars.

He exerted more influence on the public than almost all politicians. In times to come he may well be judged a hero and an unofficial politician without portfolio. Many have suggested that his bronze statue be erected next to the existing statues of Churchill or Nelson Mandela in the square as a reminder of his many sacrifices, including the resultant break-up of his marriage, and his selflessness.

# Champion and chronicler of Pakistan in turbulent times

Obituary: *Samuel Martin Burke, Civil Servant and Historian, 1906-2010*

Published in *The Financial Times*, London, November 20, 2010

Few can boast of helping to create and shape a new nation and then, instead of sinking gently into retirement, of writing acclaimed books about the turbulent times he has known. Such a man was Samuel Martin Burke, who has died at the age of 104 after a life devoted to the service of Pakistan.

As a young man he helped rule what was then British India, first as a district officer and later as a judge. At the time of partition, when millions were on the move often amid great violence, he won the respect of politicians in both India and Pakistan for his scrupulous fairness, not least in settling disputed election results. As a diplomat, representing his fledgling state to countries that had barely heard of Pakistan, he put his nation on the global map, forging strong ties with America in particular. As an academic, he wrote the biographies and the histories for which ultimately he may be best remembered.

His achievements were all the more extraordinary in that he was a Christian in an overwhelmingly Muslim country. He was born under the Raj in 1906 at Martinpur, a small Christian village in what is now Pakistan's Punjab province. His father, a headmaster, was a poet. Academically bright, Burke won a scholarship to the Government College of Lahore. After passing the Indian Civil Service exams – by then opened to Indians as well as whites – he was sent for two years' training in England, where he met his future wife Louise, whom he married in Lahore in 1933.

A non-English civil servant in the tumultuous closing phase of British rule, Burke showed a passion for fairness and impartiality.

Samuel Martin Burke: Fearless and
impartial when dealing with difficult cases

He was made chairman of the First Elections Petitions Commission of the Punjab, set up after the general election of 1945-46. When the main issue between the important political parties – the Congress and the Muslim League – was whether there should be a Pakistan at all.

Burke's first signal service to Pakistan was that he did not hesitate to give judgments in favour of the Muslim League on contentious cases. A contemporary observed: "Burke was called upon to try highly controversial cases of a political nature in an atmosphere charged with party and personal feelings, and he tackled them impartially and fearlessly."

When partition was agreed, every civil servant was asked whether he wished to serve India or Pakistan, or to retire. Many Indians looked forward to filling high positions vacated by the departing British. Burke felt he could show his unshakeable impartiality only by refusing government service in either country. He became the only Asian civil servant to opt for retirement.

His decision won him esteem from the Congress party, which assumed power in India, and the Muslim League, which took over in Pakistan. Both invited him to work for them. As he had been born in what became Pakistan, he decided to serve there and joined the newly-formed foreign service. He rose to be high commissioner to Canada. In 1952, sent to Washington, he and his wife undertook nationwide speaking tours to earn American goodwill and make the US "Pakistan conscious".

He pressed Pakistan's interests in the US even after becoming an academic; in 1970 he had an extraordinary confrontation with Chester Bowles, the US ambassador to India, who wrote in the *Minneapolis Tribune* urging the US against supplying military hardware to Pakistan. Burke took him to task in the same newspaper, sending both articles to President Richard Nixon of the US. The sale to Pakistan of 100 tanks went ahead.

After the foreign service, Burke became professor of South Asian studies at the University of Minnesota, later founding the Burke Library there. As well as authoritative works on the foreign policies of India and Pakistan, Burke's books include *Akbar, the Greatest Mogul* and *The British Raj in India*. He was approaching 100 but still writing when I last visited him at his home in England.

In his autobiography, never made public, he wrote: "If I had the chance of living my life all over again, I would like to marry the same woman and have the same careers in the same order in which they actually happened".

Louise died in 1993, aged 87. He is survived by three of their four daughters.

# Samuel Martin Burke: Jurist who helped found Pakistan's Foreign Service

Published in *The Daily Telegraph*, London, November 18, 2010

Professor S.M. Burke, who died on October 9, aged 104, was a diplomat, a historian and a rare Indian to become a judge in the Indian Civil Service during the British rule.

Born in Martinpur, a Christian village in Pakistan's Punjab province, on July 3, 1906, he was academically bright, and after his secondary education, he won a scholarship and got admission in the Government College, Lahore. He took First Class in M.A. History, and First in B.A. Honours.

In the closing phase of British rule in India, Burke was chairman of the First Elections Petitions Commission of the Punjab, following the general election of 1945-46 in which the main issue between the two principal parties – the Congress and the Muslim League – was whether there should be a Pakistan.

The commission consisted of a chairman and two members, one a practising Muslim barrister and a retired Hindu public prosecutor. All three had been appointed by the governor on the recommendation of Sir Khizer Hayat Khan, leader of the Unionist Party.

The Muslim League was convinced that the two members were yes-men of the ministry and that Burke too would not dare to offend the government of the day who controlled his prospects as a government servant.

Burke's first signal service to Pakistan was that he did not hesitate to give judgments in favour of the Muslim League when warranted. The parties to that petition were Mian Amiruddin of the Muslim League, who had been successful and Major Qizilbash, of the Unionist Party, who had been defeated. Both committee members decided in favour of the Unionist petitioner, but Burke dissented and upheld Amiruddin's victory. Because of the difference of opinion, the governor referred the case to the High Court, which agreed with Burke and Amiruddin won the day.

While the commission was still sitting, the Indian political parties agreed to the creation of Pakistan. A circular was sent to each member of the Indian Civil Service asking whether he wished to serve India or Pakistan, or to retire. The Indian members of the service looked forward to sudden promotion to high positions which were being vacated by the departing British. Burke felt that the only way he could assure leaders of all the political parties of his unshakeable impartiality was to make it plain that he was not interested in government service in either country. Accordingly, he became the only Asian civil servant who decided to retire.

It transpired that he had won the esteem of the Congress Party which assumed power in India, and the Muslim League which took over in Pakistan. Both invited him to revoke his retirement. Since he had been born in what became Pakistan, he considered Pakistan his motherland and decided to serve there.

The Pakistani government offered him a Ministry to represent the Christian minority, but he chose to join the newly created Foreign Service. He was given charge of the two most important branches: India, with which innumerable partition disputes were in progress, and the United Nations, where the Kashmir dispute was being fought in 1948.

His first appointment abroad was counsellor to the high commissioner in London in 1949. In 1952, he was transferred to Washington as counsellor, but was soon promoted to a minister. Because of recurrent crises with India, Pakistan had requested military assistance from the US. To earn American goodwill, Burke and Mrs Burke undertook nationwide speaking tours. In creating a favourable impression of Pakistan, Burke was helped by the fact that he was a Christian.

Pakistan had been painted by its critics where Christians were treated as second class citizens, but Americans could see for themselves that Pakistan had appointed a Christian minister to the most powerful country in the world.

Upon Burke's transfer from the US, the *Washington Post* wrote an article under the caption: "Good-byes mount for popular Burkes who have helped make Americans Pakistan-conscious".

Soon, his efforts to win American friendship began to bear fruit. In the food crisis of 1953, the US promptly shipped a large quantity of wheat as a gift. When signing the Wheat Bill, President Eisenhower declared: "We are proud to have such staunch friends as the people of Pakistan".

After Washington, he did stints as Charge d'Affaires in Brazil, and as deputy high commissioner in London. He became head of a Pakistani diplomatic mission – minister to Sweden, Norway, Finland and Denmark – from 1953 to 1956.

He was elected by the United Nations as a member of the Committee on Contributions for three years. There, he helped reduce Pakistan's contribution towards the expenses of the UN.

Burke's last diplomatic post was as high commissioner in Canada from 1959 to 1961. He signed an agreement for the peaceful uses of atomic energy. This enabled Pakistan to purchase uranium from Canada.

He had an extraordinary intellectual confrontation with Chester Bowles, the American ambassador in India, who wrote an article in *Minneapolis Tribune* on March 28, 1970, advising the US against supplying military hardware to Pakistan. Burke replied through a powerful article in the same newspaper and took Bowles to task. He then arranged the two articles to be sent to President Richard Nixon. The sale to Pakistan of 100 tanks went ahead.

After retirement from the Foreign Service, he accepted the post of consultant in South Asian Studies, which the University of Minnesota created for him. He later founded the famous Burke Library there, described by the university as, "the most comprehensive and systematic arrangement of material on South Asia anywhere in the world."

His books, *Foreign Policy of Pakistan,* and *Origin of Indian and Pakistani Foreign Policies,* are the most authoritative publications on those subjects. He assisted a team of scholars who worked full-time for 14 years to compile *A Historical Atlas of South Asia.*

A Ford Foundation Study Award in 1965 enabled him and his wife to make two round the world trips. This helped him to collect research material and exchange views with scholars worldwide.

Burke also wrote books on *The British Raj in India,* and *Quaid-i-Azam Mohammad Ali Jinnah, His Personality and His Politics*, in which he wrote that, "it was Gandhi, and not Jinnah, who first introduced religion into politics. This ultimately drove the Muslims and the Hindus apart and eventually convinced Jinnah, who had long played the role of ambassador of Hindu-Muslim unity, that his dream of a united India was nothing but a mirage".

Burke was approaching 100, still writing when I last visited him at his home in Surrey. In 1983, he was invited by the United Nations Institute for Training and Research to serve on a panel of experts.

In his autobiography, *A life of Fulfilment*, never made public, he says: "If I had the chance of living my life all over again, I would not like it to be different in any way from the one I have already experienced. I would like to marry the same woman, and would like to have the same careers and in order in which they actually happened."

One of his contemporaries observed: "Burke was called upon to try highly controversial cases of a political nature in an atmosphere charged with party and personal feelings, and he tackled them impartially and fearlessly, and upheld the high tradition of the service to which he belonged".

He had four daughters; the eldest predeceased him, aged 75. Louise, his beloved wife, a classic English beauty whom he met at the tennis club in Wimbledon in 1929 and quietly married in 1933 in a church in Lahore, died in 1993, aged 87. He is survived by his three daughters.

# A diplomat par excellence

Published in *TheNews*, London, October 26, 2010

Professor Samuel Martin Burke, who passed away on October 9 in his sleep, aged 104, was an internationally recognised scholar of great eminence and celebrity. His services to Pakistan as a judge, a diplomat, a brilliant academic and a highly popular ambassador remain unrivalled.

Burke, a former consultant in the South Asian Studies at the University of Minnesota, US, was a judge in the Indian Civil Service during the British rule. After the partition of the subcontinent, he held ministerial and ambassadorial assignments in no fewer than eleven countries on behalf of Pakistan.

A number of his books on such subjects as foreign policies of Pakistan and India remain incomparably authoritative to this day.

During his second career as Pakistan's ambassador from 1950 to 1975, when he retired from the Foreign Service, he had already made his mark as a highly respected international diplomat. In Scandinavia and South America, Pakistan was hardly known in those days, but through his tireless diplomatic efforts, Burke put Pakistan firmly on the world map as an independent Muslim nation. At one stage, he became synonymous with Pakistan in regions where he served as Pakistan's ambassador.

Born in Martinpur, a Christian village in Pakistan near Faisalabad, on July 3, 1906, he had his primary education in his village and secondary in a Lahore school. Being academically bright, he won a government scholarship and got admission in Government College of Lahore. He stood first in the university in B.A. Honours.

In the closing phase of British rule in India, Burke was chairman of the First Elections Petitions Commission of the Punjab. This had followed the general election in 1945-46 in which the main issue between the two principal parties – the Congress and the Muslim League – was whether there should be a Pakistan.

The commission consisted of a chairman and two members. The members were a practising Muslim barrister and a retired Hindu public prosecutor. All three commissioners had been appointed by the governor on the recommendation of the then premier, Sir Khizer Hayat Khan, leader of the Unionist Party, which was a coalition of a few Muslims propped up by the Congress Party and the Sikhs.

The commission could unseat a successful candidate and order a fresh election or declare a defeated candidate as duly elected. The Muslim League was convinced that the two members were yes-men of the ministry, and that Burke too would not dare to offend the government of the day who controlled his prospects as a government servant.

Burke's first signal service to Pakistan was that he did not hesitate to give judgments in favour of the Muslim League. An early demonstration of this came when the governor entrusted to the commission the petition challenging the election of the mayor of Lahore. The parties to that petition were Mian Amiruddin, of the Muslim League, who had been successful, and Major Zulfiqar Ali Qizilbash, of the Unionist Party, who had been defeated. Both the members decided in favour of the Unionist petitioner, but Burke dissented from them and upheld Amiruddin's victory. Because of the difference of opinion, the governor referred the case to the High Court. The High Court agreed with Burke and Amiruddin won the day.

This pre-partition contribution by Burke is by no means a small contribution in favour of Muslims and effectively for the creation of Pakistan. While the commission was still sitting, the Indian political parties agreed to the formation of Pakistan. A circular was sent to each member of the Indian Civil Service asking whether he wished to serve India or Pakistan or to retire.

The Indian members of the service looked forward to sudden promotion to high positions which were being vacated by the departing British. Burke felt that the only way he could assure leaders of all the political parties of his unshakeable impartiality was to make it plain that he was not interested in government service in either country. Accordingly, he became the only Asian civil servant who decided to retire on August 15, 1947.

It transpired that he had, in fact, won the esteem of the Congress Party which assumed power in India as well as the Muslim League which took over in Pakistan. Both invited him to revoke his retirement. Since he had been born in what became Pakistan, he considered Pakistan his motherland and decided to serve in Pakistan.

The West Pakistan government offered him a Ministry to represent the Christian minority, but he chose to join the newly created Foreign Service. He was given charge of the two most important branches: India, with whom innumerable partition disputes were in progress, and United Nations, where the Kashmir dispute was being fought in 1948.

His first appointment abroad was counsellor to the High Commissioner in London in 1949. The London High Commission at that stage was the largest foreign mission of the country. In 1952, he was transferred to Washington as counsellor, but was soon promoted to the rank of a minister. Because of recurrent crises with India, Pakistan had decided to strengthen itself by requesting military assistance from the US. To earn American goodwill, Burke and Mrs Burke undertook nationwide speaking tours. In creating a favourable impression of Pakistan, Burke was helped by the fact that he was a Christian.

Pakistan had been painted by its critics as a place where Christians were treated as second class citizens, but Americans could see for themselves that Pakistan had appointed a Christian minister to the most powerful country in the world.

Upon Burke's transfer from the US, Marie McNair, the capital's top columnist of the *Washington Post,* wrote a long article on June 5, 1953, under the caption:

"Good-byes mount for popular Burkes, Mr and Mrs Burke have helped to make this country Pakistan-conscious".

His efforts to win American friendship began to bear fruit. In the food crisis of 1953, the US promptly shipped a large quantity of wheat as a gift. When signing the Wheat Bill, President Eisenhower declared: "We are proud to have such staunch friends as the people of Pakistan".

After Washington, he did stints as Charge d'Affaires at Rio de Janeiro, and as deputy high commissioner in London. He became the first Christian head of a Pakistani diplomatic mission – Minister to Sweden, Norway, Finland and Denmark – from 1953 to 1956. In

Samuel Martin Burke, Queen Elizabeth, Prince Philip and Mrs Burke

Sweden, he negotiated technical assistance to Pakistan. When the Commonwealth Heads of Mission at Stockholm gave a reception during the state visit of the Queen Elizabeth II, they chose Burke as a leader to escort her during her walkabout. The Queen and Prince Philip also honoured Burke and Mrs Burke by calling on them at their residence.

In 1952, he was elected by the United Nations' General Assembly as a member of the Committee on Contributions for three years. He succeeded in obtaining a substantial reduction in Pakistan's contribution towards the expenses of the United Nations.

When Pakistan joined the South East Asia Treaty Organisation (Seato) Burke was appointed as the first resident ambassador to Thailand, and was accredited to Laos and Cambodia as minister, from 1956 to 1959. His colleagues elected him to preside over the third anniversary celebrations of Seato's foundation. He also negotiated and signed a Treaty of Friendship between Pakistan and Thailand. Among rights acquired by nationals of both countries under the treaty were freedom to trade, acquire property and reside in each other's country. Burke's last diplomatic post was as high commissioner in Canada from 1959 to 1961, whose technical assistance to Pakistan at that time was second only to that from the US. He signed an agreement for the peaceful uses of atomic energy. This enabled Pakistan to purchase uranium from Canada.

He had an extraordinary intellectual confrontation with Chester Bowles, the American ambassador in India, who wrote an article in *Minneapolis Tribune* on March 28, 1970, strongly advising the US administration against supplying military hardware to Pakistan. Burke, quick as a flash, replied on April 1, through a powerful article in the same newspaper, and took Bowles to task. He then arranged the two articles to be sent to President Richard Nixon. The sale to Pakistan of 100 tanks went ahead.

President Zulfiqar Ali Bhutto was delighted and wrote a congratulatory letter to him, and expressed his "deep appreciation and thanks for continuing his patriotic work of projecting Pakistan's viewpoint on important foreign policy issues". This letter by Bhutto is reproduced in Burke's private autobiography, *A life of Fulfilment,* which has not been made public. The first page of this book reads: "To My Beloved Wife Louise, Who Helped Me To Achieve Good Health, Worldly Success and Happiness". I had to beg the noble professor to let me keep this book, having lent it to me in the first place. I have been inspired by this book.

On reaching the age of 55, Burke took retirement from the Pakistani Foreign Service to accept the post of Professor and Consultant in South Asian Studies which the University of Minnesota had specially created for him. All the leading Canadian newspapers published commendatory articles. One of them wrote that, "The Canadian capital will soon be seeing one of its most esteemed couples depart."

The founder of the famous Burke Library in Minnesota is none other than this learned professor who taught at the university earlier.

President Ayub Khan recognised his unique services to Pakistan by conferring upon him the highest honour of Sitara-e-Pakistan (Star of Pakistan). The president also continued to consult him on important foreign policy issues after retirement.

Professor Burke continued to explain Pakistani policies in classroom lectures as well as in his countrywide lecture tours in the US and Canada.

His books, *Foreign Policy of Pakistan,* and *Origin of Indian and Pakistani Foreign Policies,* still hold their place as the most authoritative publications on those subjects. He also assisted a team of scholars who worked full-time for 14 years to compile *A Historical Atlas of South Asia,* which cost more than a million dollars.

A Ford Foundation Travel and Study Award in 1965 enabled him and his wife to make two round the world trips, one lasting for nine months and the other for five. This helped him to collect research material and exchange views with scholars and political leaders worldwide.

His personal library is now maintained by Hamline University, St Paul, Minnesota, under the title of "Burke Library, South Asia Collections". The Hamline University News Release of April 11, 1975, described it as "the most comprehensive and systematic arrangement of material on South Asia anywhere in the world".

For his book on *Akbar the Greatest Mugul*, published in India, he received commendation from, among others, Rajiv Gandhi, then prime minister of India.

Jointly with Salim Al-Din Quraishi, Burke has also written outstanding books on *Bahadur Shah, the Last Mogul Emperor of India*, *The British Raj in India*, and *Quaid-i-Azam Mohammad Ali Jinnah – His Personality and His Politics*.

The book on Jinnah was published in the jubilee year of Pakistan's birth and deserves special mention. By quoting chapter and verse, it is convincingly proved that it was Gandhi, and not Jinnah, who first introduced religion into politics. This ultimately drove the Muslims and the Hindus irreconcilably apart and eventually convinced even Jinnah, who had long played the role of ambassador of Hindu-Muslim unity, that his dream of a united India was nothing but a mirage. This book has been reviewed in newspapers and magazines in Pakistan, Canada and the US. It has been rightly hailed as a book for which Burke will never be forgotten. Pakistanis owe this great scholar a debt of gratitude.

Burke also wrote another brilliantly researched book, *Landmarks of the Pakistan Movement*, which I reviewed in London's two publications: *The Times Literary Supplement (TLS)* on June 14, 2002, and in *TheNews, London* on March 14, 2002.

In his autobiography, *A life of Fulfilment,* he wrote:

> "If I had the chance of living my life all over again, I would not like it to be different in any way from the one I have already experienced. I would like to marry the same woman, and would like to have the same careers and in order in which they actually happened".

So, the scenario of the pattern of his life for another century, effectively, would have meant more of the same again – the same living and loving, a brilliant student winning all the scholarships on the way to higher education, a long and satisfying career in Indian Civil Service (1931-1947), a High Court judge, Pakistan Foreign Service (1948-1975), ambassador extraordinary in eleven countries, promoting the image of Pakistan and winning the highest honour of Sitara-e-Pakistan, a highly respected professor and consultant in one of the largest universities of the United States.

One of his contemporaries observed: "Burke was called upon to try highly controversial cases of a political nature in an atmosphere charged with party and personal feelings and he tackled them impartially and fearlessly and upheld the high tradition of the service to which he belonged".

Burke displayed a rare sincerity, honesty and dedication to the task with which he was entrusted. Pakistan was extremely fortunate to have him on its side.

In a land infested with corruption and bribery, Burke remained incorruptible throughout his long public life.

President Ayub Khan saw in him a man of impeccably higher moral values, and an incorruptible civil servant.

Burke was approaching 100 years of age when I last visited him before he moved to Oxfordshire. He was still writing a new book about Maulana Mohammad Ali Johar, a subject on which very little is written. This responsibility too, seemed to fall on his shoulders. Alas, the book remains uncompleted.

He had four daughters. The eldest, Pamela, devoted her life to looking after her widowed father until she passed away, aged 75. Louise, his beloved wife, a classic English beauty with a cultured Oxbridge accent, who he met at the tennis club in Wimbledon in 1929 and quietly married on June 28, 1933 in a church in Lahore, also passed away on December 17, 1993, aged 87. Burke often said that he was blessed with a marriage made in heaven.

He is survived by his three daughters.

# Whither Pakistan cricket?

Published in *TheNews*, London, September 27, 2010

Pakistani cricket must be cleansed from corruption. Stories of spot-fixing involving the three Pakistani cricketers who were accused of taking money in an illegal betting racket must be kept alive, lest the scam should rear its ugly head in the future. Spot-betting, bet-rigging, match-fixing, catch-dropping, and betting-scam are words entered in the vocabulary of the cricket lovers that need to be made relics.

Pakistani cricket is in a deep crisis and it is not the players' fault, the whole management is open for questioning. After a 2-0 defeat in T20 matches and a 2-nil loss in One-Day Internationals so far, the team is in a dire need of revision and planning. The Pakistan Test captain, Salman Butt, who has gone back to Pakistan, is still under investigation by the ICC, which has banned him from taking part in the rest of the current tour of England. The two bowlers, Mohammad Asif and Mohammad Amir, are also excluded from playing until the ongoing inquiries are concluded. The trio plead not guilty, but the Pakistan Cricket Board would have its own internal inquest, the outcome of which will take months.

Clear evidence of spot-fixing is hard to come by. The Pakistanis have been told that they may be required to return if any criminal charges are levelled against them. Even in this highly technological age, international rackets cannot be easily detected, let alone eradicated.

Deliberately dropping catches, throwing matches, and match-fixing can be stopped if the corrupt cricketers are stopped from falling prey to the temptation of unearned money. The Pakistani public is furious. An effigy of Butt was burned in his home country. Pakistanis are saying that those predetermined no-balls at Lord's last month could not have been bowled without the consent and knowledge of the captain.

Any corrupt cricketer's manipulation can earn him a lot of money in a fast-moving money-spinning wheel, and there is no initial payment or investment required, but it is done at the cost of national honour and personal pride.

For an uninitiated spectator, a no-ball means conceding only one run to the opposition. So, what is the fuss all about? No big deal. After all, England scored 446; minus two no-balls still make them 444 and winning the match, by a heavy margin of an innings and 225 runs, but that is not the point. The fuss is really about the illegal money the bowlers allegedly may have made from their wrong footedness against the spirit of the game and honour of their country.

The bookies can recruit sportsmen for an intelligence-intensive and quick buck-making business. It is well known that thousands of pounds, dollars, and rupees change hands at the spur of the moment, according to the locations and spread of the betting network. It is a lucrative pastime like no other, with a minimum or no effort, but to succeed in this game, one or more cricketers should be willing to involve themselves. There is a safety net for these special kinds of bookies because they have no offices which can be raided, and telephone codes are difficult to decode. Visits by a newspaper reporter with a wad of banknotes do not normally occur as a trap.

In 2000, then South African captain Hansie Cronje was highly regarded as a gentleman of honour and honesty, a God-fearing, clean living, and good church going Christian. Although well paid, he succumbed to the greed. It took the authorities 18 months before he was found out. He eventually admitted receiving money from the bookies and was banned for life. The cricket world was thrown into shock and awe.

Salim Malik, then Pakistan captain who at first denied everything, was disgraced and banned for life for match-fixing by the Lahore High Court after a thorough judicial inquiry.

Also in 2000, then India captain Mohammad Azharuddin and another batsman, Ajay Sharma, were banned for life for match-fixing.

The high commissioner of Pakistan in the UK has suggested that he was convinced by the three cricketers involved that they were innocent. However, if they are found guilty of any wrongdoing, there should be an exemplary punishment to deter others in the future. On the other hand, if they are not guilty of any offence, the learned high commissioner must demand compensation from the *News of the World* for maliciously accusing the players. After further damning revelations in the same paper last Sunday, it will be interesting to see what the defenders of these players come up with.

Ignoring this match-fixing issue at this time will amount to gross negligence on the part of the cricket establishments here and abroad. This story must not be allowed to die down.

# Torture inquiry must be public

Published in *TheNews*, London, August 20, 2010

Accusations had been coming thick and fast that Britain had been complicit in tortures abroad for a better part of the last decade, during the former Prime Minister Tony Blair's regime.

The new coalition government at last had to take notice, and announced in the House of Commons on July 6 that an inquiry will be held.

Mr Blair, who had denied that British security services were involved in torture, had never wanted an investigation, but evidently both the Security Service (commonly known as MI5) for domestic intelligence gathering agency under the supervision of the home secretary, and the Secret Intelligence Service (SIS, commonly known as MI6), the agency for international intelligence gathering, overseen by the foreign secretary, collude with countries such as Uzbekistan and Pakistan, notorious for cruel and criminal practices.

The security services also allegedly cooperate with India, the so-called largest democracy in the world, where young Kashmiris are kidnapped, abused, and tortured by both the Indian occupying army and the police.

If the plans are to hold an internal secret inquiry by MI5 and MI6 then it is better not to hold it at all. The inquiry ought to be independent and transparent. If it is not open to public and politicians alike then the people are bound to criticise this as a waste of time and money. Like the on-going Chilcot inquiry it will turn out to be a futile PR exercise, and public confidence cannot be restored.

The public is not prepared to swallow yet another Chilcot type of farce. It will be an insult to injury if the guilty are found and not punished.

The horrible incidents of Abu Ghraib in Iraq and Bagram in Afghanistan had been widely reported and proven beyond doubt that torture had been committed, but nothing had been done about it at that time. Where there was an overwhelming evidence of torture by British soldiers, punishment had not been meted out for such blatantly open crimes against humanity.

This proposed torture inquiry, to be held under the very noses of the parliamentarians in Britain, must establish the truthfulness of the human rights abuses of the past nine years. The war criminals and the torturers must be punished when found guilty.

People are right to ask as to what the purpose of these inquiries is. Sir John Chilcot, you will remember, had made it quite clear at the very outset that nobody will go to prison even if found guilty of starting an illegal war against Iraq.

On the home front, the British government allowed its airspace to be used for CIA international renditions flights. The inquiry should uncover the nature of this venture and, more importantly, who authorised these flights. It also allowed its military base of Diego Garcia in the middle of the Indian ocean to be used for landings and take-offs for illegal purposes of allegedly extracting intelligence information through torture from 'terrorism' suspects. A suspect is a suspect and not guilty unless proven in an open court of law with reliable evidence.

The United Nations Charter has made it abundantly plain that torture of a detainee can never be tolerated under any, repeat any, circumstances whatsoever. Torture is a crime of universal jurisdiction.

The 1984 Convention against Torture and Other Cruel Treatment requires states to take proactive steps to prevent torture through appropriate training of all personnel involved in the custody, interrogation and treatment of detained persons. The Convention further stipulates that national courts have the power to try alleged perpetrators of torture even if neither the suspect nor the victim are nationals of the country where the court is located, and the crime took place outside that country. It imposes the obligation on all states to prosecute suspected torturers present in their territory.

The use of torture also played a significant role in the US and NATO armies' failure in Afghanistan. Intelligence information extracted through an intense torture of suspects invariably proves to be worthless. A suspect will agree to admit whatever his torturers would like to hear in order to escape the severe pain and suffering.

The Western alliance, therefore, is now divided and looking for an exit strategy after ten years of heavy fighting and alleged torture practices. The alliance is on the verge of losing an oft-repeated unwinnable war in Afghanistan. The Netherlands has already withdrawn its army.

Tony Blair's government had always denied any wrongdoing involving cruel methods of obtaining intelligence information, but video, audio and personal evidence from the former Guantanamo detainees and from their lawyers have clearly shown that torture has been perpetrated on a regular basis. The inquiry should examine all allegations of torture thoroughly.

It is of the utmost importance that this inquest be allowed to establish the truthfulness of this sordid affair. The conclusion of the inquiry, without being selective, must be made public. It must not be a whitewash. Justice must be seen to be done. Britain's reputation depends on it.

Torture has been outlawed by every country on paper, but it is unfortunately still practised by many countries around the world, in spite of the fact that they are signatories to the UN Charter, which outlaws it in their countries. The problem needs to be tackled head-on, without fuss and fury, and the lead should come from the top dogs.

Navi Pillay, UN High Commissioner for Human Rights, said on June 26, 2009 that: "Torture is a barbaric act, I believe that no state whose regime conducts or condones torture can consider itself civilised."

# Afghan policy needs change

Published in *TheNews*, London, July 1, 2010

Now that US President Barack Obama has unceremoniously sacked General Stanley McChrystal, the military commander in Afghanistan, a policy change may be in the offing. A new appointee, General Patraeus, is no less hawkish either, considering his past mistakes. The effects of this change of personnel will not be known immediately.

The other side of the story, which the US must pay attention to, carefully, is that for every Afghan, whether Taliban or not, a British or an American intruding soldier is a foreign enemy and they should be beheaded. The Afghans like to fight them to the bitter end until the occupying forces leave their country. This is a simple fact of life which the neo-colonialists must quickly digest.

The majority of Afghans, in many surveys and reports, have repeatedly made it clear that they do not need British or American military training to keep order in their country, although their puppet president, Mr Karzai, has a different opinion. The Afghans have perfected the art of fighting and winning during the past 200 years; they view all invading foreigners as murderers of women and children. Most Afghans support the Taliban who, after all, are their fellow countrymen with whom they will have to live in the future, and who are bravely fighting to expel the 42 occupying NATO countries' armies from their land, to purify the country.

Any training given by the West's Christian armies will be used against their masters in the long run. Some such instances have already occurred last year, when many off-duty British soldiers have been killed. This is not surprising, this is normal in Afghan wars over years, and the American and the Brits should understand this; if in doubt, ask the leaders of the former Soviet Union to testify this. The British at the peak of their empire were defeated twice, in 1879 and 1882, in the notorious Afghan Wars. The Brits have also known the futility of these unwinnable wars. No nation, however weak, would allow being invaded and enslaved in the modern world, and the Afghans are less tolerant of the ways of the West.

Research also shows that alliances in that part of the world change overnight. That, too, must be understood by the US and the NATO countries. A vast number of politicians, including some military commanders, now realise that this war cannot be won.

The above few lines explain why this war cannot be won. The Americans will be forced to pull out of Afghanistan just as they were forced to pull out from Vietnam 35 years ago. It is a matter of time before an exit strategy with the 'heads held high' theory comes into play. The heads held high means that the West has lost nothing and has won the war. Most people will, of course, disagree with that idea, but if the war can be brought to an end, it may be regarded a draw as in a football match; huge collateral damage is counted later.

The bloodshed of Afghans who are being killed every single day by drone bombs must end now. The news of such killings in this vast region is kept under wraps by the devious media. Drone bombings, remotely operated by the US somewhere from Nevada, are regularly killing the civilian population in and around the border areas of Pakistan/Afghanistan, where the US intelligence wrongly believes that Osama bin Laden may be found. The result is widespread anti-American and anti-British feelings running high. Last year, wedding parties and funeral processions had been bombed by NATO drones causing hundreds of civilian casualties.

British Foreign Secretary William Hague has just returned from a Pakistan visit. He could not have failed to notice the anti-British sentiments there. How is he going to respond to this anger after his return?

There is no other option for the West but to start pulling out now rather than later, and leave the country to develop its own cultural and political system.

If there is a plan to destabilise Pakistan further, then it is bound to backfire. There is also a speculation that regional powers, such as China, Russia, India and Iran, might get involved for their own interest. Who needs the third world war?

The Western alliance to remain there longer means more fatalities and unnecessary civilian deaths. The United Nations's recent reports suggest, among other things, that the presence of the British army in Afghsnistan has worsened the security of Britain.

The false but clever propaganda that occupying and fighting in Afghanistan is to safeguard the security of the West does not hold water, and no one believes in this any longer, except the invaders.

The recent incident of Times Square in New York, the 7/7 bombings in London, the so-called shoe bomb on an aircraft and the involvement of a British/Nigerian student in a failed attempt to 'blow up' a Detroit-bound aircraft were all committed by Western educated young men in revenge of the occupation of Afghanistan. None of them came from Afghanistan. So why are the American and the British armies killing Afghans? This is the question the CIA-created Taliban, formerly known as Mujahedeen when fighting the Soviets, are asking.

You can brainwash some people some of the time, but not all the people all the time. The sell by date of that delusionary propaganda has passed.

President Obama has promised that he will withdraw his troops from Afghanistan in July 2011. He had made a similar pledge to close down the Guantanamo concentration camp in January this year. He has not honoured his promise. One would expect from a man of his ability to honour his words this time round.

# An error is not a mistake until corrected

Published in *TheNews*, London, April 25, 2010

An error is not a mistake until it is corrected, so the saying goes.

The United States and Britain must correct their errors of launching an illegal war against an oil-rich country, Iraq, and a poor country, Afghanistan.

The Iraqis and Afghans are asking why their countries have been invaded and occupied for so long on the dubious pretexts of weapons of mass destruction and September 11, 2001.

None of the citizens of these countries was ever involved in the Twin Tower episode, and Iraq had no weapons of mass destruction.

After a long period of nine years, and millions of dead civilians and soldiers in both countries, the US and NATO armies show no sign of repentance, let alone withdrawing their troops.

The time has come to apologise and compensate the Afghans and the Iraqis for their huge losses.

While there is a sound and fury of election in Britain, all major political parties are guilty of brushing aside the burning issues of the illegal occupation of Iraq and Afghanistan. Why are they coy of talking about such an important issue during their campaign, and not even including it in their agenda as a topic of debate? Their silence is deafening in view of the many surveys that suggest that 73 per cent of the population of Britain is against these unwinnable wars.

Many European countries whose soldiers are in Afghanistan also show signs of fatigue. The Dutch government has already collapsed. Its political parties do not approve of Dutch soldiers killing the Afghans or being killed themselves in return. Dutch involvement in Afghanistan will soon end. Other Coalition nations are contemplating on the same lines of leaving, but some are prepared to send more troops.

In the United States, a sizeable majority disapproves of this war, but President Obama acts quite the opposite to the wishes of his countrymen. He promised to close Guantanamo by January 2010, and that pledge has not been honoured.

Most, if not all, of the detainees are innocent. They are there because of mere suspicion and have not been charged or tried. They have been subjected to brutal treatment, international renditions, hostile interrogation in the harshest conditions in violation of international law. Some like Shaker Aamer, a London resident, is still in this concentration camp after more than eight years in solitary confinement, according to his defence lawyers. He has not been charged of any offence. The British Foreign and Commonwealth Office has asked the US government to transfer Shaker Aamer to Britain so that he can join his wife and young children waiting for his return. Why is he still there?

Promise of change that Obama made before his election has changed absolutely nothing. That reminds me of another saying, attributed to former Mayor of London Ken Livingstone, that if voting changes anything they'd abolish it.

Martin Linton, MP, journalist Yvonne Ridley of *Press TV* and Ray Silk of the Stop the War Coalition are demanding the release of Aamer, who is still incarcerated in this notorious prison. They handed in a petition at 10 Downing Street yesterday.

# The Chilcot farce

Published in *TheNews*, London, February 2, 2010

No one should be surprised that former Prime Minister Tony Blair got away with war crimes at the Iraq Inquiry on Friday. He was told he was "not on trial", which gave him plenty of time to readjust himself and build up his confidence to confront his inquirers as if from the dispatch box in the House of Commons.

The inquiry gave him an easy ride, an escape route which gave the impression of being pre-planned. At times, the panellists seemed to be in the dock rather than the accused. Had he appeared in an ordinary court of law, he would have probably been convicted of starting a war of aggression which would have certainly taken him to the International Criminal Court in the Netherlands.

The Chilcot inquiry has found nothing new. Internet blogs are awash with similar information, interviews, and most are crying for Blair to be tried properly as an alleged war criminal on his own admission or evidence. He has made quite a number of mistakes in his answers which the international lawyers find amusing. He said he thought the attack on September 11, 2001, in the US was an attack on Britain, so, he decided to volunteer to get involved in the invasion of Iraq along with the US President George W. Bush, to whom he made a promise to send his army a year before the Iraq war, implying that Britain is a part of America.

Iraq had never invaded Britain and the 45-minute claim was false, so the question is: why go all the way thousands of kilometres to attack a sovereign country? That is an immoral and absolutely illegal act of a war of aggression.

There are other gaps and holes in Blair's answer which make him responsible for what he has done to Iraq. In 2003, the UN Environmental Programme identified 311 polluted sites there. Cleaning them will take at least $300 million and several years to

Demonstrators outside the Queen Elizabeth II Centre, London, where the Chilcot Inquiry was held

bring them back to the same level as before the invasion. Who is responsible for that? The Chilcot inquiry failed to ask Blair that question.

Blair seems a polemicist more than a politician. If he is being economical with the truth, then the lawyers would like to put him to test. As for the Chilcot farce, it was a whitewash from the outset, because it had made it clear that no one would be held to account for the invasion and destruction of Iraq.

Blair has repeatedly said that he wanted to remove Saddam Hussein from power. To remove by force either a dictator or a democrat of an independent sovereign country is an act of war, particularly when weapons of mass destruction, including depleted uranium, were used, killing more than a million Iraqis and uprooting four million people in their own country. Who is responsible for that?

The reason to invade Iraq by Blair and Bush may have been to please the Zionists in Britain and in the US. To protect apartheid-Israel's illegal occupation of Palestinian land has always been in the forefront of the Western foreign policy. Iraq as a most progressive state in the Middle East was regarded as an irritant by apartheid-Israel, which had to be weakened with the fall of Saddam. To achieve that goal, the West, particularly the US, where the Zionist lobby is the strongest, wants to keep any progressive Arab country permanently destabilised. Blair's war has precisely done that for his favourite Israeli entity. It wasn't for the regime change. It wasn't for the weapons of mass destruction which were not found. It wasn't even for oil, either.

The Chilcot Inquiry should have questioned Blair for his role in genocide in Iraq. This so-called 'investigation' did not ask that question, but the general public will continue to pursue that question as long as Blair lives and wherever he lives.

# Brown wants Pakistan Army to fight his dirty war

Published in *TheNews*, London, December 10, 2009

Prime Minister Gordon Brown must be naïve to think that the capture of one or two individuals such as Osama bin Laden and Ayman Zawahiri would solve the chaos created by the Western powers' armies in Afghanistan.

It must be understood that the invasion and occupation of Afghanistan has never and will never be accepted by the people of that country, whether they be Taleban or not. A sizeable population wants the foreign troops to get out of their country.

According to various surveys, 72 per cent in Britain are in favour of withdrawing their soldiers from this unwinnable war. At least one serving soldier, Joe Glenton, who refused to kill the people of Afghanistan, is now in prison. More than 51 per cent in the US, including some connected with the military and ex-CIA personnel, have suggested a total pull-out from this war with no end.

It clearly shows that the British and the American combat forces have been demoralised and virtually defeated after eight years of fighting in that region at a cost of several million Afghans dead, injured, displaced, and traumatised.

Now Mr Brown wishes to shift his desperation, if not defeat, to already over-burdened Pakistanis. He wants the Pakistani army to find Osama bin Laden and Ayman Zawahiri in the Pakistan/Afghanistan border areas. Is it a face-saving exit strategy to blame Pakistan for Western powers' ill-advised ventures? Involving the Pakistani army as Mr Brown suggests would mean unknown security problems for long suffering Pakistan, which could be further destabilised. What kind of havoc would that ensue in a large country of twice the population of Britain? Mr Brown wants Pakistan to fight his dirty war. The best thing he can do, if he wants peace and stability in all regions, is to completely and unconditionally withdraw his army and let the people of Pakistan and Afghanistan reflect in peace once the foreign invaders have left. This strategy will eventually work out itself, either by civil war or civility. After all, those countries will need to sort out their own problems internally.

One can only hope the prime minister is strong enough to follow his own instincts for the sake of saving thousands more deaths yet to occur. Is he independent enough to do this without looking over his shoulder towards the US?

Tragically, 42 NATO countries have descended on one of the poorest nations to perpetuate terrorism of the worst kind, cowardly drone bombings of both Pakistan and Afghanistan, killing women and children, dropping bombs on wedding parties and funeral processions. Is the prime minister sure that Osama bin Laden and Ayman Zawahiri are still alive, or were they killed in the first phase of bombings of Afghanistan in late 2001, when the two men were unaware of what was to come?

The prime minister must understand that indiscriminate slaughter of civilians is bound to create anti-British and anti-American feelings among the wider population of both countries, particularly when the reports have been confirmed that napalm and depleted uranium are being used on a regular basis, just as they were used in Iraq.

It is hard to judge whether the prime minister's statement at this time is a pre-election ploy or something more sinister is in the offing. One aspect of it seems certain that one cannot win hearts and minds of the oppressed people who are victims of aggression and injustice within their country, on one hand, and illegal and intolerable military occupation from outside, on the other.

All wars end on a negotiating table. This method has not been tried yet. It is better to try it now because there is no outright winner in this dirty war.

# Transforming Pakistan

Published in *TheNews*, London, October 8, 2009

Sir Hilary Synnott, the former high commissioner in Pakistan, recently delivered a lecture at the Institute of International Strategic Studies on the tedious subject of transforming Pakistan.

He discussed among other things the chronically weak institutions of the country. A frequent visitor to Pakistan, he seems to have a rare sympathy with the country and its people. He has written a book which IISS launched last night that gives an insight into Pakistan's diverse complexities, challenges of forging a national identity, and regional relationships with India, China, and Saudi Arabia.

In his book, called *Transforming Pakistan,* he describes Pakistan's three main crises: security, the age-old political turmoil at every passing phase, and crucially, the economic mismanagement.

He is not sure if Pakistan without foreign help will muddle through the three crises. He finds no easy answers that may claim the country will successfully transform itself, but he suggests effort should be made to help.

He also mentions some of the contrary or unhelpful views of other observers with which he does not agree: such as that Pakistan has shown insufficient gratitude for US help, and that therefore coercion should be used, including more proactive military action on Pakistani soil; and that history shows that Pakistan is irredeemably incorrigible and efforts to change it will be wasted.

I came away from this world media gathering that advocated help from outside with a nagging feeling that it is not foreign aid which will help Pakistan. So far this has proved the opposite. It is, I like to think, the Pakistanis themselves who should rediscover Jinnah's Pakistan. It is the Pakistanis themselves who should reinvent Pakistan and give it a united national identity that the world would truly respect, and recognise Pakistan's undoubted importance in international affairs.

# Muslim Holocaust denial

Published in *The Pakistan Times*, February 19, 2009

A scientific study, carried out by a team of researchers from John Hopkins University in Baltimore, US, and Al Mustansiriya University in Baghdad, revealed that more than 655,000 Iraqis had been killed between 2003 and 2009 after the invasion of Iraq by the US and its NATO alliance, largely through a combination of bullets and bombings. The death toll has continued to mount since then. According to an updated estimate from the organisation called Just Foreign Policy, about one million Iraqis have been killed. The estimate of a million Iraqis dead is supported by an independent confirmation from a prestigious British polling agency, Opinion Research Business, in September 2007, which estimated 1.6 million Iraqis perished extremely violently.

The researchers' findings, published in the medical journal *The Lancet*, not only lend credibility to the claims of war crimes being committed in occupied Iraq, but they are also unbearably shocking. This is an enormous number of deaths in one occupied country. The world wants to know what kind of "liberation" of Iraq was this.

The Muslim massacre is not a new phenomenon; it has been in the making for a long time and can no longer be denied.

According to Media Monitor Network, the Muslim holocaust is computed at around 550 million since 1950. The United Nations Population Statistics Department provided the key forensic evidence to certify that figure. Daily killing in Afghanistan, Iraq and Palestine by American-made-and-funded weapons of mass destruction continues unabated.

After the devastation and wholesale slaughter in the First and Second World Wars the world leaders agreed, while the mental scars were still fresh, that enough was enough and such mass murders will never happen again. Clearly, the "never again" promise has not been honoured as far as Chechnya, Iraq, Palestine, Afghanistan, Kashmir, Kosovo, Somalia, Lebanon, and Bosnia are concerned – Muslim regions all. The Russians in Chechnya, Israelis in Palestine and Lebanon, Indians in Kashmir, and Americans in Afghanistan are all committing mass murders to this day. This large scale slaughter is taking place in full view of the world. The half a billion death toll of Muslims since 1950 is one hundred times that of oft-repeated Jewish holocaust.

The sheer magnitude of this silent tyranny compels one to address the Muslim holocaust and bring to justice those responsible. The global news media, tightly controlled and manipulated by influential lobbyists in the West, are obsessed with 'the war on terror' and choose not to report accurately on crimes against Muslims. These mass murders constitute a genocide unknown in the entire human history.

Unlike the Jewish holocaust which took place only in Europe, the genocidal acts against Muslims are committed around the world. In 2006, George W. Bush's indiscriminate bombing campaign in Somalia destroyed four villages, killing 230 innocent women and children. One would be forced to conclude that the sanctity of a Muslim life is unimportant to the racists in Washington. When asked why the world hates America? The answer to the question lies in ever-expanding graveyards of Afghanistan, Iraq and Palestine.

According to numerous surveys and huge public demonstrations in Britain and in the US, a sizeable majority is against the war in Afghanistan and justice for the Palestinians. Many high ranking army officers stationed in Iraq have publicly acknowledged that the invasion/occupation has achieved nothing and is unlikely to accomplish anything.

Senator Chuck Hagel, from Bush's own Republican Party, reminded us when he said that Bush's "surge" represents the most dangerous foreign policy blunder since Vietnam. Simon Jenkins, Seumas Milne and Jonathan Steele, Britain's highly respected journalists, had said that former prime minister Tony Blair was wildly exaggerating the threat posed by terrorism, and had predicted that there was never going to be a NATO victory in Afghanistan. The fight put up by the Iraqis and the Afghans suggests that the invaders are hated, yet Bush and his chum Tony Blair failed to recognise the reality and carried on their reign of terror in those countries, creating sectarian conflict and shortages of food, medicines, electricity and water. The UN Environmental Program identified 311 polluted sites in Iraq. It will take several years to clean them at a cost of at least $170 million. Who is responsible for the Muslim holocaust? The obvious answer has to be the murderous occupiers.

There is no pressure on the war criminals to be brought in front of the International Criminal Court at The Hague. The coalition leaders seem to have no desire to uphold and respect the principles of democracy in their own countries and flout the international laws at will, but seem hell-bent on imposing an evidently unworkable system in Iraq and Afghanistan, where the political norm will need to be evolved from within.

Several hundred British soldiers and thousands more American troops have been killed fighting a purposeless war in Iraq. Civilian casualties in Afghanistan are increasing daily. What lessons can be learnt? One can look back at the Second World War criminals who had been captured, prosecuted and punished. Thirteen trials took place from 1945 to 1949 in Nuremberg, Germany. In the first, 22 defendants were tried. Twelve of them received death sentences. Ten were hanged on October 16, 1946. Apart from them, two had earlier committed suicide before they could be hanged. Others received life imprisonment. Twelve further trials took place later on, involving 185 defendants. They were charged with planning wars of aggression and crimes against humanity and received varying degrees of long prison sentences. Bush and Blair, who carry a guilty conscience, may be worried and feel uncomfortable when they hear phrases such as "planning wars of aggression", and "crimes against humanity". In the case of the Muslim holocaust, how are today's war criminals to be captured, prosecuted and punished? Meanwhile, killing is continuing as an ongoing process. It is a globally growing lucrative business for the trigger-happy warmongers. Nuremberg is a far cry.

# Media coverage and the Mumbai attacks

Published in *TheNews*, London, January 27, 2009

As the Mumbai dust settles, it looks as though India and Pakistan are not going to get to each other's throat – a great disappointment for those who orchestrated this big movie-type violent event. By the look of it this live extravaganza could easily rival any Bollywood blockbuster.

Two hundred Indian army commandos pitted against a 10-man gang, locked in fighting for almost three days.

Had it not been for the innocent people getting killed in the process, it would have been a great spectacle to watch.

The commandos seemed to have little clue as to their intended target. According to eyewitnesses the army threw grenades in rapid succession into the building randomly, without knowing who was being hurt, the gang or the guests.

Attention remained focused on the Mumbai massacres, so some may have missed the interview of Larry Pressler on the BBC Radio programme World Tonight recently.

The former senator was in his element, again saying the US tolerated Pakistan to have a nuclear bomb, but the device in the hands of Pakistanis is too dangerous. He said nuclear bombs in India are in safer hands because the civilian government has control over them.

Challenged by the presenter Robin Lustig that Pakistan also has a civilian government, he replied it made no difference if there was a civilian government in Pakistan, the military has overall control.

In 1985, Mr Pressler proposed a legislation banning military assistance to Pakistan. Under the so-called Pressler amendment, the US denied Pakistan the purchase of F16 fighter aircraft unless Pakistan stopped piling nuclear arms.

Regarding the print media coverage of the Mumbai assaults, one notices Mr R. Vaidyanathan, professor of finance and control, Indian

Institute of Management, proposing steps to shock and awe Pakistan's economy, said "it is imperative that India seize this opportunity to destabilise Pakistan. A stable Pakistan is not in the interest of world peace. Identify the major export items of Pakistan (like Basmati rice, carpets etc.) and hurt Pakistan on the export front, and arm-twist countries providing arms to Pakistan". So much for promoting friendly relations between the two neighbours.

Shashi Tharoor, former Under-Secretary General of the United Nations, was more diplomatic. He admitted occasional Hindu violence against Muslims which made Indian Muslims to call for arms.

He says in India, the state has an army; in Pakistan, the army has a state. If it turns out that the massacre was planned from Pakistani territory, the consequences for Pakistan are bound to be severe. "India would be likely to find practical support from the countries of other victims".

Responding to Mr Tharoor's charges, a Mr Adnan Gill writes: "In his haste to demonise Islam in general and Pakistan in particular, Mr Tharoor's sweeping statement deserves a reminder of India's chequered past painted red by the Hindu extremists:

> In 1971, at the cost of thousands of deaths, India maliciously severed Pakistan.
> In June 1984, the Indian army massacred more than 7,000 Sikhs during Operation Blue Star.
> In November 1984, 3,000 Sikhs were butchered by the Hindu mobs in New Delhi.
> In 1992, VHP and Bajrang Dal men demolished the 500 years' old Babri Mosque.

During the past 20 years alone, thousands of Christians have been slaughtered by the Hindu extremists. A gruesome example of such atrocities stood out when Bajrang Dal's activists burnt alive the Australian missionary and his two young sons.

In 2002, Hindu fundamentalists butchered 2,000 Muslims in Gujarat. Sickening confessions of the VHP's leaders, responsible for the attacks, are available on YouTube.

Since the early 1990s, the Indian military systematically exterminated about 80,000 Kashmiris.

In 2007, more than 60 Pakistanis were burnt alive in India. The massacre was the handiwork of Bajrang Dal's shining star Lt. Col. Prasad Shrikant Purohit.

Last September, VHP terrorists destroyed dozens of Christian churches and also set a Christian orphanage on fire, and burnt to death a 20-year-old Christian teacher.

Ironically, despite the blood-letting of hundreds of thousands of minorities, not a single Hindu could be found on the UN's, EU's and on US lists of terrorists. Nothing could be heard from the so-called fair and balanced Western media over the genocide in Kashmir.

# Pakistan in a great political turmoil

Published in *TheNews*, London, October 5, 2008

Pakistan is in deeper turmoil now than ever before. The huge bomb explosion at the Marriott hotel in security-conscious Islamabad says it all. The agony with which the ordinary citizens suffer from their own politicians and from foreigners alike is not a new phenomenon, but recently it has been exacerbated by a new twist in the US foreign policy in this region. Involving the Pakistani army to do the dirty work of the racists in Washington may not have the desired effect or intended result.

That only means, in essence, a Pakistani killing a Pakistani to please the Americans, a perfect recipe for weakening and destabilising the country.

After a prolonged interval, Pakistan has had a sort of general election, and the parliament appointed a new civilian president. One would have thought then that there would be a long-term stability and an economic growth that people most desperately need. This has not turned out that way.

The US has launched regular raids into Pakistan in hot pursuit of the Taliban, killing hundreds of women and children. Well-equipped NATO and US soldiers with the help of air power have been slaughtering innocent people on both sides of the Afghan/Pakistan border for the past eight years.

Pakistanis from Khyber Pass to Karachi are up in arms against the US for its violation of the sanctity of their country. A cry of anguish against the West is becoming louder and louder. Under the United Nations Charter, this kind of utterly disturbing behaviour amounts to war crimes. Visual and print media reports in Pakistan suggest that the Security Council indict the culprits for their reign of terror and punish them.

European countries and Canada, Australia and New Zealand also don't criticise the US for its policy towards Muslim countries. They are all the same stock – Europeans both ways – home and away. Some EU countries have withdrawn their soldiers from the war zones because they were being killed by the hundreds.

President George W. Bush said the other day that he wants to protect Pakistan. He did not say from whom. If he means to protect Pakistan by bombing its citizens day and night, then one would not think Pakistan needs 'protection'.

India is sitting on the sidelines, waiting not altogether anxiously, but gleefully, for its chance to pounce. The risks are increasing every week.

Meanwhile, Prime Minister Yousaf Raza Gilani would not pick anyone for his Cabinet better than himself. His international political skill and intellectual capacity were exposed, particularly after his awful performance when he recently met Bush in Washington.

At the press conference he could not respond intelligently to any of the questions asked by the world media. He could have made his mark. What a lost opportunity. He could not even understand what question was being asked in the first place. So Pakistan is lumbered with a kitchen cabinet.

Most US presidents proved themselves power drunk; during the past 60 years they have attacked without shame a weaker sovereign country. The most recent victim is Pakistan, besides Iraq and Afghanistan. The superpower has not learnt any lesson from its humiliating defeats in the Korean, Cambodian and Vietnam wars.

According to political observers and media watchers, those defeats are bound to be repeated in the present wars that the US is engaged in.

It has been argued by many journalists and scholars of history that there can never be an American victory in Afghanistan unless there is another Hiroshima and Nagasaki type of bombing. The word 'never' is not mine. It has been used by the most respectable journalists in Britain and the US, in this context, to describe an impending US defeat.

The politicians in Pakistan may be encouraged to ask Americans why they are still occupying Afghanistan when their mission of capturing Osama bin Laden on one hand, and winning the hearts and minds on the other, has miserably failed.

The leaders of Islamic countries, such as Saudi Arabia, Egypt, Jordan, Libya, are sold out, or rather bought outright like slaves by their masters in Washington. Who said slavery was abolished in 1840?

At least these kings and presidents, who by the way are not interested to raise their voice on behalf of their own people, can humbly ask their masters how long the US soldiers are going to stay in Afghanistan and Iraq. What is the end game? What would the US be satisfied with? How can the US win the battle of hearts and minds through the barrel of a gun?

How many more women and children must die under the pretext of the war on terror? They may also tell their masters in no uncertain terms that there is no such thing as al-Qaeda; this is a misnomer for Mujahedeen, the same people who fought against the Soviet Union, a superpower only 20 odd years ago. That battle lasted for ten years from 1979 to 1989 and the Afghans dragged the Russians out of their country, resulting in the breakup of the USSR Empire.

These are the same people who the late US president Ronald Reagan and the late British prime minister Margaret Thatcher applauded as Mujahedeen in their conversations and speeches. These are the same people who were described as the defenders of their faith and protectors of their land by the same president.

These are the same people who fiercely fought from 1839 to 1842 and defeated the army of the British Empire at its peak, in what is known as the Anglo-Afghan wars from 1878 to 1881 when the British had to run in disarray to escape being beheaded. These are the same people who will not be subdued by the greatest military might today.

So, in the 19th century the Afghanistan/Pakistan region could not be occupied by the British. In the 20th century Afghanistan could not be occupied by another great power, the Soviet Union.

Now in the twenty-first century the people of this region, Afghanistan/Pakistan, are ever more determined to get rid of the invaders from their land.

A tiny minority of right-wing supporters of George W. Bush and Tony Blair may still continue to argue differently, but it is no gainsaying that the US with its allies have virtually destroyed Iraq by creating a sectarian divide on Shia and Sunni lines, fomenting trouble by supplying arms to both sides. Many people do not know that Shias and Sunnis lived in Iraq peacefully for more than 1,000 years with cosy inter-marriage relationships among them. A tried and tested policy of divide and rule worked in Iraq in a notoriously colonial fashion.

Bush's argument in occupying Afghanistan is that he is trying to prevent another 9/11 attack in his country.

On paper this looks a good line, and many people may be taken in, but let us look at this argument:

A person in Afghanistan first fills in forms and applies for a passport, then he goes to the American embassy in Kabul and fills in more forms in order to get a visa to enter the United States. After that preliminary hard work of obtaining a passport, visa (if he can get one), and air tickets, he travels and lands in one of the airports in the US.

On arrival, he will be thoroughly examined by immigration officials who apply stringent rules for entry. Permission to stay is granted. So far so good.

Next, he would apply for training as a pilot of an aircraft (preferably a jumbo jet). Having been trained as a competent pilot, depending on his ability and aptitude, and length of training, he will now hire a plane or highjack one, and manoeuvre it towards the Pentagon or the Oval office. If this is the argument Mr Bush is using to occupy Afghanistan then it would not hold water and it would certainly not be very convincing. Or, is he saying that Afghans might invade and damage his country through terrorism? Both scenarios would take hell of a lot of convincing.

There is a widespread conviction among the thinking people that the war on terror is stupendously overplayed and there is no audience for this drama any longer. The best thing for the US, one would imagine, is to withdraw its army from the occupied lands.

The next president of the United States can start thinking now of ending these wars rather than contemplating pouring in more soldiers to be killed.

# Ex-convicted prisoners up to the same old tricks

Published in *The News*, London, February 28, 2008

Asif Ali Zardari and Nawaz Sharif, the two party dictators who have not participated in the General Election of Pakistan and therefore have not been elected by the people, are up to the same old tricks for which they are globally notorious.

Sharif, who was kicked out twice as prime minister for incompetence and corruption charges, seems to have a one track mind of revenge politics and clash of personalities with his former chief of staff, and has nothing new to offer to the nation.

Both of these guys, tried and tested earlier, are now haggling over who will get what. They owe their freedom to the benevolence of General Musharraf who kept his promise of a free and fair election and kept them out of prison.

Musharraf also gave Imran Khan an opportunity to take part and face the nation in the general election, but he turned it down. What a lost opportunity; he shot himself in the foot. What sort of politician is he? The nation may be glad that Mr Khan will not sit in the National Assembly. The so-called cricketer-turned-politician, a phrase coined and proudly used by the British media because of his education in Oxford University and county cricket performances. Divorced from his English wife, left cricket, he has lost even this title on the way. He is no longer a cricketer, neither a national politician, his contribution in eight years has been a slogan of one sentence that reads: Musharraf should resign.

Musharraf, who wisely saved Pakistan from annihilation from the wrath of the angry Bush and determined Rumsfeld after September 11, 2001, unlikely to resign under pressure and would complete his term of office for which the previous parliament elected him as president of Pakistan. Pakistanis have a short memory and are ungrateful to their president.

What kind of democracy would it be when party leaders who are not even elected, and a former cricketer, demand that the president of Pakistan resign? That will amount to stifling the meaning of democracy.

Musharraf, no more in a military uniform, has proved time and time again that he is a worthy leader of Pakistan, capable of dealing with dodgy foreigners, and at home he is prepared to cooperate with members of the new Assembly. The free, fair and transparent election under him proves his sincerity when he says, "First of all Pakistan". Proof of the pudding is in the eating.

Pakistanis must not confuse the electoral system with democracy. If the new rulers can avoid revenge politics or a clash of personalities, particularly between Sharif and Musharraf, and instead focus on policies and reconciliation, then Pakistan has a fighting chance of survival as truly proud and an independent country. The next few months will be crucial for Pakistan.

# Khuda Kay Liye: In the Name of God

Published in *TheNews*, London, June 7, 2007

There was a time when the Pakistani film industry was merrily engaged in making escapist films with variations on the same theme: a young girl and a boy chasing each other round a leafy tree and bursting into singing playback songs away from their parents in a film studio.

Now the mould seems to have been broken, and Pakistani film makers have come of age and belatedly realised that there is a real market for political films without the help of dozens of songs and dances every ten minutes.

Shoib Mansoor, a film director of great renown, accepted the challenge of making such a film. It is called *Khuda Kay Liye* or *In the Name of God*. His film shows the torturing of a suspected "terrorist" by the Central Intelligence Agency in America on one hand, and on the other, ironically, the same suspect's brother who is constantly goaded by a religious leader to raise arms against the United States, which is relentlessly bombarding Afghanistan post-9/11.

There are some of the scenes which etch out in one's mind instantly, mainly because of heavy doses of extreme violence on both sides of the equation. The Americans are trying to stop being attacked again by so-called al-Qaeda, and the Afghans, with the help of their Arab brothers, are trying to stop the US colonising and occupying their Muslim lands.

The film vividly throws light on both political factions as fanatics. The clear message therefore, undoubtedly, seems that no solution would be found in violence.

The film is also to a greater extent about a forced marriage with a religious, racial and colour divide as an added ingredient.

A British girl of a Pakistani father and an English mother wishes to marry a Christian English guy. Her father instinctively opposes this union and takes the girl away to Pakistan, and marries her off to a Muslim boy of her age.

This is where the dreadful trouble starts, and what happens next is to be viewed to be believed. Accusations of rape, kidnapping, deception, trickery and double dealing are played out in the highly charged atmosphere of a High Court drama in Lahore.

Two Muslim scholars, one played by the famous Bollywood actor Naseeruddin Shah, are diametrically opposed to each other's interpretation of Islam. It is all-absorbing watching.

Shoib Mansoor keeps you awake, if you blink you miss the point. There is no chance of falling asleep, either. This is the first time I have ever seen a full-length film from the Indo-Pakistan subcontinent without falling asleep half way through.

Already shown in Pakistan and the Gulf states, *Khuda Kay Liye* deals with current international issues such as fighting in Afghanistan, Islamic ideology, torture of suspected inmates by the US, and a forced marriage.

I, for one, was gripped by an intriguingly gruesome scene of an innocent Pakistani student in the US who was chained and regularly interrogated, character assassinated, humiliated, badly beaten by FBI agents repeatedly hitting the student's head against the concrete wall until blood spills all over.

This one is a grim, emotional, and highly disturbing scene, not for the faint hearted, but powerfully acted by all concerned.

The people who ask why the world hates America will most definitely find the answer in this frightening scene.

Shoib Mansoor's film beautifully tackles love, hate, extreme violence, forced marriage, religious bigotry, political blackmail, and above all, a clash of civilisations in action.

Much of the credit goes to the superb acting under a flawless directorship. The film raises, though, as many questions as it answers.

The Press Preview was ably organised by the active help from the Geo Television chief in London, who, in spite of his other duties, took time off to look after the media types. If you go to see this film you will not be disappointed; take with you a proverbial pocket handkerchief.

# High Sheriff of Greater London promotes multi-faith observance

Published in *TheNews*, London, July 9, 2006

Dr Khalid Hameed, High Sheriff of Greater London, hosted a reception in the College Garden, attended by Benazir Bhutto, Maleeha Lodhi, Lord Nazir Ahmed, Lord Dholakia, Baroness Flathers, Prince Mohsin Ali Khan, Mr Hinduja and Madhava Chandra, among others.

Apart from Jews, Christians and Muslims, other religions such as Zorastrian, Jain, Hindu, Sikh, and Buddhist were represented, reflecting in their speeches universal values endorsed by those faiths: justice, compassion, tolerance, peace, love and brotherhood of mankind.

The high sheriff is normally associated with a law-enforcing officer in a US county, usually elected by the local people. Dr Hameed is not elected by the people of London in the same way as the mayor of London is, but is appointed for a year by the head of state.

It is this man who keeps order in his county. It is not known how Dr Hameed, in spite of his fabulous credentials as a high profile medical doctor and an appointed CBE, is going to keep order in the county of London, or Greater London to be precise.

In ancient times, the high sheriff's duties used to entail, among other administrative responsibilities, attending courts, visiting prisons, executing judgments, keeping the Red Indians and marauding cowboys in check, and where possible, introducing reforms. Under Dr Hameed's sheriffdom, one hopes that racist murders such as that of young Zahid Mubarek in prison would never be repeated.

The most famous high sheriff in the UK was John Howard, born in London in 1726. He was shocked at what he found in prisons. He visited every prison in the country four times. He also visited hospitals throughout Europe, inspecting kitchens and talking to inmates to gain first-hand knowledge.

After a long and deep study, he wrote a book called The State of Prisons in England and Wales in 1777, which led parliament to correct many abuses. Had Howard been alive today, Belmarsh prison in east London, popularly known as 'Hellmarsh', would have been a different place. Zahid Mubarek would still be alive today.

It is most unlikely, however, that a modern-day high sheriff will find time to visit all the prisons, let alone inspecting kitchens in hospitals and prisons to bring about reforms. One might hope, nevertheless, that Dr Khalid Hameed keeps order in his county of London, now that he is the chief officer of the crown and has a legal territorial claim to his name for his newly-found Sheriffdom.

Would he cooperate, one wonders, with the mayor of London, who is bent on extending congestion charges farther afield, or would he agree with the high priest of the Metropolitan Police on his shoot to kill policy?

# Community leaders stress respect for faiths

Published in *TheNews*, London, June 6, 2006

Community leaders called for peace, tolerance and unity among different faiths at a special service ahead of the anniversary of the July 7 terror bombings in London.

Speakers from nine religions stressed the importance of respect among different faith communities, and condemned the evil-minded few who had terrorised London last year. Guests including Metropolitan Police Commissioner Sir Ian Blair and former prime minister of Pakistan Benazir Bhutto attended the multi-faith service at a church next to Westminster Abbey last night.

The event, the first multi-faith service at Westminster Abbey, was the brainchild of the new High Sheriff of Greater London, Dr Khalid Hameed, whose appointment was also marked by the ceremony. Dr Hameed, the first Muslim to take up the role, said before the event that he wanted to send out a message in London and beyond, that 'We will not be intimidated by terrorists'.

The service featured speeches by representatives of faiths, including Sikhism, Hinduism, Islam, Judaism and Christianity.

Dr Khalid Hameed and wife; former prime minister of Pakistan Benazir Bhutto next to Metropolitan Police Chief

# Palestinians appeal to the world to bring down apartheid wall

Published in *TheNews*, London, May 12, 2006

While the world's attention remains focused on Iraq and Iran, the Palestinians are reminding the world media about the latest atrocities committed by Apartheid-Israel's land grab on the West Bank and the killing of innocent women and children on a regular basis. They want Israel to abide by the international law, recognise the democratically elected Hamas Government, dismantle the Apartheid Wall, and remove settlers from the illegally occupied Palestine.

To help achieve that goal the Palestine Solidarity Campaign organised a seminar at the Friends Meeting House, Euston, London, to highlight the dire situation in Palestine; starvation may soon be the order of the day because of sanctions imposed by the European Union, Apartheid-Israel and the US.

Journalist and author Victoria Brittain, who chaired the conference, said that no one can explain the plight of the Palestinians better than the veteran campaigners Tony Benn and the author and journalist Tariq Ali.

Mr Benn started by saying that coverage by the media about the latest atrocities committed by Israel is appalling and totally unacceptable. The use of starvation for Palestinians is a new weapon of war, favoured by Israel and its friends. There should be more reporting on this, he suggested. The US president George W. Bush claims to be a born-again Christian, and says he is doing this for his God.

Benn pointed out that Zacarias Moussaoui, who was recently sentenced to life imprisonment in America, said the same thing to the judge in the court that he was doing this for God. Benn advised Bush to refrain from using religion as a reason for war. The president should know that the crusade wars lasted 140 years without achieving

*Evergreen Tony Benn and Tariq Ali: Israel must stop atrocities against Palestinians*

anything, and Muslims all over the world hate to hear about those wars.

He demanded complete withdrawal of Israeli forces from occupied land. "Attacking Iran would be a terrible mistake. If action is taken against Iran, exactly the same action must be taken against Israel", he roared, to the delight of the approving capacity audience.

Tariq Ali, who has lost none of his traits as a powerfully captivating public speaker from his earlier days of the Vietnam War, wanted to know how long the Palestinians have to suffer from the Israeli bombings while the world turns a blind eye.

He said Hamas has shocked the West by winning the general election. That result was a recognition that absolutely nothing was done for the Palestinians by their own previous leadership and the Oslo accord. The so-called roadmap was a great deception by the Israelis, and now the power base has been ultimately transferred to the people of Palestine.

This is the reason why the Bush administration is scare-mongering against Hamas and does not want democracy in Palestine. Tariq Ali said this is the democracy paradox for the West. Democracy itself is changing its character.

The Israeli dictator Ariel Sharon should have been tried as a war criminal before he went into a coma, he said, because he had committed more crimes against the Palestinians than the Serbian president Slobadan Milosovic against the Bosnians.

He said the US and British warmongers use the Security Council for their own dirty tricks, and if that fails they try NATO, and if that does not work out then they attack unilaterally any country of their choosing.

Lindsey German, convener of the Stop the War Coalition, said that Bush and Blair say that if they attack Iran they can solve the terrorism problem in the Middle East. These hypocrites should know that this has had an opposite effect after the invasion and occupation of Iraq and Afghanistan. A suicide bomber is called a terrorist, but if Israel, a rogue state, attacks and bombs by air and kills Palestinians, how come that is not called terrorism, she asked.

Keith Sonnet, deputy secretary of trade union Unison, said Hamas should be recognised and allowed to run the country the way it wants. "We should ask our government to take strong action against Israel and boycott Israeli goods in Britain." He said most of terrorism in the region is the result of the British and the American foreign policies. The Apartheid Wall should be demolished, he added.

Karma Nabulsi, an exile, said that occupation has strangled the economy and now Israelis want Palestinians to starve to death. Refugees are created every day and there is no end to the suffering in sight. She appealed to the outside world to help end the occupation of her ancestral land and bring about the demolition of the Apartheid Wall.

# March from London to Karachi

Published in *TheNews*, London, March 3, 2006

March 18 will be a unique day of anger against the occupation of Iraq. Protests from London to Karachi and beyond in more than 80 countries will be joined by mass demonstrations in Baghdad and Basra, all calling for British and US troops' withdrawal from Iraq.

The Iraqis, Shias and Sunnis together, will be uniting with protesters in Amsterdam, Ankara, Athens, Barcelona, Bogota, Boston, Cairo, Caracas, Copenhagen, Denver, Dublin, Geneva, Helsinki, Istanbul, Jakarta, Karachi, Kuala Lumpur, Lisbon, Ljubljana, London, Madrid, Managua, Manila. Melbourne, Memphis, Minneapolis, Montreal, New York, Odense, Oklahoma, Ottawa, Seoul, Stockholm, Sydney, Tarragona, Toronto, Vancouver, Vienna, Warsaw and many other towns and cities.

March 18 is the third anniversary of the unprovoked attack on Iraq by the warmongers in Britain and the US. This war, with no end in sight, has been opposed consistently by the vast majority of British people, millions of whom have been actively involved for four years in what is the biggest protest movement in British social and political history.

Throughout the country, seminars, street stalls, film shows, distribution of leaflets and other events are being organised by Stop the War Coalition, in association with both the Campaign for Nuclear Disarmament and Muslim Association of Britain, to help build support for the London part of the demo.

Already, people opposed to the slaughter of the innocents and tortures by foreign soldiers in occupied Iraq are busy spreading the information about this demonstration through family and friends, in workplaces, and in communities.

Coaches to bring demonstrators to London are now being booked in most areas of the United Kingdom. No one should be able to say after March 18 that they were not on the march because they did not know about it.

In addition, the government of Hugo Chavez, socialist president of oil-rich Venezuela in South America, has given a green light for its people to demonstrate against the continued oppression by the US in Iraq and elsewhere. Many people would recall that Chavez had publicly accused the United States of planning an invasion of Venezuela after he had been democratically elected.

So, the scene is set for a huge turnout around the world in one day. For peace loving people of the world it will be an inspiring occasion, but for Blair, Bush and his Defence Secretary Donald Rumsfeld, it will not be so good for they would have been found out and exposed once again about their barbaric activities in the Middle East.

As you read this, tortures continue apace at Guantanamo Bay concentration camp, and this worries the whole of humanity except Bush and Rumsfeld, both of whom claim to be defending 'democracy' by locking up defenceless innocents indefinitely.

The inmates at Guantanamo Bay are now force-fed by a plastic tube inserted through the nose, causing the detainees to vomit blood.

The UN General Secretary Kofi Annan says: "Guantanamo Bay should close. It is just flat wrong." The International Red Cross finds: "The interrogation techniques are tantamount to torture." Amnesty International, which has been campaigning for years for the closure of Guantanamo, demands: "Detainees must be released immediately unless charged with recognisable criminal offences and brought to fair trial." Bishop Desmond Tutu of South Africa says: "It is horrendous," and one of Tony Blair's cabinet ministers, Peter Hain, says: "I would prefer Guantanamo was closed."

There are other torture chambers, apart from Guantanamo, namely, Abu Ghraib, Bagram, Diego Garcia, Yemen, and numerous other secret prisons. The European Union nations which proclaim freedom of speech, democracy, and fair play, can play a greater part in bringing about the closure of these evil torture camps.

A number of conferences have been held in the meantime to discuss Guantanamo prison and the pull-out of troops from Iraq, but these have gone unreported. Even the very big one, organised by the United Nations Association, at Central Hall Westminster, London, last month, which was addressed by Kofi Annan and foreign secretary Jack Straw, was neither reported in the print media nor shown on television, despite its strong appeal to the public at large.

At these meetings, people usually ask tricky questions such as whether the CIA and M16 were behind the attack on the Shia shrine to stir up trouble between Shias and Sunnis to show to the world that because of this in-fighting the West's presence in Iraq was necessary.

Anas al-Tikriti, president of the Muslim Association of Britain, an Iraqi, did not have a straight answer in "Yes" or "No" to the above question, but he stressed that the destruction of the Shia holy place last week, a calculated act, seemed a bigger job and certainly some unknown "dirty hands" could not be ruled out. That left the audience to reach their own conclusion.

He added that the two communities had been living together in peace and close brotherhood for more than a thousand years. He was shocked and dismayed that this conflict has erupted as a direct result of the invasion and occupation of Iraq by foreign armies, which are more likely to exploit the situation to their own advantage.

# "Don't Attack Iran"

Published in *TheNews*, London, February 3, 2006

The above headline would be fluttering on hundreds of thousands of placards on March 18 protest march against the likely attack on Iran by Britain and the US, and against the illegal occupation of Iraq.

This international day of action is going to be the beginning of a new wave of demonstrations on the onset of a summer which may prove uncomfortably rather hotter for Bush and Blair; the duo may not have had a single night of uninterrupted sleep without pricking their consciences since the assault on Iraq.

If an aggression against Iran is being plotted in London and Washington, although the foreign secretary has said that attacking Iran is not on the table, what can then be on the table? The national organisers of this forthcoming protest have given strong reasons to demonstrate on that day. One of the reasons given is that so far 100 British soldiers have been killed in Iraq in Blair's war, and hundreds others severely injured, and this killing process on both sides has to stop.

The campaigners say that Blair's foreign policy is making Britain a terror target, as the attacks on July 7 last year proved, and as a result civil liberties are being torn up by the government. They also claim that British Muslims are under threat and are being targeted by Islamophobic racists, and communities need to be protected for the sake of unity and decency of this country.

They also complain that the government deliberately told blatant lies before the attack on Iraq, misled the parliament and can no longer be trusted. As a consequence, Iraq has suffered far too long from sanctions and occupation. It is time the troops come home. They want Blair to be held to account for his decisions which undermined democracy, and wasting billions of pounds in the occupations of Iraq and Afghanistan. John Reid, the Defence Secretary, announced that he is about to send an additional 3,700 soldiers to teach the Afghans to be democrats at a cost of one billion euros. He is unaware of the fact, though, or perhaps he could not care less, that in Afghanistan, risks of more troops being killed are higher than in Iraq. Already 92 British soldiers have been killed there. The taxpayers' money could be used for pensions and public services in Britain.

Alan Watkins in *The Observer* sums up the situation and shape of things to come: "Blair hopes that the anti-war movement would fade from view. March 18 demo is likely to show him how mistaken he is. Peace supporters will continue campaigning for as long as the occupations of Iraq and Afghanistan continue, and the best antidote to Bush and Blair's missile rattling over Iran will be to make this national demonstration in London as big as ever, reflecting the anti-war views of the vast majority of British people".

Meanwhile, there is so little information about Guantanamo Bay tortures and hunger strikes, and the "international renditions" flights through European airports. People are now questioning what the EU countries and the Security Council of the United Nations are going to do about that. This, and other similar serious issues, will constantly occupy the campaigners, demonstrators and human rights activists throughout the year. Demonstrations are already planned worldwide, including one in Iraq.

So the Bush-Blair-Rumsfeld triad has much to ponder over. Iran is not Iraq in military strategy, but to George W. Bush and Rumsfeld these are only the same rhyming words. Iranians as a nation are absolutely right behind their leaders and are concerned about Israel's hundreds of nuclear warheads. Israel has refused any inspection of its nuclear plants; it has considerably more weapons of mass destruction than Iraq could ever have.

In such an atmosphere, Iran has a right to defend itself with whatever weapons, conventional or nuclear, it deems fit. A pre-emptive strike, if such a stupid idea is contemplated by the US or Israel, will most certainly backfire and bring the whole world to the brink from which it will not recover.

Moreover, Iran is a very important country for the world. It has more energy resources than Iraq. The world needs its energy resources. Ukraine, for instance, recently had asked Iran to supply gas after a pipeline from Russia had been exploded. Any thought that Iran could be subdued, let alone occupied, by any foreign power, super or sinister, is a notion not to be entertained by the above triad or Pentagon.

# Dr Moazzam Ali Alvi

Published in *TheNews*, London, December 23, 2005

The news of the death of the founder-president of the movement of Khilafat-e-Rashida was eclipsed by the earthquake in Pakistan and was not widely reported. Many people still do not know that he has died.

Pakistan has lost in him a scholar, a reformer, a great educationist and a political figure in both England and Pakistan for more than 50 years.

A legend in his own right, synonymous with the movement, Dr Moazzam Ali Alvi passed away peacefully in Islamabad on October 9 – one day after the earthquake.

On hearing about the disaster, he rushed from Islamabad to Mansehra the same morning to help the survivors, disregarding his age and health. He was 85 years old and fragile. The two-way long journey and shock took its toll.

A thoroughbred political activist, he practised what he preached; he held honesty, integrity and hard work closer to his heart in a world full of corruption, greed and moral decay.

He was born on September 9, 1920, in a noble family at Thana Bhawan District, Muzaffarnagar, U.P. India. He migrated to Pakistan with his entire family of doctors, teachers and politicians, who helped establish the new country. He mentioned this quite often and took a lot of satisfaction from this achievement.

After his interrupted education in Ali Garh Muslim University, he completed his BSc degree from Karachi's famous D. J. College. While there, he founded the All Pakistan Muslim Students Federation and encouraged students to work for a truly just society in Pakistan.

Having instilled the reforming revolutionary zeal among the activists in Karachi, he travelled to Britain for further education and research.

Dr Moazzam Ali Alvi: He never lost passion for a better Pakistan

He observed that successive martial law on one hand and corrupt civilian governments on the other could not deliver, and was convinced that the system of Khilafat-e-Rashida was the only cure for Pakistan's political ills.

In 1991, when the US attacked Iraq, he was extremely upset that Muslim countries did not protest, and was depressed because of the destruction of Baghdad by the US and British bombings and sanctions on Iraq. He twice went to Afghanistan to meet Mullah Omar and the Taliban to render his help and advice.

He wrote to General Pervez Musharraf asking him to consider his six-points plan for Pakistan. His letter reads:

*Dear General Musharraf, Assalam-o-Alaikum,*

*I would like to congratulate you on your bold and daring action against the previous corrupt government and saving the unity of our armed forces.*

*"I do realise that it is very difficult for a soldier, however bold a person he may be, to run a civilian government, but if he sticks to the orders of Allah and follows in the footsteps of our Holy Prophet, Allah will grant him success and protect him from those who hinder progress.*

*"Now, I send to you a workable plan for your kind consideration, hoping that these points would help in solving the problems faced by our nation:*

1. Military rule is not a solution for our country. Law given by Prophet Muhammad is the only law and therefore this must be implemented immediately.
2. Islamic welfare system needs to be introduced straightaway as was done by our Prophet to solve the social problems. For instance, Islamic justice system should be provided and no court fees should be charged. This can be done easily through a justice committee in local mosques. Medical treatment should be free for those in need. Food should be available for each and every person, this can be done without any difficulty, provided the system of Zakat is properly established and is run on the principles of rehabilitation and not on a charity basis.
3. The money which is taken out of the country must be brought back. The persons who robbed the country be put behind bars at their own expense until they return the entire money.
4. Foreign accounts must be reinstated, so that foreign currency starts flowing back to the country.
5. Prisoners who have not been tried for years must be brought before the courts according to the basic Islamic justice and human rights. By doing this we can get places in jails where new criminals who corrupted the nation can be kept.
6. There is no need of borrowing from outside. The nation can generate enough money to run the government.

It seems that Dr Alvi wanted Musharraf to implement the principles of Khilafat-e-Rashida in Pakistan rather than Khilafat itself. He emphasised the value of justice in a society which alone can free the country from corruption. He used to say that without social justice communities cannot progress, and nations disintegrate.

He wrote a book, called *System of Khilafat-e-Rashida – The Only Way*. At its launch in Lahore, in 2002, most prominent politicians and cultural leaders of Pakistan attended the function.

Dr Alvi says in the foreword that the book is dedicated to the nation and he is not interested in royalties whatsoever. His free lectures on mind-making at the Islamic Cultural Centre in London's

Regent's Park mosque, from 1982 to 1999, were very popular among all strata of society.

The late President Zia-ul-Haq was quite impressed by Dr Alvi's ideas. He invited him to Islamabad and appointed him Chairman of Zakat Fund Committee. Dr Alvi seized the opportunity and decided to do something useful with the money. He immediately established a school for women who missed out on education, along with a sewing academy. He employed the best teaching staff. He paid a salary to the under-privileged women to educate themselves.

Thousands benefited from this method of vocational learning. Dr Alvi attributed the legendary success of this school in Islamabad to the system and principles of Khilafat-e-Rashida.

He dedicated his life to this movement of helping others. Unlike most politicians, he was rarely seen in front of a camera. Very few photos were taken of him for such an important public figure. He was always a source of inspiration, particularly when delivering speeches at meetings and seminars.

Dr Alvi will be greatly missed by those who knew him in London, Lahore, Karachi and Islamabad, where he had finally settled.

# Blair's role in Iraq caused the bombings in London

Published in *TheNews*, London, September 11, 2005

A hard hitting anti-war message linking the London bombings with the Iraq invasion was heard at the Baptist Church in Balham, south-west London late on Thursday.

The former *Sunday Express* journalist Yvonne Ridley, who was arrested in Afghanistan by the Taleban and now has converted to Islam, spoke passionately about the bombings of Iraqi civilians by Britain and the US. She said there is an irrefutable link between the bombings in London and the occupation of Iraq by Britain and the US.

The Muslim community is being ordered what to read and think, and be like the British. Islamic bookshops are threatened to be closed down permanently. The Scots, the Irish, and the Welsh celebrate their nationality and do not like to be pigeon-holed as British. Muslim people should be allowed to be Muslim. What is being British, anyway? she asked.

"I am a journalist by profession. If I see injustices, threats to civil liberties and freedom of thought and speech, resistance is my duty". She said Tony Blair should be kicked out for his war crimes and a shameful reign of torture and terror in Iraq. His acts are of a despotic dictator, reminiscent of Pol Pot who killed thousands of people in Kampuchea.

Jeremy Corbyn, Labour MP for North Islington, said that Bush has "unleashed the dogs of war in Iraq and our prime minister has followed him blindly. Through our demonstrations we are now winning the public opinion in America against this illegal war.

"The whole issue of weapons of mass destruction was whipped up to justify the attack on Iraq. British and American troops are not part of the solution they are part of the problem. Britain has intervened

Yvonne Ridley spoke about Blair's indirect role of bombings in London

in Iraq as an aggressor twice before and on each occasion failed to achieve anything.

"The bombings in London in July were wicked and horrible. Twelve people from my borough died. International publicity was enormous. I would like to have seen this kind of coverage for the innocent 100,000 civilians who perished at the hands of the British and the US bombings. The US can start a war anywhere in the world, but cannot help its own people within the country, as the New Orleans hurricane disaster has clearly shown".

Where was the superpower for the whole week, he asked. In this country, he pointed out, "people crave for a real Labour Party government which can represent them and not a sort of Republican dictator in the US".

Lindsey German, National Convener, Stop the War Coalition, said: "When Bush and Blair attacked Afghanistan in October 2001 to capture Osama bin Laden, we said then that they would create hundreds of bin Ladens around the world. Events since then have proved that, including the London bombings.

"Now Bush and Blair are telling us even a bigger lie than the lie of 'weapons of mass destruction', that Iraq is a better place after the invasion and occupation. In reality, the country is in a more terrible mess now than it was under Saddam.

"The US has no right to tell the Iraqis what kind of constitution they should have and how to elect their parliament. They should get out of Iraq," she demanded.

All the speakers, without exception, agreed that the bombing in London in July was linked with the war in Iraq, and Tony Blair is telling a blatant lie when he simply says it is not.

Stop the War Coalition will organise a big march on September 24 in central London.

# Livingstone urges Londoners to shop at Palestinian Trade Fair

Published in *TheNews*, London, December 5, 2004

London Mayor Ken Livingstone, who opened the Palestinian Trade Fair at the Arab-British Chamber of Commerce on Monday, has urged Londoners to buy more Palestinian goods to support their economy.

The mayor said with half the population unemployed and 60 per cent surviving on a poverty-line income of just one dollar a day, the situation in the Palestinian economy could not be more grim. This trade fair aims at improving links between the UK and the Palestinian economies and to help expand the British market for imported Palestinian goods. "I hope that many Londoners will choose to do so some of their Christmas shopping at the Palestinian Trade Fair, where they will be able to find some unique gifts such as embroidery, olive, wood carvings and Hebron glassware". The Fair, supported by the European Union, seeks to improve trade between the UK and Palestine. Mr Livingstone spoke passionately about independent Palestine. "We want a free and a dynamic Palestinian state, a state with diplomatic relations with the outside world".

Sir Roger Tomkys, left, and London Mayor Ken Livingstone, right, in conversation with Palestinian Consul General in London, Afif Safieh

He said the Government was playing a double role in relation to help free Palestine, and the British media are not far behind.

Sir Roger Tomkys, Chairman of the Arab-British Chamber of Commerce, said the motto of the chamber is friendship through trade.

# A day in the life of Conway Hall

Published in *TheNews*, London, October 3, 2004

The Conway Hall in central London has celebrated its 75th anniversary on September 23. The invited guests, Professor Laurie Taylor of the BBC, Polly Toynbee of *The Guardian,* Barbara Smoker, and Richard Dawkins, all spoke on the subject of free speech and answered a number of tricky questions from the audience. Celebrations included exhibitions, tour of the halls, live music, and refreshments.

In 1971, at the peak of a horrible conflict in East Pakistan, the then Foreign Minister Zulfiqar All Bhutto, on his way to the United Nations in New York, came to address a meeting at this hall. The Mukti Bahini, a secessionist faction opposed to the Pakistan Army in what is now Bangladesh, made it clear that they came to protest and disrupt, but the West Pakistanis came to listen to their foreign minister, affectionately called by his admirers as 'Zulfi'. Throng of people were trying to get in from both sides of the building entrances.

Bhutto had an unenviable task of defending the military ruler Yahya Khan in West Pakistan on one hand, and his military emissary Tikka Khan on the other who was engaged in controlling the eastern wing, where he was extremely unpopular among the Bengalis.

The atmosphere was emotionally charged, and after an initial scuffle outside the hall a vicious and violent fight erupted between the Punjabis and the Bengalis, the type of fighting that this hall had never seen before in its entire history. Only the hecklers in the past have been known to have won their day after shouting at the speakers from the floor, but no physical injury resulting from wild aggression or the pitched battle like the one on this occasion.

It was bitter hate war between the Punjabis and the Bengalis with no borders and no mediators. It was free for all who dare. There were many bleeding noses, black eyes, people kicked on the ground mercilessly, and blood splattered on shirts all over. It was mayhem.

In those days the security used to be lax compared with today, and the fringe meetings attracted no police or public attention. The perpetrators of violence fled before the police arrived. Mr Bhutto had to be bundled out of the building in a hurry for safety. A few months later Bangladesh was established, but not before Conway Hall lost its innocence, as it were.

This episode was not widely publicised in the mainstream press, most probably because of its minority interest and also to maintain the reputation of Conway Hall as a peaceful, civilised, tolerant place where free thinkers, trade unionists and humanists could assemble for serious discussions on basic ethical principles, and organise conflicting views in the spirit of the original idea.

Conway Hall, completed in 1929, is renowned as a hub for free speech and progressive thought. In recent years we have seen on the platform speakers such as Salman Rushdie, Imran Khan, Tony Benn, Tariq Ali, Will Self and Mary Robinson to name but a few. The hall is named after Moncure Daniel Conway, born on March 17, 1832 in Stafford County, Virginia, the son of a prominent slave-holder in that county.

Conway became increasingly disillusioned with the Unitarian Church and fellow abolitionists and moved to London in 1863, having virtually no ties left to the United States. England afforded Conway, the anti-slavery advocate, the intellectual and spiritual freedom for which he had always yearned. He became involved in artistic, non-conformist, free-thinking and humanist circles of London that he held most dear.

He returned to the United States in 1884 after the death of his father, but when his wife died in New York on Christmas Day, 1897, and again becoming disillusioned with politics in his home country, he left in 1898, this time for France, where he devoted his life to the peace movement. He died on November 15, 1907, alone in his Paris apartment. The Conway Hall named in his honour remains as a leading internationally renowned centre of intellectual, political and cultural life and hosts a wide variety of lectures, performances and community events.

The Pakistanis have also used this hall for their meetings and conferences on a regular basis without an incident such as the one on that day in 1971.

# Islam Under Siege

Book review published in *TheNews*, London, September 12, 2004

At a time when most politicians are worried about what the US is doing around the world in the name of a conveniently chosen word, 'democracy', Professor Akbar S. Ahmed, standard-bearer for all causes Islamic, has written a new book, *Islam Under Siege* about the world's major civilisations and their interaction with one another in modern times.

The book is based on his lectures, speeches, articles, and academic research in the United States and Britain. An engaging paragraph in it, therefore, sets the scene of pre-September 11 perception of the West in the minds of Muslims all over the world which reads:

"Bill Clinton reaffirmed the Muslim reading of the American society, particularly after Clinton admitted his affair with Lewinsky to the grand jury in Washington. The West had little to offer the world except sex, violence and greed. If the president of the United States was a man without honour, his people could not be different. It seems clear to me that Osama bin Laden misread Bush on the basis of Clinton's behaviour. To him all American presidents behaved in a feckless and dishonourable manner. Bush responded to the attacks on his nation as a man of honour bent on vengeance."

The above paragraph works wonders if analysed further, where there are curiously many assumptions, presumptions and perceptions. Another book perhaps could be written to explain all that. A dialogue and a never-ending debate is bound to ensue, and this is probably the intention of the author, to bring all of these contentious issues in the open for debate.

The book is a scholarly inquiry into a likely clash of civilisations in our time, when several societies on this planet simultaneously feel threatened and fearful of one another. It is meticulously researched, and written in such a way that no major religion or a political party can accuse him of being biased. Remarkably, then, he has succeeded in steering clear of the controversy himself.

The author has quoted the Egyptian activist Sayyid Qutb who inspired Osama bin Laden and Al Qaeda. He had visited the US and had come back repelled by its culture and described it in this way as follows:

> "Humanity there is living in a large brothel. One has only to glance at its press, films, fashion shows, beauty contests, ballrooms, wine bars and broadcasting stations. Observe its mad lust for naked flesh, provocative postures, and sick suggestive statements in literature, the arts, and the mass media. Add to all this, the system of usury which fuels man's voracity for money and engenders vile methods for its accumulation and investment, in addition to fraud, trickery, and blackmail dressed up in the garb of law".

After reading the above piece, one realises why that Muslim scholar with a vision had been executed by the pro-American Egyptian government in 1966.

A chapter discusses the failure of Muslim leadership and ideal. He cites the sight of palatial mansions guarded by security guards carrying automatic weapons and, nearby, the miserable squalor of shanty towns teeming with poor children, which is common in Muslim cities.

Another chapter expresses the fear that a dialogue between the West and the Muslim world is unrealistic in the face of the global hostility to Islam, and also the difficulties in Muslim societies at a time when the Muslim leadership appears bankrupt of vision and indifferent to the condition of its people. "Redistribution of wealth must remain a priority of any Muslim government. Central features of Islam will re-emerge only with justice, fair play and respect for knowledge and individuals", he writes.

With a sense of detachment, mindful perhaps of not upsetting the US too much, which is trying to democratise the whole world in its own image, Professor Ahmed says that after September 11, 2001 it is a dangerous time in world history, when several societies and civilisations feel threatened and uncertain about their future.

His interfaith activities in America with Jewish and Christian scholars had given him a unique experience and a platform from where his opinions and thoughts are partially derived. So much so that the book is dedicated to his close friend Lawrence Rosen of Princeton University, as he puts it, in acknowledgment of his scholarship and friendship.

Many people may wonder why the book was not dedicated to his wife who, according to Akbar Ahmed himself, played a crucial role in publishing it, as he admits: "As always my wife, Zeenat, inspired me with her commitment to my work, oversaw the writing of the book, and helped me in refining my ideas".

It will be interesting to see whether his Jewish and Christian friends reciprocate by dedicating their books to him for his friendship and scholarship. After all, Professor Ahmed is a world renowned dedicated interfaith scholar and an important Muslim academic and anthropologist. It is rather more tricky to please rivals in international affairs than to please one's own.

Professor Ahmed left his post as Pakistan's high commissioner in the United Kingdom after a stint of only nine months in the wake of a wrangle over his involvement in *Jinnah,* a film about the founder of Pakistan. This project, quintessentially Pakistani and about Pakistan's charismatic leader Muhammed Ali Jinnah, failed to hit the box office in a significant way and not many people took notice. It made no impact as was expected, and this was partly because so many aliens instead of Pakistanis got involved in producing it.

His book, on the other hand, which is a serious political commentary on world affairs, particularly on the Islamic affairs, is more likely to prove a success story where his film could not. I enjoyed reading it. A professional politician, a student, or anyone interested in current affairs, can benefit from its easily graspable language and content. The book comprises several suggested solutions to the world's political and religious problems.

Professor Ahmed is now ibn Khaldun Chair of Islamic Studies, American University, Washington, DC, United States.

*Islam Under Siege* by Professor Akbar S. Ahmed (Polity Press, 2004)

# Is the clash of civilisations inevitable?

Published in *TheNews*, London, July 23, 2004

Professor Akbar S. Ahmed, a former High Commissioner of Pakistan to the United Kingdom and now a professor of International Relations at the American University in Washington, DC, delivered a lecture last night at the London School of Economics and Political Science. He discussed his new book *Islam Under Siege,* from clash to dialogue on civilisations. He said many countries today simultaneously feel under siege. The Muslims feel aggrieved because of what is happening in Iraq, torture in Abu Gharib prison, Palestine, Kashmir, Chechnya, and Guantanamo Bay.

The Israelis say that they are surrounded by Arabs, and they are afraid of being eliminated if the Arabs have an upper hand. The Indians say that on each side of their border there is a Muslim country – Pakistan and Bangladesh – and beyond that more Muslim countries, and therefore, they are under siege. The Americans have expressed more frequently their opinion and fear about Muslims being a threat to them globally and that they are not safe anywhere, and therefore the US is under siege.

Professor Ahmed says it is a dangerous time in world history when several civilisations and societies on this planet simultaneously feel threatened and fearful of one another.

He asked the audience to ponder over the word 'simultaneously'. There seems no compromise, but cyclical terror against terror. He said this anarchy and turmoil must end if humankind is to survive.

This school has a reputation of being a left-wing political hotbed for more than 50 years. It was here that most plans, or rather plots, were hatched for demonstrations against the United States during the Vietnam War in the late 60s and early 70s. The place seems to have lost its former touch and glory since the heady days of such revolutionary student leaders as Tariq Ali. Jack Straw (later to become foreign secretary) was seen in those days with open neck, long hair and open mind; and Professor Fred Halliday, co-editor with Tariq Ali of the radical weekly *Black Dwarf.*

The main single issue then, apart from Vietnam, was apartheid in South Africa and also the struggle for the release of Nelson Mandela. Since then, Tariq Ali has gone on to write books on modern political history and became a broadcaster for Channel 4 Television, among other things. Fred Halliday has become a professor at this very school, so he has not gone far away to reminisce his past.

We all know of course what the one and only Jack Straw is doing now. He has put collar, tie and suit on, and has become Foreign Secretary of Great Britain; the lefties feel that they have lost an excellent brain to the establishment.

Many people now ask if the school with such a remarkable political activism has run out of causes. It so happens that last night out of a blue moon the roving Islamic scholar and critique, Professor Akbar Ahmed, got the ball rolling and enlivened and enlightened the audience at this school with a greater cause, the survival of the human race when billions are in the process of being brainwashed into believing that the clash of civilisations is to come and is inevitable.

The learned anthropologist strongly argued in his lecture against that worrying prediction, whether it comes from Professors Samuel Huntington, Bernard Lewis or Osama bin Laden. He believes that a serious dialogue between the Muslim world and the West is not only possible but inevitable in order to counter misunderstandings, suspicions, and fear of each other. This can be done, he says, by encouraging friendship among the Abrahamic sister religions: Christianity, Judaism, and Islam.

Prof. Akbar said the West cannot afford to ignore the wishes of 1.3 billion Muslims around the world, many millions of whom live in the US and Europe; they are citizens of those continents. Muslims, on the other hand, cannot afford to isolate themselves from the rest of the world because of their religion; they will have to live in the twenty-first century and not outside of it. Without a desire for change, reform and education within Islam, Muslims would be left behind, the learned professor said.

# Prince Mohsin's idea of solving the Kashmir problem

Published in *The Pakistan Times*, February 26, 2004

Through a telephone interview with me yesterday, Prince Mohsin Ali Khan, the founder-president of the Society of British Muslim Elders, has suggested that India, Pakistan, Bangladesh and Sri Lanka (IPBS) could be brought together under one political umbrella without losing regional or geographical autonomy.

"In each of these countries", he said, "there are substantial numbers of Muslims, and by forming a confederation they can benefit from one another's cultural and religious experiences, free from external threats and leading to permanent peace in the entire area. Thus the Kashmir dispute will disappear altogether in the IPBS evolving process".

This idea seems to have been based on the European Union type of regional and economic unit. The prince, who has been propounding this version of unity in the whole region for almost quarter of a century, believes that the people of these four countries are able to unite and fight their common foe in illiteracy, injustice, poverty, and political terrorism.

He congratulated the government of Pakistan and the President Pervez Musharraf for successfully organising the recently concluded SAARC conference in Islamabad, and also praised the Indian Prime Minister Atal Behari Vajpayee for his desire for peace with Pakistan, including talks on the disputed issue of Kashmir. India's offer of contributing 100 million dollars towards poverty alleviation in the seven SAARC countries is also an indication of good omens for its smaller neighbours.

He emphasised that united Indo-Pak sub-continent, free form ill-will and suspicion, can achieve, in the long run, economic and social reforms much quicker.

# German stalwart values cosmopolitanism in Europe

Published in the *Daily News*, Karachi, and *TheNews*, London, December 2, 2003

Dr Helmut Kohl, the former Chancellor of the Federal Republic of Germany, on a rare visit to London, described cosmopolitanism in Europe as an undeniable fact of life.

The architect of the demolition of the Berlin Wall in 1989, which paved the way for the reunification of Germany, was joined by hundreds on this special occasion in the splendid setting of London's Victoria and Albert Museum yesterday. He said that European Union is expanding, which is very much a desired development. He discussed at length many of the global issues, including smaller nations' role as participants in order to maintain law and order and peace in the world.

He justified his joining the Euro and luckily he did not have to look for the majority. The Euro is now one of the most important currencies in the world and would be a stable currency in the future. He estimated that 27 European nations would be using it very soon. The German Ambassador to the United Kingdom, His Excellency Thomas Matussek, said that Germany and Europe have been the two focal points in the life of Dr Helmut Kohl. In 1989 when the opportunity to unite the two parts of Germany arose, Dr Kohl seized it without hesitation despite much resistance from home and abroad. With his impressive political courage and great vision, he succeeded in achieving what many had for decades only dreamed.

The ambassador said Helmut Kohl is not only the champion of German unity, he is also one of the most devoted stalwarts of new Europe, shaped, no doubt, by the experience of the Second World War and with a profound understanding of Germany's history. Dr Kohl stated that friendship for him was not to give commands to

Helmut Kohl: "We must have genuine tolerance for other religions and cultures."

friends. "We must respect differences of opinion among friends and genuine tolerance for other religions and cultures".

During his tenure of office from 1982 to 1998, he struck in his own peculiar way friendships with Margaret Thatcher, John Major, Ronald Reagan and Bill Clinton, and the late French President Mitterrand, while remaining at the centre of European politics and quietly moulding the EU as we see it today.

He repeatedly emphasised the importance of levelling out big and small nations in order to maintain peace in the world.

Hubert Schulte Kemper, Chairman of the Board of Managing Directors, Hypothekenbank in Essen, and Mehmet Dalman, Director of Commerzbank AG, who organised this dinner at this world famous venue, said that their bank is now heavily involved in London capital and bonds markets and doing a good business with Great Britain. Nothing was said of if and when Turkey might join the EU.

# Schimmel eulogised at German embassy in London

Published in *Diplomatische Magazin*, Germany, November, 2003

AUSSENPOLITIK

# Erinnerung

Die deutsche Botschaft in London erinnerte mit einem Seminar an die Islamwissenschaftlerin Prof. Annemarie Schimmel.

Zur Erinnerung an die im Alter von 80 Jahren im Januar dieses Jahres verstorbene Professorin Dr. Annemarie Schimmel hatte der deutsche Botschafter in London, Thomas Matussek, zum ersten Schimmel-Seminar in seine Residenz eingeladen. Prof. Annemarie Schimmel war eine der bedeutendsten Islamwissenschaftlerinnen des 20. Jahrhunderts. Sie lehrte in Ankara, Bonn und an der weltberühmten Harvard University. Ihr Spezialgebiet war die islamische Mystik. Wegen ihrer Verdienste erhielt sie 1982 das Bundesverdienstkreuz Erster Klasse, 1995 den Friedenspreis des Deutschen Buchhandels und 2001 den Reuchlinpreis. Prof. Saeed Durrani von der Iqubal Academy (Großbritannien), der zahlreiche Konferenzen in Lahore (Pakistan) organisiert hatte, an denen Prof. Schimmel teilnahm, bezeugte seinen Respekt. Mohammed Aman Herbert Hobohm, Direktor der Bonner König-Fahd-Akademie, sagte: „Als Annemarie Schimmel am 26. Januar dieses Jahres starb, verloren der Islam und die Muslime einen Freund und Fürsprecher." Der Bischof von Rochester, Dr. Michael Nazir-Ali, reflektierte die Arbeit Annemarie Schimmels ebenso wie Dr. Leonard Lewisohn vom Institute of Ismaili Studies in London. Dr. David Matthews von der Iqubal Academy, sagte, dass Schimmel und der Dichter und Philosoph Iqubal viel gemeinsam hätten. Beide bewunderten Jalaluddin Rumi und wurden von ihm inspiriert. In seiner Rede sagte Prince Mohsin Ali Khan: „Wir sind auf deutschem Boden und ich bin der deutschen Botschaft dankbar dafür, uns alle heute Nacht hierher einzuladen, um uns einer großen Dame zu erinnern, die so hart arbeitete, um diese Welt ein wenig besser zu machen." Burzine Waghmar erinnerte, dass Schimmel einen großen Beitrag zur indopakistanischen Kultur und Religion geleistet habe. Auch Javed Akhtar von der pakistanischen Botschaft und Rev. Peter Berry gedachten Prof. Schimmel. Botschaften von Prince Al-Hassan bin Talal von Jordanien und des High Commissioners von Indien wurden verlesen, in denen sie bedauerten, nicht persönlich an dem Seminar teilnehmen zu können. *Nisar Ali Shah*

Prince Mohsin Ali Khan, Botschafter Thomas Matussek und Botschaftsrat Max Maldecker (v. l. n. r.). Foto: Nisar Ali Shah

# Summary

The German Ambassador in London, Thomas Matussek hosted a reception at his residence in memory of Europe's greatest Islamic scholar, Professor Dr. Annemarie Schimmel. He said that she was trying to bring the Muslim world closer to Europe through her knowledge and belief in Islam. Dr. Annemarie Schimmel died on January 26 this year. Glowing tributes were paid by Professor Saeed Durrani of Iqubal Academy (UK), who organized many conferences in Lahore (Pakistan), when Schimmel was the chief speaker. Pakistan Embassy was represented by Javed Akhtar. Messages of apology from Prince Al-Hassan bin Talal of Jordan and the Indian High Commissioner were read who both could not attend. The Bishop of Rochester, Rt Rev Dr. Michael Nazir-Ali, delivered an illuminating speech reflecting Schimmel's work and discipline. Mohammed Aman Herbert Hobohm, Director of the King Fahd Academy Bonn said: "When, on Januar 26 this year, Annemarie Schimmel closed her eyes for ever, the Islam and the Muslims lost a sincere friend and advocate." Also Dr. Leonard Lewisohn from the Institute of Ismaili Studies, London, Dr. David Matthews of Iqubal Academy, Prince Mohsin Ali Khan, Rev. Peter Berry, vice-chairman of Iqubal Academy and Burzine Waghmar, reflected the life and work of Annemarie Schimmel.

# First Schimmel Memorial Seminar held in London

Published in *TheNews*, London, October 31, 2003

The German Ambassador in London said that Professor Annemarie Schimmel was trying to bring the Muslim world closer to Europe through her knowledge and belief in Islam, right up to the time of her death.

Speaking with feelings and gusto, His Excellency Mr Thomas Matussek, who hosted a reception at his residence in Belgrave Square in memory of Europe's greatest Islamic scholar, said that it was an honour for his embassy, that so many scholars of different faiths have assembled here.

Emphasising the importance of being a Schimmel, he said that in Germany people often quote Goethe (poet/philosopher) who was inspired by Eastern faiths and philosophies. Prof. Schimmel was similarly bridging the gap between the Muslim world and her native Europe.

His government was committed to tolerance towards all comers. People of different cultures come to live in Germany, but the political climate in the world and particularly the situation in the Middle East has not helped much. Mr Max Maldacker, First Counselor, German Embassy, said that he was proud as a fellow German of Schimmel's unique contribution.

Earlier, glowing tributes were paid by Professor Saeed Durrani, a scientist at Iqbal Academy, UK, who organised this and many other conferences in Lahore, when Schimmel was the chief speaker and guest of honour.

The Pakistani Embassy was represented by Mr Javed Akhtar, the press minister. A message of apology from Prince al-Hassan bin Talal of Jordan was read, who could not attend because of the Iraqi political crisis. In another message the Indian high commissioner also expressed his regret not to have been able to attend.

The Rt. Rev. Dr Michael Nazir-Ali, Bishop of Rochester, spoke at length but confined himself to Annemarie's mystical approach to Islam. Himself an authority on both Christianity and Islam, he delivered an illuminating speech reflecting Schimmel's work and discipline.

Mohammed Aman Herbert Hobohm, who embraced Islam in 1939, Director of King Fahd Academy, Bonn, said: "When, on January 26 this year, Annemarie closed her eyes forever, the world of oriental learning lost a great scholar. Islam and the Muslims lost a sincere friend and advocate, and I personally lost in her a person with whom I had been closely associated for more than 50 years". He said a campaign of vilification had erupted in the German media against her because she had allegedly defended the Fatwa against the author Salman Rushdie.

Dr Leonard Lewisohn from the Institute of Ismaili Studies, London, who translated classical Iranian Sufi poetry into English and wrote a book about Schimmel, also kept his speech closer to her mystical dimensions of Islam. He said Annemarie could write in 17 languages. When offered a laptop by her Turkish friend she said if she can write in 17 languages, why would she need a computer?

Dr David Matthews of Iqbal Academy, UK, and a lecturer in Urdu at the School of Oriental and African Studies, said that Schimmel and Iqbal had much in common. Both liked Jalaluddin Rumi and were inspired by him.

In his speech, Prince Mohsin Ali Khan said: "We are lawfully on German territory and I am grateful to the German Embassy for inviting us all here to celebrate and remember a great lady who worked so hard to make this world a better place to live in. Annemarie Schimmel was such a scholar that she will always be remembered".

Burzine Waghunar, a research fellow of Iranian Studies, said that Schimmel had made a unique contribution to Indo-Pakistan culture and religion.

Rev. Peter Berry, vice-Chairman of Iqbal Academy (UK), said that Muslims have been humiliated during the past century, but the twenty-first century is going to belong to them. Dr Razia Sultanova, Visiting Professor, Goldsmiths College, London University, played the dutar (two wires), a traditional Uzbek lute.

In keeping with the spirit of the seminar, Durdana Ansari from the BBC World Service, beautifully sang a mystical poem with an Islamic overtone that Schimmel would have approved of. Mrs Pakeezah Baig sang a ghazal of Allama Muhammed Iqbal, the poet and philosopher of Pakistan.

# Hawks pounce on Iraq to redraw its map

Published in *TheNews*, London, September 11, 2003

Wesley Clark, the former NATO Supreme Allied Commander in Europe during the Kosovo campaign, had suggested early last year at the Royal Institute for International Affairs meeting in London that the war in Afghanistan was "a war for the heart and soul of Islam". So, the top general may have unwittingly let the cat out of the bag. In an entirely different message involving religious wars, using the word 'crusade' was conveyed by the newly elected George W. Bush who targeted Iraq first thing in the morning as soon as he became president. This was before September 11, 2001. The fact that the West has completely lost credibility among Muslims around the world is not new or surprising.

On this side of the Atlantic, for example, an IRA rocket attack in February 1991 on Downing Street was launched and a piece of shrapnel lodged in the ceiling of the Cabinet Room. Six years earlier in 1985, a powerful bomb exploded in the Grand Hotel at Brighton where the Tory Party conference was being held, nearly killing the whole Cabinet; the then Prime Minister Margaret Thatcher miraculously escaped. She did not dare ask the Irish living in this country to apologise for the bomb explosion. She was understandably too scared to upset the Irish, but she had recently sprung out of retirement to complain that Muslims living in this country did not condemn enough the Twin Towers attacks in New York, even though those incidents occurred outside of her own country in a far-flung foreign land.

That 'hijacking', if it was, took place in the United States; American aeroplanes were involved; American airports were used; and no other country's airspace was violated, certainly not Britain's. Most people who died were not British. Citizens from 80 countries, including Muslims, were killed. Muslims living in this country had nothing to do with that, so why should a former prime minister ask the Muslims to apologise? It is still not clear as to who was behind those attacks in the US; there is no evidence as to who did that.

Mrs Thatcher was prime minister at the time of Ariel Sharon's engineered massacre in the Sabra and Shatila refugee camps in 1982, where 17,000 Palestinians were slaughtered in cold blood, and since then more Palestinians have been murdered by apartheid-Israel. She never asked the Jews living in this country to condemn those crimes committed by the Jews in the occupied West Bank. No sanctions were imposed on Israel. Apartheid-Israel has intensified its firepower against the innocent civilians and bulldozed more Palestinian houses to make room for Jewish settlements. There is no end to the double standards applied by both the US and British politicians when dealing with the law-abiding Muslims.

Today, where does Mr Blair come in line with the responsibility for his country? If he is serious about a 'war on terrorism' he should look away now towards apartheid-Israel, which has been terrorising the Palestinians and other Arabs for the past 50 years with no questions being asked and no apology demanded. Israeli actions in the occupied Palestinian lands fit the definition of genocide in international law as "acts committed with intent to destroy, in whole or in part, a national, ethnic, racial or religious group".

Bush and Blair ought to start bombing Israel instead of Iraq if they mean to end terrorism, and follow the path of peace with justice. Both politicians have some responsibility for misleading their own respective nations.

The US has propped up Israel by pumping in billions of dollars' worth of weapons of mass destruction, mostly free of charge or paid for by the Zionists in the US and Europe. No politician dares talk about Israel's weapons of mass destruction. To add insult to injury, the US claims to be even-handed regarding its Middle East policy, so why not supply the same kind of weapons to the Palestinians? When the Palestinians and other Arab countries can match the military might of Israel, only then may the Israelis be prepared to talk peace and come to the negotiating table on an equal footing. Some Arab countries can also help the Palestinians build their armed forces by providing them with planes, tanks, training, and missiles. The US will oppose such a move because this issue is inter-connected with the Iraq situation.

The West dare not try a regime change in North Korea, which has expelled weapons inspectors from its shores, but Iraq, which has let the inspectors in, is under constant bombardment. The US chooses only weaker targets, and having burnt its finger in Korea once before in the early 1950s, it has a nasty memory of that misadventure. Therefore, North Korea is a different kettle of fish and is not a Muslim country, anyway. This is not true of Iraq where the US had a successful run during the 'desert storm' in 1991.

When an Arab country, such as Iraq, tries to become stronger and decides to defend itself, the US immediately intervenes and the problem of Arabs/Zionists in the region remains unsolved. This is the crux of the matter in the Middle East, where the West is trying to redraw the map of this region. Many Arab countries are also conspicuous by their silence on Iraq.

Meanwhile, Israel defies all UN resolutions demanding the withdrawal of its troops from the occupied territories and continues to disregard world opinion which is in favour of establishing a Palestinian state. The US keeps repeating the same old tired phrases, war on terror and weapons of mass destruction. War on terror is a euphemism for war against Islam. Mr Blair is equally guilty with Mr Bush of killing thousands of Muslims in Afghanistan, and the hawks are now engaged in killing thousands of innocent Iraqis yet again. Mr Bush's wondrous proposition to 'smoke these folks out', in cowboy language perhaps, is incomprehensible.

If I were a leader of a Middle Eastern country I would not allow any unwanted and unidentifiable foreigners in my country, let alone inspect my nation's private and public possessions. I would have argued that weapons inspectors in my country are illegal immigrants without work permits or visas from my embassies abroad. I would have proclaimed that the so-called weapons inspectors in fact are spies, advised and inspired by my country's enemies. I would have emphasised that no country in the world would willingly allow its sovereignty to be violated in such an open and offensive way. I would have insisted that every country has an inalienable right to defend itself with whatever means it thinks appropriate.

I would have readily agreed with those who say that the US is a superpower, but only in kid-glove methods and not a superpower in morality. I would have reminded the public of the United States' long list of misadventures overseas and how badly it dealt with those delicate international issues. I would have conceded that in spite of its superbly high-powered technological advancements, the US, paradoxically, has nothing to offer to the world, except hatred, international tension, warmongering, crude propaganda techniques, and diabolically inhumane conditions of its captured citizens of many countries in Guantanamo Bay prison. I would have accepted that the Muslim world rightly believes that racist-Israel and the US are hellbent on destroying the Muslim culture and civilisation slowly, as the great Native American civilisation in the old North America had been destroyed.

Finally, I would have given a strong warning to the US and Israel that Islam is not merely a religion or a code of conduct for life, but an emotion to the Muslims. You can separate a man from his wealth, but you cannot separate him from his emotion. Communism collapsed because it was a jumbled-up commercial/financial theory without emotion as part of it. Islam is not collapsible. It spreads rapidly in adversity, just as it did for the past 1,400 years.

# An Islamic scholar made in Germany

Published in *TheNews*, London, July 13, 2003

The life and work of Professor Annemarie Schimmel, one of the greatest Islamic scholars of the past century, were eulogised at the memorial service at St James's Church, Piccadilly, London, on Thursday. Prince Charles was represented by his Private Secretary, Sir Stephen Lamport.

Prince Hasan bin Talal of Jordan, brother of the late King Hussain, read from the pulpit to honour her as a bridge between the West and the Muslim world.

Ralph Pinder-Wilson, former curator of Islamic Collections in the British Museum, was present, and so was Pakistan's High Commissioner, Abdul Kader Jaffer, who took time out to attend this important ceremony.

In the true spirit of interfaith ideals, the service took place in both Christian and Muslim traditions.

The Reverend Charles Hedley read from the Bible: 'Let us love one another, for love is of God and everyone that loveth is born of God and knoweth God'; while Ahmed Moustafa quoted from the Quran: 'Guide us on to the straight way – the way of those upon whom Thou hast bestowed Thy blessings, not of those who have been condemned by Thee, nor of those who go astray'.

Annemarie Schimmel (April 7, 1922-January 26, 2003) was very fond of Islamic music, so it seemed apt that a ghazal in Uzbek was sung by Razia Sultanova of the Russian Academy of Music, one in Urdu (written by Allama Mohammed Iqbal) by Dr Ziauddin Shakeeb, and another in Sindhi called Universalism was sung by Karuna Loomba.

An Ismaeli devotional poem, sung by Naaz Jiwan, and an Iranian ghazal recited by Shusha Guppy, were well received.

Two Iranian musicians played classical music in a constant euphony. Iraj Emami played on the *ney* (flute).

Professor Annemarie Schimmel

Ayse Parman beautifully recited a Turkish poem which was translated by none other than Annemarie Schimmel herself.

Mohammed Aman Herbert Hobohm, a fellow German and a friend of Schimmel for 50 years, who accepted Islam in 1939, paid glowing tributes to her achievements and passion for learning:

"She started learning Arabic when she was only 15 and obtained her first PhD degree at a tender age of 19, followed by a second PhD in History of Religions from Berlin University.

"She was invited to teach at Ankara University in the Faculty of Islamic Theology. This was by no means a small achievement for a Christian, a German, and a woman".

Having made her mark as an unrivalled authority on Islam and Islamic Studies, she was soon headhunted for the Chair of Indo-Muslim Culture at Harvard University in 1967. She held that position until 1992.

Muslim and non-Muslim scholars who knew her through her books and lectures in Turkish, Urdu, Persian, Arabic, Sindhi, German and English were impressed with her scholarship. She also endeared herself to the ordinary people, who had unfailingly shown love and affection for her wherever she went.

Schimmel was no ordinary scholar. She spoke as fluently in those languages as her own native German, and lectured not only in Arabic, Farsi and Urdu, but in all other languages linked with Islam. She was an expert on the great Persian poet, Jalaluddin Rumi, and was greatly inspired by Sufism.

She made an enormous impact in the Muslim world where she extensively travelled and lectured in the local languages with an awe-inspiring ease.

She received three honorary degrees from Pakistani universities and was awarded the highest civil honour of Hilal-e-Pakistan.

A major boulevard was named after her in the city of Lahore.

She wrote more books than an average person reads in his whole life.

Not only did she help Muslims understand their religion better, but also showed in a convincing way that Islam is different from the adverse picture the Western media so often depict.

Among her admirers present were Professor Yacoub Zaki, a Scot, who embraced Islam and himself a great scholar; Mr Maidacker from the German Embassy; Sheikh Hussan al-Sabah from Kuwait; Prince Mohsin Ali Khan; Ms Gerda Vedder, a close friend specially flown from Germany for this occasion; Maria Robinson; Philippa Vaughan; Mr Ashraf Qazi, former editor of *Daily Jang,* London; Farhad Hakeemzade; Ali Nanji; Nicholas Barrington from the Foreign and Commonwealth Office; Shamsuddin Agha of Indo-Muslim Federation, UK; Bob Aldeman; and more than hundred others.

# Turkey at a crossroads after Iraq War

Published in *TheNews*, London, June 29, 2003

Turkey's Ambassador to the United Kingdom, His Excellency Mr Akin Alptuna, was the guest of honour at a reception and dinner-debate at St Ermin's Hotel in central London on June 25.

He spoke about Turkey's future and consequences of the Iraq war. He said Turkey has a common vision with Europe, but the country is facing innumerable problems at the moment, partly because of the Iraq war.

These problems are not insurmountable and would be ironed out by the time Turkey joins in. He thought Turkey's roadmap to join the European Union had already been mapped out and negotiations would take place in 2004 to decide the eventual date of joining.

"Turkey played a crucial part," he said, "in stabilising the whole area from the very beginning, and supported the territorial integrity of Iraq, but unfortunately this part of the world is undergoing a considerable change and there is an uncertain future and Turkey is rightly concerned about it, and the international community would be faced with this new development for a long time to come".

He mentioned his concern specifically about the influx of refugees from places bordering Iraq and the menace of PKK terrorism through which thousands of people have lost their lives. Consequently, Turkey had to send troops to the south-east of the country to stop the flow of refugees, he said.

Although no friend of Saddam Hussein, the invasion of Iraq came to him as a shock. In any case he did not like to see the humiliation of a neighbouring Muslim country.

Asked if the coalition forces should withdraw from Iraq, he replied that to do so now would be a worst case scenario because the law and order situation would worsen.

Turkey is frustrated, he said, when wrongly criticised by some European countries on moral issues. These are interrelated issues and find their parallel elsewhere in Europe, but the country is rapidly changing, he added.

Earlier, Sir Michael Burton, President of the European Atlantic Group which organised the dinner, enlightened some 300 diners by his thorough knowledge of the history and political and culturally rich life of Turkey.

Diplomats from Europe as well as from around the world attended this lively debate. The local dignitaries included Sir Eldon Griffiths, Elma Dangerfield CBE, Director of the European Atlantic Group, Prince Mohsin Ali Khan, Sir David Logan, Ms Demetra Christodoulou, Cyprus Embassy, Colonel Zhao Zhi Qiang, Chinese Embassy, Dr Seyed Vahid Karimi Councillor, Islamic Republic of Iran, Captain Sala Al-Mousa, Saudi Embassy, Mr Radomir Kosie, Embassy of Bosnia and Herzegovina, and Baroness Hooper.

# Hyde Park rally exposes war of conquest not "Liberation"

Published in *TheNews*, London, April 14, 2003

The Stop the War Coalition, the organisers of Saturday's march and rally in Hyde Park, gave reasons why such demonstrations must continue with more vigour and resolve, saying that Iraq has been invaded in a war of conquest not liberation.

Tony Benn, former cabinet minister, said America has conquered Iraq and turned it into a colony. He assured Muslims that millions and millions of people in this country are their friends.

A loud thunder of joy burst among the large audience (estimated 250,000) who greatly admire Mr Benn for his forthright and outspoken condemnation of Tony Blair and his government's actions.

The only power to control America, he said, was the power of the people of the world, and we must continue to oppose this war.

Jeremy Corbyn, MP, said: "In Iraq 5,000 people have died so far. Many more will die. We oppose war because the price of war is paid by the poorest people. This is a war for no reason other than pumping out Iraqi oil for the benefit of the US and Britain.

"America spent 81 billion dollars and the British three billion pounds on this war so far. This money could have been spent on hospitals, education and for the starving millions in Africa and other parts of the world. We condemn the actions of the British and American aggression. We will outlive the militarists", he concluded.

George Galloway, MP said: "We would not be silenced by the Labour Party leadership". He appealed to every single participant to write to Tony Blair that this war is immoral, and the blood of the Iraqi people will remain on his conscience forever.

The disturbing photo we have all seen of limbless Ali in his bed is not going to go away from Tony Blair's conscience."

He asked: "Is that what you mean by disarming Iraq? Real looters are still to come. Be under no illusion that this is not the end of beginning, but the beginning of the end," he said.

Dr Ghayasuddin Siddiqui of the Muslim Parliament, said: "This war is about control of resources." By occupying Iraq and handing it over to the arms manufacturers and oil companies in the US, Bush wants to ensure his genuine re-election as president next year.

Lindsey German, the convener, said Iraq is going to be taken over by a retired general, Jay Garner. "This war is waged by the rich against the poor".

A young Iraqi activist, Wasan Alfikriti, spoke on behalf of the youth of Iraq about the destruction of Baghdad, a city of culture and two beautiful rivers. She advised Blair, Bush, Hoon, and Rumsfeld – a gang of four – to leave Iraq immediately.

# BBC One's 'Question Time'

Published in *TheNews*, London, April 4, 2003

It was disgusting to watch the way Mr Dimbleby conducted his usually orchestrated Question Time on BBC One on Thursday. He seems to have moulded this programme in his own political image, or rather this episode was. His behaviour was appalling towards Yasmin Alibhai-Brown, columnist of *The Independent*. I only guess he might have apologised to her after the show went off air, but it would have been better had he done so while live.

This slot used to be in a different format and slightly more probing under its former presenters, the late Robin Day, and BBC newscaster Peter Sissons. One cannot bring back Robin, but come back Peter, all is forgiven. On this occasion, airily everybody was interrupting everybody else, including Mr Dimbleby himself and a Kurdish woman from the floor.

When Yasmin Alibhai tried to put a word in edgeways against the invasion of Iraq by Britain and the US, a point of view with which Mr Dimbleby did not seem to agree if his body language was anything to go by, he rudely interrupted her sentence and put his boot in. This is freedom of speech in practice! You have to be sympathetic with the warmongering aims of Bush and Blair before you can be heard uninterrupted on television.

Most people who saw this programme will agree that Dimbleby gave Yasmin little chance to speak in comparison with other panellists: Geoff Hoon, Defence Secretary; Oliver Letwin, Shadow Home Secretary; and Charles Kennedy, Lib-Dem Leader, who appeared to have the same, if not worse, colonial mentality.

That Kurdish woman who was against the Iraqi regime and in favour of the British and American assault on Iraq had more repeated time to speak than Yasmin was allowed, and she was not even on the panel.

Mr Dimbleby never interrupted her and no one asked her any questions. One would doubt if it was a selected audience to match the other three panellists to please George W. Bush, who is engaged in killing innocent Iraqis with a bit of help from his cheerleader Blair, who has involved Britain unnecessarily and is sticking behind his master to trounce 'Eye-rack' (Mr Bush's pronunciation for Iraq) for 'however long it takes'.

# Galloway explains his expulsion after thirty-six years

Published in *The News*, London, March 11, 2003

In his first major speech after expulsion from the Labour Party, George Galloway said that he was expelled from his party after 36 years because he opposes the Bush-Blair axis plans for endless war of imperial conquest and occupation. Because he was most critical of Tony Blair's Iraq venture, and because he refused to be intimidated, he was considered as an obstacle, he said.

Referring to the Iraq war, he chided the prime minister by saying that this appalling blunder which has scarred the face of the world for a generation to come would be the political death of Tony Blair. "I believe he is on the ropes, and we may be able to knock him out in the coming year. So let the bell ring and let us come out fighting."

A huge audience at the Friends Meeting House, Euston, London, on Wednesday, gave him a standing ovation lasting a few minutes. He will stand as an independent candidate for a seat in the House of Commons from wherever it is thought his candidature would be helpful.

He also criticised the government's economic policies on privatisation of essential services, public utilities, and the growth of uncontrollable corporate power without any thought for social consequences.

Salma Yaqoob, of Stop the War Coalition, said that trade unions have been treated with contempt by this government. Most people want good health and good education and both are mismanaged by the Labour Party. She said despite opposition against the Iraq invasion, where thousands of civilians have been killed by Bush-Blair bullets, the government ignored the collective wisdom of millions of people. What is the alternative? she asked.

Ken Loach, a well-known film director, said that a hundred years ago the Labour Party was created to organise and analyse the day to

George Galloway

day issues, but now it is a party of contradictions. Blair certainly puts the employers first. We have to follow the principles of socialism. Do we want a Labour Party of Harold Wilson, Jim Callaghan or Tony Blair? We do not need those Labour parties any more, we have to start afresh, he advised.

By this time of the proceedings, an announcement was made that Iain Duncan Smith had lost his Tory leadership vote, and the author and environmentalist George Monbiot started his speech by saying that IDS has been put to rest. However, turning to the main business of the evening, he deplored that Labour was not working and was not compatible with its original ideals. It is a facade of democracy when people lose in democracy; 'it is a scam', he added.

Bob Crow, General Secretary of the RMT union, expressed his concern about the safety on the Underground. His union might ballot his members for strike action unless things improve. He blamed privatisation for shoddy workmanship where 'profits before people' is the norm. He offered Galloway sponsorship by his union as an independent candidate for parliament.

John Rees, vice-chair and staunch supporter of Stop the War Coalition, warned Tony Blair thus: "You can invite Bush to this country by all means, but he cannot move while he is here". He attacked the Labour agenda of cuts in services and expressed horror on Iraq's daily killing of civilians by the coalition forces.

Linda Smith, of Fire Brigades Union, said her members' 85 years of relationship with the Labour Party is at a crossroads. "Because of ill-conceived policies of the government towards trade unions, I can confirm as a treasurer that not a single penny has gone to the Labour

Party from our political fund. We have suspended all affiliation fees and donations. The expulsion of George Galloway after 36 years of membership was disgraceful," she said.

A representative from the postal workers union, Communication Workers Union (CWU), whose unofficial strike action continues and is spreading, said that this dispute was engineered by Trades and Industry Secretary Patricia Hewitt and the Government; last year the CWU cut its financial contribution to New Labour.

# African Union to sort out the killer loan sharks

Published in *West Africa Magazine* and *Aimet*, Travel & Tourism Magazine, January-March, 2003

When the Organisation of African Unity (OAU) was relaunched at a gathering of 40 African countries in Durban, South Africa, on July 9, in its new name of the African Union (AU), it had embarked on an ambitious plan of creating a Pan-African parliament and a central bank similar to the World Bank. The whole world would be watching as to what decisions the AU takes in its next deliberations in the new year.

Established in 1963 in the times of Dr Kwame Nkrumah of Ghana, Gamal Abdul Nasser of Egypt, and Haile Selassie of Ethiopia, it served its purpose while it lasted, but outlived its tenure without achieving a significant political unity.

It follows the same rhyming trend as the EU, which had also changed its few other names before finally settling for the European Union. South African president Thabo Mbeki is the current chairman of this newly renamed organisation.

The continent of Africa is big and rich. It contains the world's largest reservoir of diamond and gold mines and other mineral resources which are not found elsewhere, but ironically half the population lives below the poverty line, less than a dollar a day. Sixty thousand people in Africa die of starvation every single day. In the richest area of the world more than half are deprived of the basic necessities of life, and millions live in sketchily built mud huts. Life expectancy fell by 20 years in the last decade in the whole of Africa. It reaches an average 48.9 years, compared with 77.7 years in developed countries. A recent OAU survey shows that in the last decade, 28 murderous conflicts were fomented in Africa, affecting 474 million Africans, that is 61 per cent of populations. No region escaped. These countries have to pay 30 billion dollars yearly to service the foreign debt, imposed by institutions such as the World Bank, International Monetary Fund, World Trade Organisation, and some European countries.

The African Union is greatly worried about the economy and security of the continent. The new resolve and motto in Africa, therefore, is "Africa for the Africans". The late Dr Nkrumah's vision of Pan-Africanism has not been carried forward because of the internal divisions. Now this organisation with more members in it has a major task of countering this instability. Ex-colonial powers such as France, Belgium and Britain are still active in controlling the mineral and human resources of Africa for their own benefit rather than for the poorest in the continent. Independence for most African countries brought no solace because the international political and economic conspiracy is still at work in exploiting the poor miners and farmers through the local dictators and stooges who are supported by the European businesses. The International Monetary Fund and the World Bank have also played the dirty tricks of lending money to these poor nations which are unable to repay the interest, let alone the capital. This keeps them in perpetually growing debts, resulting in poverty, lack of educational facilities, and shortage of food and medicines. The African Union needs to sort out, if it can, and wipe out the killer loan sharks from Africa.

# Multi-faith conference condemns State terrorism

Published in *TheNews*, London, January 18, 2003

While Afghanistan burns, a multi-faith conference condemned terrorism, whether perpetrated by a state or by a disgruntled individual. A seminar at Lambeth Town Hall, London, on the subject of The Role of Religions in Diminishing Terrorism heard Mr Taha Qureshi, Director of Khatme Nabuwat Centre, say that Islam does not support terrorism. He pointed out that millions have been spent on building mosques where most of these places are used only for three to four hours a day. He said he wanted to use some of the money on educational institutions and social well-being of the poorest in our society. He urged the local authorities and mosques to work together to keep vulnerable youth away from harmful anti-social activities.

Kate Hoey, MP, said that she strongly believes in justice, human rights and religious diversity. "There is a need for interacting with the Islamic community and promote confidence and initiate open discussion".

Yvonne Ridley, the *Sunday Express* journalist who was arrested in Afghanistan, said she was treated with courtesy and respect by the Taleban. "A journalist's job is to expose and explore truth. I put on a Burka and went into Afghanistan. I wanted to speak to ordinary Afghans. I had full two days before my arrest. The Taleban have been demonised by the Western media.

"They were first demonised because you cannot drop bombs on nice people. The village I was in had no military value, yet it was completely destroyed by America. One American life is no more important than an Afghan life". She was loudly applauded for saying this. She asked, "What has this bombing achieved?" So far 9,000 people have died. She did not like prisoners being shackled and transported to Cuba and kept in cages like animals.

Dr Jenny Tong, MP, spoke about the plight of the poor in the world. "September 11 has demonstrated that you do not have to be a nuclear power to inflict damage to a superpower". The World Trade Centre is for the benefit of the US and the poor nations are ignored, she said. Dr M Ashfaq said that Islamophobia is not new. It will not disappear overnight. We must continue to educate our people for advancement in the society.

Cllr Lal Hussain, former Mayor of Sutton, made a short, sharp incursion into the fray and put the cat among the pigeons by saying that those who are in the forefront of accusing Islam of terrorism are in fact greater terrorists themselves. Today, the Soviet evil empire has been replaced by another evil empire in its place, he maintained. He quoted a Quranic verse which says that "in Islam, killing one person is like killing the whole mankind, and saving a life is as if saving the entire mankind".

Rev. Jeffery Wilcox, a priest, said that alienation of young Muslims in our society is worrying. "I have every sympathy with my Muslim friends who feel distressed after September 11 with which they are unjustly associated."

Imam Qasim Rashid, from Croydon Mosque, said colours and languages must not drive us apart. Allah has created us differently which is a blessing in disguise. Tom Franklin, Leader of London Borough of Lambeth, said that September 11 is etched out in our mind and left us with major challenges. People who died in the Twin Towers were from all religions and none. Islam, Judaism and Christianity promote peace and harmony.

Barrister Ahmad Thomson, a convert and author of many books, wondered why so many people have been killed in Afghanistan for nothing. Daisy cutter bombs have caused havoc in Afghanistan. "Those who kill are evil and they will come off worst in the end. If we can have unity in this hall, why can we not have unity of different races outside of it?"

Dr I. Anwar, from Glasgow, said: "We should interact with the local community and learn from one another and devise a caring and happy society."

# War on terrorism is no way to end terrorism

Published in *TheNews*, London, December 2, 2002

At a time when tension between Pakistan and India is ever more threatening, a mixed audience of Indians and Pakistanis gathered at Gustave Tuck Lecture Theatre, University College London, yesterday, and listened to a lively discussion about religious fundamentalism in their countries.

The principal speaker, a rare visitor to this country, was Arun Gandhi, the grandson of the assassinated leader, Mohandas Karamchand Gandhi, who had long struggled for independence from Britain.

Mr Gandhi, now Director of the Gandhi Institute for Non-Violence, Memphis, US, said that war on terrorism is not the answer for today's violence. "How do we define terrorists?" he asked.

"Terrorists may be living among us. It is very easy to blame Islam, but it is not the fault of Islam." He did not believe that September 11 was the result of Islamic adherents.

"We are still living in an ancient cave type existence when people used to kill one another with clubs and now they have developed more sophisticated weapons to continue killing. The methods are the same, only the weapons are different".

He said he was greatly shocked and dismayed when he saw the Israeli prime minister's interview on CNN television saying that he will eliminate not only the terrorists, but the countries which harbour them.

"The US has come to a point where it should not be looking for what is good for the US, but what is good for the whole world. Unless we tackle the divide between rich and poor, violence will continue unabated.

"We may have to reduce our standard of living in order to increase the standard of living of the poor. The economic equation needs to be changed," he added.

He quoted a teaching from his grandfather as follows:

> Keep your thoughts positive;
> Because your thoughts become your words;
> Keep your words positive;
> Because your words become your behaviour;
> Keep your behaviour positive;
> Because your behaviour becomes your habits;
> Keep your habits positive;
> Because your habits become your values;
> Keep your values positive;
> Because your values become your Destiny.

Dr Ram Puniyani, of the International Institute of Technology, Mumbai, India, said that victims of terrorism in India and Pakistan have been the innocent people.

Christians in India and Pakistan have been killed for nothing.

Hinduism, he said, was not a religion in the traditional sense of the word, but a conglomerate of disparate streams of cultures. He deplored what happened in Gujarat during the past few months when a lot of innocent people lost their lives.

Professor Khalid Masud, of the International Institute for the Study of Islam in the Modern World, University van Leiden, Netherlands, delivered his speech from a Muslim and Pakistani perspective, and defended fundamentalism in Islam as positive. He thought that Islam is demonised by the world's media and mainly encouraged by the United States.

# Congo exploited – right, left and centre

Book review published in *The Voice*, London, November 16, 2002

A new book about Congo reveals how its huge reserves of wealth were plundered by its present and former rulers.

The present-day Democratic Republic of Congo was ruled by King Leopold II of Belgium like a private plantation for 23 years. This nation, 80 times bigger than Belgium, was named the Congo Free State – free, that is, to be exploited for its vast reserves of zinc, gold, ivory and rubber by Leopold and assorted traders from all over Europe.

He handed over the colony to the Belgian government in 1908 after millions of Congolese had been worked to death. It was one of Europe's darkest hours. The government then ran the country until independence in 1960, exploiting its riches, though in a less murderous way.

In his new book *The Congo from Leopold to Kabila,* highly respected academic Georges Nzongola-Ntalaja, former Professor in African Studies at Howard University, Washington, points out that independence brought no comfort to the people of Congo because of interference by the ex-colonialists and the US on the one hand, and dictator Mobutu Sese Seko on the other. Mobutu ran the country, which he renamed Zaire, like a personal fiefdom for more than 30 years, heaping yet more disaster on it.

The book traces the national liberation struggle in the Congo through many decades. Later chapters examine the Mobutu years, the corruption, the mismanagement and political repression that characterised them. It ends with an attempt to understand how the democracy movement deals with new forms of dictatorships internally.

The author, a significant player in the country's political struggle, shows how the huge wealth extracted from the country over the past

King Leopold II, left, and Mobutu Sese Seko

hundred years was never used for the benefit of the Congolese people. In one of many examples, he describes how Congo rescued Belgium from financial troubles during and after both First and Second World Wars. Robert Godding, the Belgian Colonial Minister, admitted as much in 1946 in the following words:

"During the war, the Congo was able to finance all the expenditure of the Belgian government in London, including the diplomatic service as well as the cost of our armed forces in Europe and Africa, a total of some 40 million Pounds.

"In fact, thanks to the resources of the Congo, the Belgian government has not had to borrow a shilling or a dollar, and the Belgian gold reserves could be left intact."

This is probably the best book about Congo's past and present out at the moment, and it does help place its current troubles in the wider context. It also gives a hint of how such a huge country might achieve its true potential.

*The Congo from Leopold to Kabila* by Georges Nzongola-Ntalaja (Zed Books, 2002)

# Scholars see no quick fix of Kashmir dispute

Published in *TheNews*, London, October 28, 2002

The Kashmir dispute between Pakistan and India has been lingering on for the past 55 years and there is no sign of its being solved in the foreseeable future. This was the conclusion of four prominent scholars and experts on the Kashmir question when they defined the complexities surrounding this dispute.

Speaking at the British Local History Room, Institute of Historical Research, London University, on October 24, Dr Pervez Iqbal Cheema, President of Islamabad Policy Research Institute, said that the Kashmir dispute is much more of a territorial dispute than a terrorism issue. It is of self-determination of the people of Kashmir.

On the contrary, the Indian government is taking refuge under the United States' war on terrorism, and thus confusing the issue and hiding its own state terrorism.

He regretted that India has been calculating from the very beginning and concentrating entirely on retaining Kashmir illegally while flouting the United Nations resolutions. Pakistan, on the other hand, proved no match for India's guile and has been naive in relying only on the UN to solve the problem.

He was well supported by Richard Bonney, Professor of Modern History, Institute for the Study of India-Pakistan Relations, University of Leicester, who said that he had no difficulty understanding the Kashmir dispute. He thought the problem could be solved either through fear of nuclear war, or through peaceful negotiations.

In 1951, the British Prime Minister Clement Attlee said to Nehru that India was divided on the two-nations principle; how about implementing the UN resolution on Kashmir? Nehru replied that he did not believe in the two-nation theory. So now India does not believe there is a dispute, and has a heavy-handed control over the people of Kashmir.

Maria Sultan, of Bradford University, discussed decolonising Kashmir on the same pattern as East Timor, which gained independence from Indonesia recently. She said India can take a first nuclear strike and survive because of its size, but Pakistan can be greatly damaged by India's response.

Professor Alistair Lamb, an authority on the Kashmir dispute and holder of Star of Pakistan, did not believe this issue will be solved in his lifetime.

He had known the first prime minister of Pakistan, of whom he spoke very highly, and said Liaquat Ali Khan was one of the greatest politicians of south east Asia, but unfortunately he is not much remembered in Pakistan after his assassination.

Prince Mohsin Ali Khan, a well-known London luminary, suggested that China, with which both India and Pakistan have a common border, should be brought in to get involved as the UN has dismally failed.

# Old Ethiopia recalled

Book review published in *West Africa Magazine*, Sep 30-Oct 6, 2002

Ethiopia has its origins in centuries before the birth of Christ. It was also known for centuries, at the time of Italy's occupation 1935-41, as Abyssinia, while its ancient name was Lopia.

Although not strictly a Christian country, it nevertheless derives its moral and social values from Christianity, Islam and Judaism. Rastafarians in Jamaica and elsewhere in the West get their inspiration from the glorious past as represented by His Imperial Majesty Haile Selassie, seen by them as their spiritual leader.

When Dr Kwame Nkrumah, first President of Ghana, visited Addis Ababa for the first conference of the Organisation of African Unity (OAU) in 1963, the pet lions which the Emperor usually kept at his side roared at Nkrumah as he approached the monarch. The Emperor instantly stomped his foot firmly on the ground and ordered the huge felines to be quiet, much to the relief of the president and other guests. One wonders what would have happened had the angry lions disobeyed. The history of Africa might have looked very different today.

At that time all and sundry obeyed His Imperial Majesty's orders. In Ethiopia's national flag of three horizontal bands in green, yellow and red, there was a crowned lion at the centre. Haile Selassie used to be called Lion of Judah, Lion of Abyssinia, Lion of Ethiopia, and so on. Rastafarians' dreadlocks may well have something to do with the lion's mane. King Solomon also kept lions at the side of his throne.

*Majestic Tradition of Ethiopia,* written by Dr Miguel F. Brooks, born in Panama of Jamaican parents, is a fascinating book about Ethiopian history and culture. It contains unique photographs, drawings and maps. There is a remarkable painting depicting the visit of the Queen of Sheba to King Solomon at Jerusalem, a visit

*Majestic Tradition of Ethiopia* by Dr Miguel F. Brooks
(LMH Publishing, 2002)

which, according to Ethiopian legend, led to the birth to them of a son who became Ethiopia's first ruler.

Under the monarchy, Ethiopians claimed that their emperors for more than 2,000 years – using the title Negus – were descended from King Solomon in this way. The size of the Ethiopian state varied greatly over the centuries, before being greatly expanded under Ras Tafari who became Haile Selassie, but whose earlier name was adopted by Jamaican admirers.

*Majestic Tradition of Ethiopia* grips you into a feeling of being in the whole of humanity's historical legends and drama. Dr Brooks deserves praise for collecting the material for his book from all over the world, which gives us an insight into why the modern political movements such as "Back to Africa" and "Reparation" have come about.

Ethiopia had been an inspiration for many pan-Africanists in Africa and the Caribbean (not only for the Rastafarians), long before the choice of Haile Selassie's capital Addis Ababa for the headquarters of the OAU in 1963.

# Landmarks of the Pakistan Movement

Book review published in *The Times Literary Supplement*,
London, June 14, 2002

In 1867, Sir Syed Ahmed Khan, who believed in reviving the fortunes of the Muslims of India, urged his people to "educate, educate, educate", thus prefiguring by 135 years Tony Blair's election slogan. Professor S.M. Burke's new book, which traces the origins of Pakistan through such landmarks as the Indian Councils Act of 1909, reveals that Sir Syed also learnt Hebrew, set up a printing press with English, Urdu and Hebrew typefaces, and employed an Englishman to translate from Urdu into English. He opened a school at Aligarh on June 1, 1875, with eleven students, which later developed into a prestigious university in 1920.

The founder of the Indian National Congress in 1885 was Allan Octavian Hume, a Scotsman, who had retired from the Indian Civil Service to devote his life to Indian political regeneration. He told a member of the Council of the Secretary of State for India in 1892 that it was Sir Syed's book, *Causes of the Indian Revolt*, that inspired him to establish the Congress. Burke writes that Hindu-Muslim differences had existed long before Mohammad Ali Jinnah, the founder of Pakistan, was born. Again, Syed Ahmed illustrates the point: while he was in the Civil Service at Benares in 1867, some Hindus decided to abolish Urdu in law courts and replace it with a mixed sort of Hindi. A sudden change came over Syed Ahmed's attitude towards the other community.

The great Urdu poet Altaf Hussain Hali observed: "This was the first occasion when Syed felt finally convinced that henceforth it would be impossible for Muslims and Hindus to cooperate as one nation and for anyone to serve them both simultaneously." Sir Syed is also portrayed as the first Muslim leader in India to conceive the idea of creating Pakistan. If Jinnah was the father of the nation, Sir

Syed was the grandfather. When he died on March 27, 1898, after a life, and earnings, dedicated to the service of others, even his funeral expenses were paid for by his well-wishers. This book, which comes in the wake of the subcontinent's nuclear war posturing and the March riots in Gujarat, helps us to understand the political triangular landscape among the British, the Muslims and the Hindus, from which today's problems arise. Historians, diplomats and lay readers alike will benefit from S. M. Burke's meticulous research.

# Bush needs to concentrate on causes of conflict

Published in *TheNews*, London, September 26, 2001

There is a greater fear now that the world may unwittingly drift into a war and cut itself into pieces. Television pictures showed scores of bodies falling down from the blazing World Trade Centres in New York in order to escape from being burnt alive through intense heat on so many floors. There were no visible staircases and elevators were dysfunctional. The only way to come down was the way those people had chosen, knowing that they were to fall to their certain death from such an altitude. It was a classic case of out of the pan and into the fire. Either way they would have lost their lives. It was not a question of to be or not to be. It was simply to be.

A great deal has been written about the US producing some kind of Hollywood type of presidents lately, with a fundamentalist cowboy mentality to shoot first and ask questions later. The US president is horribly out of touch with political reality outside of his own shores.

At first, initial suspicion fell on a fringe Palestinian liberation group for the responsibility of attacking the Twin Towers, and the Pentagon in Washington. Palestinians' capability of staging such a truly spectacular act of daring do had been in doubt anyway. It was so sophisticated and skilful that the ordinary Americans were shell-shocked into disbelief. Palestinians' ability to amaze the whole world for this kind of unusual cool efficiency, discipline and execution of the plan to that perfection remains doubtful. If the Palestinians had applied these attributes in such a measured way as the "hijackers" displayed, they would have liberated their occupied land by now.

As for Osama bin Laden, the US would indulge in wishful and misguided thinking that he may be behind it. Again, the same criteria apply. First of all, it would have been difficult to find at least four young, fit and highly educated men to be trained as pilots who are also prepared to give their lives after training. From the technical aspect of hijacking, the men were required to take control of the planes in mid-air, then piloting and manoeuvring the planes to the right targets by dodging and zigzagging through difficult terrain in two major cities full of skyscrapers. That requires a great deal of patience, cool-headedness, drilling and constant practice. The third and the most important requirement must have been that the mission must not fail in any circumstances. All of this would seem beyond the abilities of the Taliban and bin Laden.

The third possibility as to who could do this risky, daring bravado act in the most powerful country of the world with airspace-protected remains unexplored. Is it an inside job with the usual suspects, a CIA/Mossad combination? Are there dissidents in the US Air Force who could not live with their conscience after what they had done to destroy Iraq during the Gulf War? Was it a revenge on the Pentagon by those who are against globalisation of political, military and economic powers of the US? In any case, the US must not attack any country out of hate or suspicion, because only the innocent and more civilians would be slaughtered for no fault of their own. A whole country must not be held responsible for the misdeeds of a few of its citizens. Does the United States know beyond doubt which country or countries the hijackers belonged to? Has anyone found the passports from that rubble where even the bodies have not been recovered? How can the US say that this was masterminded by Osama bin Laden? The kind of hasty action the US and its allies are thinking of taking might backfire and may have far-reaching repercussions throughout the east and the west.

The Americans have seldom won a war abroad, and at home they dragged the indigenous Indians out of cities and confined them on reservations. This may account for a victory on their own soil. Kidnapping President Noriega from sovereign Panama can be seen as some sort of win abroad.

The world was surprised to learn that the president was advised to hide in an anti-nuclear bunker until ordered by the CIA to come out. The CIA, DIA, FBI, Secret Services, US National Security and Police were all stunned. None of the institutions had any knowledge of what was to come. As if the disaster was not enough, the Fire Brigade and rescue and emergency services could not function properly. All of this is the biggest psychological blow to the pride of the superpower's ego. No one up to now knew that superpowers can be so vulnerable.

As a result of what happened on September 11, the US would not be the same country again. It has been a catastrophe for all concerned. Some good must come out of this tragedy for the betterment of mankind and world peace. Those who are supposed to have piloted the aeroplanes were young, rich, and had everything to live for, but they gave their lives for a cause they passionately believed in, and if connected with the Middle East, then they also believed that the United States aided and abetted Apartheid-Israel in committing atrocities against the Palestinians. It is a tragedy for their families and friends. It will be a mistake to think that those hijackers were "lunatics", "deranged", "enemies of civilisation", "Muslim fundamentalists" and half a dozen more labels attached to them; they had a cause and they died for it, so it looks. If the US has really changed now and is in favour of world peace with justice, it must change its foreign policies in the near, middle and far east. The US has dismally and totally failed in its role as an impartial policeman for the past sixty years. There is no need for a policeman to patrol the world. If a Muslim country is attacked and a protracted war ensues, that will trigger off the wrath of Muslims everywhere.

When the West derides Muslims as fundamentalists, it does them a favour. Muslims, incidentally, desire to be fundamentalists. That is to say living a life according to the moral teachings of the Quran: justice, peace, brotherhood of mankind, and respect for human life. Muslims believe death is no big deal. Allah had given life and Allah had taken it away. In a Western opulent society where man is attracted and fascinated by worldly goods and comforts, death means something, on pain of losing life. It is not easy to sacrifice one's life. This is where defeat and victory come in between the prosperous Christian West and the mainly poor Muslim world. The West has absolutely no chance of winning here, unlike against Communism.

Mr Bush's words that this act of a few desperate young men was the first war of this century, which clearly he lost, implies that he has more wars on his mind which would follow. How many? This trend of thought and language from a "peace loving" president may engulf the whole world in a permanent state of war for the rest of the century.

Instead, Mr Bush should concentrate on the root causes of the problems of this nature. Most people around the world would disagree with Mr Bush if he is hell-bent to follow his theory of war and peace on his terms. The mind boggles when the most powerful country takes on the poorest country in the world, Afghanistan. It must never be forgotten, however, that while Christians are not prepared to commit suicide for Christianity, Muslims, by their nature of being, are prepared to die for Islam and damage their enemy on the way out.

John Ashcroft, the US Attorney General, told the House Judiciary Committee, on September 24, that the FBI had arrested 350 people in connection with the September 11 incident in New York and Washington. How many innocent people may have been detained, one knows not.

# Beating about Bush

Published in *TheNews*, London, February 19, 2001

President George W. Bush is sending General Colin Powell, Secretary of State, to the most troublesome spot of the Middle East to urge the newly elected prime minister of Israel, Ariel Sharon, and the Palestinian leader, Yasser Arafat, to resolve their disputes according to the peace process.

Political observers around the world, however, are smart enough to know how serious the US is in resolving the conflict between the two factions. In the past the US has tried its tactic by dispatching a high-profile politician to this area to help solve the problem peacefully, but war almost certainly followed. A further worrying point this time is that the 'desert storm' General has declared on his own, or perhaps after consulting the president, that he would give priority to enforcing United Nations moves to deny Iraq the opportunity to acquire weapons of mass destruction. This is a classic case of the pot calling the kettle black after what havoc the US had caused in Iraq in 1991. How come the US of all countries should talk about weapons of mass destruction lightly, after having been a participant on numerous occasions of crimes against humanity? Even without mentioning Hiroshima or Nagasaki and forgetting about the Korean War and Vietnam War, and leaving aside the ever present but potentially dangerous Arab/Jewish war by proxy, where mass destruction is the order of the day, the US continues to accuse Iraq whose infrastructure has already been completely destroyed by the West, and the country is suffering from UN/US/EU economic sanctions. There are no signs as yet of Iraq's economic recovery for a long time to come.

What is more worrying, moreover, is that younger George Bush seems to be following in his father's footsteps, and utterly confused as to what his military strategy should be when he says on one hand that he is determined "to develop a national missile defence" as a shield against attack from 'rogue' states, and on the other, he states to establish a "long range vision for the military." The new Bush administration is intent on reviving the so-called Strategic Defence Initiative by another name. The new name is National Missile Defence (NMD). The purpose of the NMD would be to include satellite readiness to complement the Star Wars idea. The meaning is the same, but the philosophy is different. One wonders if this is for an exhibition only or intended for mass destruction. The US has now far fewer foreign bases around the world than previously, so it wishes to control this planet globally from above, for instance, by putting these missiles at strategically designated areas overlooking Iraq, North Korea, Libya, Cuba, and Iran, or wherever the devils are found. The message and the hint seem clear: no beating about Bush.

Would the democratic president concede the same right to Iraq as any other country in the world to defend itself?

# Islam's contribution to Western civilisation

Published in *TheNews*, London, April 10, 2000

Professor Akbar S. Ahmed, the High Commissioner for Pakistan, while speaking at a conference organised by Stockwell Green Cultural and Community Centre to mark its launch, said that Islam first gave mankind liberty and free speech, which the West now preached. He reminded the audience that *ilm* or knowledge is the second most often used word in the Holy Quran.

Recalling his experiences at Cambridge University, he observed that many faculties there came through Islamic ideas. It was for this reason that the West respected books, debate and knowledge. The Quran also addressed the same issues.

While the High Commissioner lamented that Islam was not being practised in its true spirit in most places, he advised to continue to develop cooperation and harmony within the local community and offered his support, and assured the Muslims that there was a friend in the Pakistan High Commission. The two greatest attributes of Allah, he reminded, were the Compassionate and Merciful (Rehman and Raheem).

Ms Kate Hoey MP, Minister of Sport; Jim Dickenson, Leader of Lambeth Borough Council; and Dr Z.U. Khan, formerly a race relations commissioner, also attended.

Dr Khan, in his speech, highlighted the role of Islam's influence on other civilisations. Islam was the first religion to have laid down anti-discrimination laws for mankind 1,400 years ago. In this country, anti-discrimination laws were enacted only in 1976. The West had learnt a great deal over many centuries from Islam, as Islam learns now the Western ways of doing things. Both civilisations had borrowed ideas and sciences from each other and neither should be regarded as inferior or superior. Why has the West suddenly become Islamophobic? He called for a partnership between the West and Islam on an equal footing.

Dr Mohamad Ashfaq, a financial analyst, outlined the need for improving educational opportunities for youngsters whose parents did not speak English as a first language and, therefore, could not give much help with homework. This project, he said, would prove beneficial for them. He believed this would serve as a pilot scheme for serving the community at grassroots level with quality and equality.

A distinguishing aspect of this Islamic centre is that it is run by a scientist who holds two degrees, one in Physics and the other in Electronics and Electrical Engineering with Management. Although social welfare and education are the main objectives of this organisation, an ambitious plan for providing facilities for basketball, football, tennis and cricket is being keenly pursued and would soon be implemented, the centre informed.

# Seminar calls for an end to feudalism

Published in *TheNews*, London, October 26, 1999

In the wake of sudden and dramatic political change in Pakistan, a roomful of Pakistani intellectuals once again gathered at the School of Oriental and African Studies in London to discuss the future of their country.

Mujahid Tirmizey, Director of the Pakistan Institute of International Affairs and representative of Lahore High Court Bar Association, who organised this meeting on October 22, had made it plain at the outset the objectives of the debate.

In his opening remarks he stressed that they were there only to discuss the future of Pakistan in the light of recent events with an open mind, and without holding any brief for any individuals or political parties.

Dr Amir Ali Majid, a lawyer and political commentator, opened the debate by saying that democracy was a buzz word and was not the most suitable system for every country. Independent judiciary was the key to good governance, but it was rather sad that deposed Prime Minister Nawaz Sharif was trying to make the judiciary compromise – he should not have touched this sacred cow. The new regime can make this a propitious moment and make efforts towards a smooth transfer to a civilian government. He advised that if Pakistan wants to go forward, it must reduce its reliance on foreign loans.

Zahoor Butt, a well-known barrister and writer on Pakistani politics, began by quoting that democracy was better than martial law and martial law was better than anarchy. He wanted this meeting to discuss whether there was democracy in Pakistan at all. The mafia in Pakistan had been ruling the country under the cloak of democracy.

Nawaz Sharif's regime was not a democratic one. Pouring scorn on Pakistan's political past, he was ashamed to say that in the past few months more than 700 people have committed suicide in Pakistan. This was not a Pakistan that Quaid-e-Azam envisaged, he remarked.

Sirdar Mazhar Ali Khan, a prominent political figure in Tehrik-e-Insaaf, said that whenever army rule is imposed in Pakistan, it turns out against the interests of the working class in the country. But the alternative seems also tragic, because under the civilian governments the civilian rights are usurped all the same. Decentralisation may be the answer when decisions can be taken at a local level.

He commented that deposed Prime Minister Nawaz Sharif used to boast on the floor of the National Assembly that he was there to fulfil the mission of his mentor, the late military dictator Zia-ul-Haq. Under Zia, no dissent was tolerated and severe punishments, such as floggings and locking up in jails without trial, were the order of the day.

Mushtaq Lasharie, Labour Councillor from North Kensington, London, said that he disagreed with Dr Majid's viewpoint that democracy does not survive in Pakistan. He said what happens in Pakistan is a new ruler comes along and takes over power, criticises his predecessor and leaves the country in a worse state than before. The army should go back and hand over the charge to a democratic government as soon as possible.

In spite of differing opinions, Mr Tirmizey and others had observed that there was a consensus on three officially sponsored resolutions on accountability, decentralisation and eradication of feudalism. The resolutions were adopted by the seminar.

# Legal and political sides of the Lockerbie affair

Published in *TheNews*, London, December 20, 1998

For almost a decade the United States and Britain have been accusing two Libyan citizens of involvement in the bombing of Pan Am Flight 103, which took place on December 21, 1988, over Lockerbie in Scotland.

Despite the fact that those who unleashed these accusations never submitted any proof to support their claim, Libya declared its readiness to find out all the facts relating to the incident and started its own investigations, and called on the governments of both of these countries to assist Libya with inquiries.

Instead of responding to this request, which falls within the legal framework of the dispute, these countries politicised the issue, resorting to the United Nations Security Council to impose resolution 731 (1992), which orders Libya to uncover all the relevant facts concerning the incident. After two months, the Security Council brought out a new resolution 748 (1992), which imposed an arms and air embargo against Libya. The country announced its acceptance of that imposition and took practical measures in response to it, and condemned international terrorism in all shapes and forms and declared its commitment to any measures to be decided by the international community to combat it. Libya also called for the convening of a special session of the General Assembly to study the causes and dimensions of terrorism and devise the means that would eliminate it.

The question arises, what can be the role of the Security Council with regard to the Lockerbie case? According to the UN Charter's article 24, the Security Council has the primary responsibility which includes the following:

To maintain international peace and security in accordance with the purpose and principles of the United Nations. The specific powers granted to the Security Council for the discharge of these duties are laid down in Chapters VI, VII, VIII, and XII.

To submit annual and special reports to the United Nations General Assembly.

Under the Charter, the role of the Security Council, when dealing with the pacific settlement of disputes under chapter VI, is not the same as when it is considering enforcement action under chapter VII. With regard to the former, the council has no power of making decisions binding on the member states.

It must be made clear that it is not the function of the Security Council to look into any dispute, but it cares only for those disputes that subject international peace and danger to security. It was understood from this principle that disputes which do not fall in this category are beyond the scope of the Security Council as far as direct intervention is concerned. In the Lockerbie case, the Security Council has been totally oblivious to the possibility of invoking any of the pacific modes of settlement, outlined in Chapter VI. Therefore, it is not within the mandate of Security Council to look into the claims of the US and UK to hand over the two Libyans who have been suspected of blowing up the Pan Am aircraft.

Even if we suppose that this subject is within the competence of the Security Council, is it permitted to issue a resolution, requesting an independent country, which is a full member of the United Nations, to hand over its citizens in order to be tried before another country's court? From the legal point of view it seems that this is prohibited.

The resolution 731 is the first to be issued at the request of a member country of the United Nations to assist in an international legal dispute like this, where this is considered as an intervention in the internal affairs of a sovereign state. This resolution is an arbitrary decision, violates the international legal basis and breaches the sovereignty of a country. This matter is not only restricted to this limit, but it is considered as a violation of international charters and conventions, and consequently, leads to loss of trust in the international organisation which many feel is increasingly becoming a vehicle to execute the politics of the United States.

The subject of accusation is a penal case that should be determined by legal means through the courts, and it is not within the mandate of the Security Council, as it is also not permitted to raise accusations without evidence.

The laws of all countries, including these two countries' laws, prohibit handing over of their citizens to other countries, unless there is a bilateral agreement between the two. Libya has no such agreement with any one of the above mentioned countries.

The Libyan law takes the principle of regionalisation of law based on the sovereignty of Libyan country over its territories. In other words, Libyan law applies on all people existing on its territories, whether Libyans or foreigners, and not outside Libyan territory even for Libyans. Libyan law prohibits the handing over of Libyan citizens to foreign countries. Therefore, the law that should be applied is Libyan law, and this is a legal right confirmed by all international laws and charters. The moment Libya allows or shows its readiness to hand in its citizens, this would show its generous intentions, but such a generosity would be a violation of citizenship rights. That is to say that it is the obligation of the Libyan state to protect its citizens and not to hand them in to be tried by any means.

Libya proposed several solutions for the trial of the two Libyans suspected of involvement in the Pan Am crash. It proposed that the two can stand trial before a court whose venue should be agreed upon. It also suggested that the concerned parties should resort to the International Court of Justice after the US and the UK had refused to apply the convention on the suppression of illegal acts against the safety of civil aviation, the 1971 Montreal Convention, in spite of the fact that the countries are parties to this Convention. Libya has also accepted the proposal submitted by the League of Arab States, which calls for a compromise for trying the suspects at the headquarters of the International Court of Justice. These proposed solutions, either submitted or accepted by Libya, have been confirmed before several fora, including the United Nations' General Assembly.

Britain, the US and France are permanent members of the Security Council. How could they be the litigants and the arbitrators at the same time? They are the ones who design the law and interpret it and also criticise it. How did these countries give themselves the right to participate in voting on resolutions, contradicting subparagraph 3 of article 27 of the UN Charter?

Moreover, the authority of the Security Council is not absolute, but is restricted by the objectives and principles of the United Nations. If it does not observe these principles, the General Assembly has the power of supervision on the resolutions of the Security Council, according to article 24(2) of the UN Charter. The Libyan handling of the dispute has been widely supported at international level by African and Arab countries. The Organisation of the Islamic Conference has declared its solidarity with the Libyan position. The Non-aligned Movement supported it in Jakarta in 1992, and reaffirmed its support in Cartagena, 1995. Libya was strongly supported by the Arab Summit in Cairo in 1995, and by the Organisation of African Unity in Yaounde, Cameroon, in 1996.

Britain and the US have attempted to depict the dispute as one between Libya and the international community. But how can the dispute be one between Libya and the international community, when international support is increasing daily for the Libyan position? This is embodied in the support of regional and international organisations, the population of whose members exceed two-thirds of the world's population. The accusing countries must realise that the international community does not comprise only the US and Britain.

# Quaid-e-Azam Mohammad Ali Jinnah: His Personality and His Politics

Book review published in *Crescent International*, Toronto, June 16-30, 1998

Whenever India's independence from Britain is mentioned, two names connected with the event dominate: Mohandas Gandhi and Jawaharlal Nehru. Meanwhile, Mohammad Ali Jinnah, the founder of Pakistan, is either mentioned only in passing, usually as a separatist, or totally ignored.

Such is the prejudice Jinnah experienced from both British and Hindu politicians in his life. This prejudice existed before, during and after the independence of India. Jinnah was undermined by Hindu politicians to their own loss because the pretence not to understand him led to the partition of the subcontinent.

The ultimate result was that the country was carved out in such a haphazard manner that its consequences still linger on.

This new book, *Quaid-e-Azam Mohammad Ali Jinnah – His Personality and His Politics*, part of the Oxford University Press' Jubilee Series, analyses how a new country on the globe, Pakistan, was created. It reappraises the personality and politics of the country's founder. Both authors seem sympathetic and knowledgeable on Pakistani affairs. Professor Samuel Martin Burke is a former professor and consultant in South Asian Studies at the University of Minnesota, US, and his co-author is another scholar, Mr Salim Al-Din Quraishi, Head of the Modern South Asian Section of the British Library in London.

Among the history makers of this century, Mohammad Ali Jinnah is the most misunderstood politician. The reasons for this are twofold. First, the history of Indian independence, partition, and Pakistan, has been dominated by Hindu writers, who inherited the kind of animosity against Muslims usually reserved for their perceived enemies.

Mohammad Ali Jinnah

Second, the British historians, who wrote about Jinnah, Pakistan, and Muslims, went one better. The British did not write much about him because he stood up to them on an equal footing. Jinnah presented his irrefutable arguments with courage and correct manners. Lord Mountbatten, Britain's last representative in India, found him more than his match because of Jinnah's upright, transparent personality and a good barrister's unambiguous approach.

Had Jinnah adopted a Gandhi style of living, for instance, scantily-clothed, intentionally homeless, hunger strikes, travelling in third class railway compartments rather than in first, as Jinnah always did, his value and status in the British colonial eyes would have been different.

But Jinnah was his own man; he never felt compelled to resort to such a theatrical act, and reduce himself to a degrading position as Gandhi and some other Hindu politicians did. Jinnah did not lead a double life; his greatness as a leader lies in the fact that at all times he presented himself as he really was, irrespective of how others may have wanted him to behave.

Ironically, Pakistanis themselves have not written often enough about either Jinnah or Pakistan to redress the imbalance. So, the gap was filled by outsiders and foreigners with little sympathy or knowledge for these subjects.

The result is that Pakistan and Jinnah are universally misunderstood, even by his fellow Muslims in the Arab world. His critics' dislike of him also emanates from a misunderstanding that he wanted to divide India to satisfy his own ego.

Jinnah denied this time and again. He was determined, though, to fight for the civil and political rights of Muslims within the union of India; his concentration on this point was unbreakable. His long membership of and active participation in the Indian National Congress Party testify to this.

During his dealings with the Congress, he thought of himself as an Indian nationalist and a believer in Hindu-Muslim unity.

After working within the Congress Party for many years, he became disillusioned with the machinations of Gandhi and was disgusted with Nehru and other Hindu leaders' prejudices. The Hindus at no time showed any sympathy towards their Muslim fellow citizens. This made it difficult for Jinnah to maintain his faith in the possibility of a permanent amicable relationship between India's two major communities.

Jinnah's relations with the Congress lasted only long enough for him to discover its true nature, which he found incompatible with the aspirations of the Muslims who longed for their civil rights to be protected under constitutional and electoral guarantees.

Disillusioned and disappointed, Jinnah finally realised that the parting of the ways was unavoidable and made a clean break from the Congress.

These are some of the historical points elaborated in this book which give the reader a greater insight into what really happened and what could have been averted.

Gandhi himself admitted that religion was the inspiration of his politics long before Jinnah started to demand a separate homeland for Muslims. Gandhi frankly declared in his autobiography in 1927: "I can say without the slightest hesitation, and yet in all humility, that those who say that religion has nothing to do with politics do not know what religion means."

In another book, Gandhi is quoted as saying: "If I seem to take part in politics, it is only because politics today encircles us like the coils of a snake from which one cannot get out no matter how one tries. I wish to wrestle with the snake. I am trying to introduce religion into politics".

Nehru, too, concedes that Gandhi introduced religion into politics. He says in his autobiography, "Gandhiji, indeed, was continuously laying stress on the religious and spiritual side of the movement. His religion was not dogmatic, but it did mean a definitely religious outlook on life, and the whole movement was strongly influenced by this and took a revivalist character so far as the masses were concerned."

Jinnah, on the other hand, was convinced that Hindu-Muslim cooperation was a noble and achievable aim, provided the political and religious rights of the Muslims could be safeguarded. A united India, free from tensions and social chaos was Jinnah's original dream. An ideologically united, politically integrated, constitutionally secure India could not be achieved as Jinnah envisioned, because Gandhi and Nehru never reassured the Muslims that they would he safe in a Hindu-dominated country.

The final chance for India-united came in 1945 when the Cabinet Mission Plan was accepted by Jinnah but rejected out of hand by Nehru.

If Gandhi and Nehru had had their way, the Muslims would have suffered permanent Hindu majority domination in the name of democracy. A Pakistan, albeit truncated, mutilated or moth-eaten, was the only option Jinnah could accept. The book is so persuasively written and painstakingly researched that it is difficult to argue with its convincing evidence that Gandhi left no option for Jinnah but to demand a separate State for Muslims.

It is most unfair that Jinnah is often described by some Indian and British writers as arrogant and unfriendly. The authors of this book have diligently researched Jinnah's past to discover the sort of person he really was. Their findings after meticulous appraisal belie this description. Even the television footage, shown in Britain on his birth anniversary on December 25, does not support that idea of Jinnah.

On the contrary, he is shown smiling at Gandhi, receiving him at his Bombay residence with good grace. His character assassination may be based on the belief that if enough mud is thrown at him, some is bound to stick.

Had Jinnah been dealing with such Hindu leaders as Bal Gangadhar Tilak, who understood the fears of the Muslims and an accord at the Lucknow Pact of 1916 between the Congress and the Muslim League, or Gopal Krishna Gokhale, another realist who got on well with Jinnah and understood Hindu-Muslim aspirations well, India would be one country today, and a more powerful and prosperous one.

It was after Gokhale's death in 1915, and Tilak's in 1920, that the political atmosphere changed radically. Had either or both lived a bit longer, and with Jinnah at the helm of Muslim affairs, not only might India have remained undivided but independence may also have come much sooner.

The two communities would have had a shared priority: to win freedom for their country. There would have been a will to succeed and a meeting of minds among the leaders of all factions. Instead, the situation rapidly deteriorated into virtual warfare.

Although Gandhi comes in for a great deal of criticism, the authors make it plain that their purpose in discussing the extraordinary aspects of Gandhi's political tactics is not to question his status as a venerated Hindu.

This book is not on the lofty subjects of religion and ethics, it is on the down to earth subject of politics. The authors needed to explain their view that Gandhi was not a practical politician and that he, and not Jinnah, was really responsible for wrecking the chances of Hindu-Muslim unity.

Attention is usually focused on Gandhi's theory of non-violence. Jinnah's actions were essentially non-violent too, but nothing is written about this. One of the greatest violent acts in the history of mankind was committed in India when approximately two million civilians were slaughtered under the very noses of Nehru and Gandhi. The authors have undertaken a difficult task of explaining the duplicitous character of Gandhi's political activity, and Jinnah was made to look like a communal leader. This sham was also promoted by the Hindu media barons who dominated the press.

The authors have quoted from some Hindu writers and politicians who did not approve of Gandhi's politics either. Tilak is quoted as saying, "I have great respect and admiration for Gandhiji, but I do not like his politics. If he would retire to the Himalayas and give up politics, I would send him fresh flowers from Bombay every day because of my respect for him."

On May 9, 1933, a joint statement by Subhash Chandra Bose and Villabhai Patel declared: "We are clearly of the opinion that as a political leader Mahatma Gandhi has failed. The time has, therefore, come for radical reorganisation of the Congress on a new principle and with a new method. For bringing about this reorganisation a change of leadership is necessary".

The writers' knowledge and incisive analyses of the events are explained in a way that there is no confusion or ambiguity as to what they mean. This book is a compelling reading for historians, teachers and journalists. After reading it, the reader will come to the same conclusion as the authors have discovered – that both Gandhi and Nehru were not farsighted politicians and that it was they, and not Jinnah, who shattered the unity of India.

*Quaid-e-Azam Mohammad Ali Jinnah: His Personality and His Politics* by S.M. Burke and Salim Al-Din Quraishi (Oxford University Press, Karachi, 1997)

# Reflecting on Pakistan's lost years

Published in *Eastern Eye*, London, October 3, 1997

Five years after Partition, when Pakistan and India were locked in fighting a bitter battle on the Kashmir border, some of Pakistan's prominent residents were busy thinking of how to re-create a new dynamic Pakistan.

Half a century on, in the midst of independence celebrations, a group of 40 professionals – scientists, engineers, lawyers, accountants, historians and academics – gathered at the School of Oriental and African Studies, London, for discussion.

The seminar organised by the Pakistan Institute of International Affairs was a large gathering of members of the Pakistani community in this country.

The three keynote speakers chose to speak on the unwritten history of Pakistan, illiteracy in the country, provincial and ethnic strife, and the nation's relationship with India.

Professor K.K. Aziz, from Cambridge, the first of the main speakers, spoke about the lack of interest shown by Pakistanis as a nation in their history. He stressed that if Pakistanis disown their past, it will be difficult to improve the future. He suggested that most political systems in Pakistan have failed because the people have little or no sense of their past.

Mahammad Naim Ullah, a former civil engineer and now a campaigner and political activist, said the problem of illiteracy in Pakistan is serious.

He highlighted the failure of the literary centres called *Nai Roshni*, set up in 1987, which were a good thing, but had been closed down after only two years by the incoming Prime Minister Benazir Bhutto. He lamented that not enough protest was launched against its closure. He cited former President Ayub Khan, who had once decreed that social sciences be taught in schools in favour of history.

The third key speaker in this series was Dr Ishtiaq Ahmed, who briefly spoke about the role of Islam and what it should be in the way of improving the system of education. He said Pakistan is neither an Islamic nor a secular state, and suggested that in the light of the country's recent history, it should be possible now for Pakistanis to incorporate secular aspirations into their value system.

The United Kingdom was also well represented by the notable writer on Pakistan, Victoria Schofield; the former Deputy Head of the BBC Eastern Service; David Page; and historian Richard Talbot.

Summing up on behalf of the chair, Dr Iftikhar Malik said that Pakistan has gone through many difficult phases during the past 50 years, and that Pakistan was not an open society where serious issues could be discussed. Many intellectuals do not accept pluralism, and the state does not want its affairs devolved either.

# The legacy of Dr Kalim Siddiqui

Published in *Crescent International*, Toronto, and *TheNews*, London, May 15, 1996

The death of Dr Kalim Siddiqui, the Leader of the Muslim Parliament of Great Britain and Director of the Muslim Institute in London, is undoubtedly a great loss to the Muslim community in Britain as well as the world of Islam.

He made an immense contribution to the political life of Muslims in Europe for which he will be remembered by Muslims everywhere. He was a proactive intellectual and scholar, a man of letters, journalist, politician and the author of many books. He was also a revolutionary, reformer, scourge of the establishment, defender of the faith of Islam and a first class brain. Many also saw him as a spiritual leader though not in the same mould as Imam Khomeini.

His work kept him in the public eye for more than 30 years. In his political and journalistic career, at times, he stood alone, opposed by some ill-informed mullahs on the one hand and the British press on the other, especially in the wake of the Salman Rushdie affair.

His undaunted courage in the face of a persistently hostile campaign in the British media, who lost no opportunity of denigrating him to the point of verging on character assassination, was remarkable. A man of lesser ability and calibre would have collapsed under that kind of aggressive propaganda, but being a staunch believer of Islam, he never wavered.

Whoever heard him once in a seminar or a television debate immediately recognised his great leadership qualities: clear thinking, straight forwardness and simplicity.

Dr Kalim cut no corners. He wrote with a clarity of thought so there was no confusion left in the reader's mind. His words and phrases fitted like a glove in the hand. He had an astonishing gift for communication skill. His enemies, mostly in the British

Dr Kalim Siddiqui: "The ink of a scholar's pen is holier than the blood of a martyr."

establishment and media, listened to him carefully, for he could not be ignored.

Producers of panel discussions on television or chat shows on radio programmes seemed reluctant to have Dr Kalim on their programme because they had had a taste of his sharp tongue and critical eye.

He had a masterly habit of letting the cat out of the bag when appearing on television shows. He had his own Kalimistic manner of exposing a politician or a panellist as hypocrites when he saw one and gave them a clear answer.

Several of his co-panellists were no intellectual match for Dr Kalim in television debates. Many people must have heard him one morning on a popular BBC Radio 4 programme called 'Moral Maze' when he was hounded, as usual, by several journalists and panel invitees. The subject under discussion was Islam versus Christianity, dating back hundreds of years, about the crusades and the wounds inflicted by Christians on Muslims. Dr Kalim was habitually very sharp and incisive. He took them on, one by one, answered all their tricky questions amid shouting and abuse, and overcome the collective hostility by giving them irrefutable historical facts.

On another day, this programme seemed to run quietly without any shouting or verbal violence, but because Dr Kalim was on the show the panellists wanted to make his life difficult. Their idea was to score a point or two over him without serious debate or discussion of the subject. Instead, Dr Kalim turned the tables and made them look like silly mischief-makers.

After that broadcast debate, I have not seen him on any audio or visual channel for more than 9 years. With people like him around, it was difficult for the media to distort the news about Islam and Muslims because Dr Kalim always countered them in the same language. There exists an intense hostility towards Muslims here and also in continental Europe.

Dr Kalim tried to redress this imbalance in the European society, first through the Muslim Institute, which he founded in 1972, and then through the Muslim Parliament which was established in 1992, purely in order to represent the views of Muslims in Britain, which he articulated magnificently.

Deputy Leader of the Muslim Parliament Jahangir Muhammad has promised that the work of Dr Siddiqui will be carried forward more vigorously from where he left off.

Dr Muhammad Ghayasuddin, the new leader of the Muslim Parliament, a close companion and right-hand man of the late leader, has also expressed similar sentiments. So it would seem that his lifelong work will not be in vain.

Those who opposed the Muslim Parliament obviously did not like the parliament, and argued that a parliament already exists in this country, so there is no need for another one. The Muslim Parliament of Great Britain is a pool of a debating group comprising more than 150 members, among them are doctors, lawyers, solicitors, accountants, barristers, journalists, artists, businessmen, school teachers, university lecturers and laymen. This is a platform where Muslims discuss their problems among themselves.

This parliament does not pretend to have a parallel parliament to the one that already exists in this country. It is neither in competition with nor complementary to any other institution. This is made up of only those Muslims who respond to one identity at all times. Dr Siddiqui wanted to promote debate about the economic, social and political life that Muslims in this country may adopt. He was offended by the negative media coverage since the uproar over the Rushdie affair and over the Muslim Parliament.

On March 14, 1996, he wrote a detailed letter to British Prime Minister John Major, expressing his deep concern at the current media hype against Islam and Muslims in Britain. Explaining briefly what the meaning of jihad in Islam is, he wrote:

> "In writing this letter I am also engaged in jihad. It is a centuries-old tradition in Islam that 'the ink of a scholar's pen is holier than the blood of a martyr'. Scholarship, and by extension all forms of journalism, writing, publishing and the spoken words are dimensions of jihad. The setting up of the Muslim Parliament of Great Britain in 1992 and our long standing commitment to punish blasphemy against Islam are all within the purview of the meaning of jihad.
>
> "I have no hesitation in putting on record our view that the West is currently engaged in a programme of aggression and oppression against Islam and Muslims in many parts of the world, including Bosnia and Palestine. The British Government is, and has always been, an active participant in this anti-Muslim campaign."

Dr Siddiqui was greatly annoyed by the Zionists' claim in this country that some of the charities are being used to finance Hamas in Palestine. He said he did not know of any one in Britain who has raised funds for Hamas. But what was widely known, he said, was that the Zionists and their 'charities' routinely raise billions of pounds a year to finance the Zionist movement and to shore up the illegitimate entity of Israel.

He gave a piece of advice in his letter to John Major:

> "We are also committed to maintaining good community relations in Britain. This is not easy when the Zionist lobby uses its influence in the media and in the Government to try to demonise Islam and Muslims in the manner we have seen and experienced in the past few weeks. I understand you have a regular monthly meeting with the chairman of the Board of Deputies of British Jews. At your next meeting, kindly consider advising him that in the long run, their campaign of demonising Muslims and Islam may well backfire. History has a habit of overturning roles and power balances among communities."

Dr Siddiqui was open about everything he did. No form of official pressure or media witchhunt could deflect him from what he did and what he said. He continued his work till death, despite several previous heart attacks and two bypass operations.

Dr Kalim Siddiqui has laid down firm foundations through creating the Muslim Institute and the Muslim Parliament of Great Britain. The least the Muslims of this country can do is to organise a memorial lecture each year to remember him and his work as a debt of gratitude to his legacy.

# Media in a trap

Published in *TheNews*, London, August 18, 1987

Last week a tragic news story had broken about a man who committed suicide near London's Regent's Park Mosque. The man cut his throat and leapt from a 160 feet high crane to his death.

Police did not know who he was, where he came from and why he had to do this.

What drove this man to such an extreme act remains a mystery.

Society ought to see that no man should be driven to that desperation. In an ideal world that could not happen, but unfortunately we do not live in an ideal world.

When the news first broke, it gave the impression that the crane was fixed within the boundary of the mosque, which it certainly was not.

In fact the crane from which the man fell to his death was quite away from the mosque, towards the roundabout linking Park Road and St John's Road but overlooking the mosque.

It is possible the Muslims travelling by buses and nearby Tubes for prayers for their annual festival of Eid-ul-Azha, gathered at the scene. That does not mean that the tragedy was anything to do with the Muslims or with the Islamic Cultural Centre.

Linking the mosque with the man's fall seems a far-fetched idea.

It is not known, however, whether the man 'with a Middle Eastern appearance', as the police describe him, whatever that may mean, was a Muslim. Could he be a Middle Eastern Christian? Or a Jew? If so, then would a church or a synagogue in the vicinity have been implicated?

Almost all the national newspapers have fallen into the same trap. None of them questioned the relevant facts either of the man or of the area.

A simple fact was that a sick or depressed man, who did not look like an Englishman, and in peculiar circumstances, took his own life. Full stop.

Prominence, however, was given to the nearby mosque which had nothing whatsoever to do with the tragic death.

That can mean only one thing: anti-Islam and anti-Muslim sentiments are expressed in a subtle way in the mainstream media.